PRAISE FOR

THE RAGING

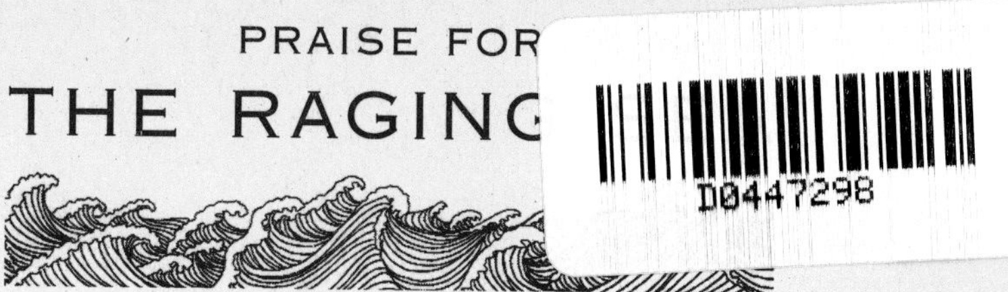

D0447298

"Man's worst nightmare—a wall of ocean in the middle of the night—really happened in Crescent City, California. There are tales in this book that will curl your hair."

—Jim Carrier, transatlantic sailor and author of *The Ship and the Storm: Hurricane Mitch and the Loss of the Fantome*

"Dennis Powers tells the story of a Good Friday that went terribly bad when off-the-scale natural forces converged on a small coastal town in northern California. He also reminds us that tragedy often brings out the best in people, and that's a story I never get tired of reading."

—Willie Drye, author of *Storm of the Century: The Labor Day Hurricane of 1935*

"Fascinating, chilling . . . An excellent book that describes a tsunami's affect on a coastal community, and residents' reactions during and after this disaster. A must-read."

—Tom Sokolowski, director (retired) of the West Coast & Alaska Tsunami Warning Center

"What a great read! *The Raging Sea* is an accurate account, told through the experiences of people who went through this catastrophe. I know all this to be true—I was there."

—Carol Cleveland, director, Del Norte Historical Society

"A gripping tale of nature on a rampage . . . Powers carefully documents how human courage and the will to survive can overcome even a wall of water crashing through the streets."

—David G. Brown, author of *White Hurricane* and *The Last Log of the Titanic*

"A must-read because nature is capable of a repeat performance."

—Rob Mundle, author of the international bestseller *Fatal Storm*

"As an emergency director I have read many details of disasters, floods and tsunamis, but never has anyone covered the details of one disaster so completely. It is an exciting true story and a wake up call to all coastal communities."

—Bill Parker, director of Civil Defense, County of Del Norte, City of Crescent City, California

DEL NORTE TRIPLICATE/DEL NORTE COUNTY HISTORICAL SOCIETY

THE RAGING SEA

THE POWERFUL ACCOUNT OF THE WORST TSUNAMI IN U.S. HISTORY

DENNIS M. POWERS

CITADEL PRESS
KENSINGTON PUBLISHING CORP.
WWW.KENSINGTONBOOKS.COM

CITADEL PRESS BOOKS are published by

Kensington Publishing Corp.
850 Third Avenue
New York, NY 10022

Copyright © 2005 Dennis M. Powers

All rights reserved. No part of this book may be reproduced in any form or by any means without the prior written consent of the publisher, excepting brief quotes used in reviews.

All Kensington titles, imprints, and distributed lines are available at special quantity discounts for bulk purchases for sales promotions, premiums, fund-raising, educational, or institutional use. Special book excerpts or customized printings can also be created to fit specific needs. For details, write or phone the office of the Kensington special sales manager: Kensington Publishing Corp., 850 Third Avenue, New York, NY 10022, attn: Special Sales Department; phone 1-800-221-2647.

CITADEL PRESS and the Citadel logo are Reg. U.S. Pat. & TM Off.

First printing: April 2005

10 9 8 7 6 5 4 3 2 1

Printed in the United States of America

Library of Congress Control Number: 2004116398

ISBN 0-8065-2682-3

This book is dedicated to the people of Crescent City and Del Norte County, California—especially Wally and Lillian Griffin and those who experienced the 1964 tsunami.

CONTENTS

PREFACE

FORTY YEARS AGO as a senior at the University of Colorado in Boulder, I remember reading with awe the stories and national headlines about the tsunami that had coursed down the U.S. West Coast and slammed into Crescent City, California. As I read the survivors' accounts, I was struck by their descriptions of the devastation and very curious as to what had really happened. When bodysurfing large waves, whether off California or Hawaii, I wondered just how somebody could survive that raging ocean that I had read about.

Much later in my life, a friend of mine, Patt Wardlaw, and I were talking about the ocean and boating ventures and the topic soon became tidal waves. Patt recommended that I chat with a friend that he knew, Bill Stamps, who owned and operated a radio station in Crescent City. I called up Bill, introduced myself, set an appointment for the following week, and drove five hours from my home to see him. I had a sense of adventure as I first drove down from the surrounding mountain ranges of pine, spruce, and redwood on the 101 Coast Highway and watched the long, sandy beach of Crescent City curve around into its famous "crescent" bay. Once I reached Bill's radio station and he started telling me his tsunami stories, I soon became awed at the tales of courage, of overcoming hard times, and of the rebuilding that took place after this disaster.

Bill then told me about Wally Griffin, who had written a book about the tsunami entitled *Dark Disaster* that I could purchase at the local historical museum and society. Since it was already late, I stayed over at a local motel and in the morning wandered over to the Del Norte County Historical Society. I there met Carol Cleveland—a very knowledgeable lady who gets things done—and she opened up the society's voluminous files about the city and the tidal waves. After I had reviewed several mounds of newspaper clippings, Carol said, "You ought to talk with Wally. He knows a lot about this." She pointed down the street and said that he owned a printing shop just two blocks away.

At the Crescent City Printing Company, the business that Wally and Lillian Griffin have owned for years, I met Wally for the very first time. I found him to be interesting, fun, knowledgeable, and generous with his time, sharing with me an equal and strong interest in this natural disaster. After talking with Wally and listening to just a few of his stories, I knew I had to write this book. The year was 1990—fifteen years ago.

Thanks to Wally's introductions, I began meeting people, interviewing them, and gaining more and more facts. I couldn't believe that I was now talking with some of the people whose chilling stories I had read about when I was young. I had seen many marinas on the coasts of California and Oregon, from Venice, Santa Monica, and Half Moon Bay to San Rafael, Eureka, Crescent City, Brookings, Coos Bay, and north. All had experienced the effects of this sea wave. Now, I stared at the mouth of the Klamath River where Sergeant Stuart Harrington had his ride in Hell, and imagined the effects of the tsunami when it crushed up the mouths of the Chetco, Rogue, Umpqua, Suislaw, and other rivers in Oregon.

I hunted libraries from Marin County close to San Francisco to the cities of Sonoma and Santa Rosa in Sonoma County. I inspected microfiche from the Del Norte County Library in Crescent City as well as newspapers ranging from Eureka in Humboldt County, California, to Brookings, Eugene, Portland, Medford, Florence, Coos Bay, and other cities in Oregon. I scrutinized the national accounts from newspapers ranging from the *New York Times* on one coast to the *Los Angeles Times* on the other. Of all the reports, Wally Griffin's accounts of the disaster in his own newspaper, the *Crescent City American*—publishing these vivid stories from the very first day afterwards—were the most striking.

While researching the tsunami, I wrote manuscripts on other subjects, then left my Kenwood, California, home and law practice to move to Ashland, Oregon, and become a professor at Southern Oregon State College (now named Southern Oregon University). During this time, I published five other books, all the while working on this labor of love.

During summers and breaks from my responsibilities at Southern, I would continue interviewing people, trying to locate others. Four years ago, I was fortunate to track down and interview Gary Clawson, whose acts of courage had become the topic of national interviews and magazine coverage after the 1964 disaster. Through my research, I marveled at Sergeants Donald McClure's and Stuart Harrington's incredible bravery—riding the tidal wave two miles up the river, then back in the dark of night. Hearing Gary's stories, I was struck by the uncommon courage of ordinary people who rose to extraordinary heights. I then toured and inspected both the Pacific Tsunami Warning Center in Ewa Beach on Oahu, Hawaii, and the West Coast/Alaska Tsunami Warning Center in Palmer, Alaska. Here I met with its director, Tom Sokolowski, regarded as one of the founders of modern tsunami forecasting.

I began writing portions of this book in 1992, referring to it with my friends as my "Project X," as I fleshed out the stories. My friend and agent, Jeanne Fredericks, agreed with me from the start that this would be an important and worthwhile story to tell. We then were fortunate to have the best publishing company for this project come forward, through the presence of Kensington Publishing's Editor-in-Chief, Michaela Hamilton.

It is now my privilege to relate to you the story of the tsunami of 1964 that savaged the United States West Coast and of those whose fortitude and courage were tested to an extent beyond which, we hope, most will never need to experience.

ACKNOWLEDGMENTS

THIS BOOK would not have been possible without the friendship, help, and generous support over the years of Wally and Lillian Griffin and their business, Crescent City Printing Company. In addition to providing pictures for this publication and releasing photographs not seen before by the general public, as well as recommending people to interview, Wally Griffin was very gracious in his support, including allowing me full access to the information contained in his book, *Dark Disaster*, copies of which are also available from the Del Norte County Historical Society in Crescent City.

Carol Cleveland and the Del Norte County Historical Society receive high marks, as well; I thank Carol for her friendship and help in acquiring photographs and their release for publication. Bill Parker stands out, not only for his interviews, but also for reviewing portions of this manuscript and giving appreciated advice. Tom Sokolowski, the long-time head of the West Coast/Alaska Tsunami Warning Center in Parker, Alaska, and Paul Whitmore, its present chief, were helpful with their input on the WC/ATWC's operations. Tom also made appreciated suggestions on the manuscript. A professor in Environmental Studies, Eric Dittmer, of Southern Oregon University provided valuable assistance in understanding tsunamis, especially with respect to Crescent City and its vulnerability. And my appreciation is extended to a friend, Chris Honore, who also reviewed portions of this manuscript and made helpful comments.

I thank Gary Clawson and his wife, Carole, for their time, graciousness, and help. It was my pleasure to get to know them. I appreciated interviewing and/or meeting: Bill Peepe, Bob and Mary Jean Ames, Bill Stamps, Guy Ames, Ernie Pyke, Doug Pyke, Don Mather, Ruth Long, Joan and Bud Clark, Merv and Margo McGuire, Ray Shalk, Roy Magnuson, Richard Weir, Jim and Sophia Hooper, not to mention again Carol Cleveland, Wally and Lillian Griffin, Gary Clawson, and Bill and Boots Parker. With sadness I note that Jim Hooper, Ernie Pyke, and others passed away after my interviews with them. Jim Hooper and his wife, Sophia, met me for lunch in Ashland, and Jim sent me copious notes and information concerning the rebuilding of Crescent City.

I grew fond of the people I met during my research for this book, and of Crescent City itself—it is a city with which we all can identify, as older residents hand over their knowledge and experiences to new generations. I take my hat off to all of you and send you my very best, as always.

I must thank the staff, publishers, and editors (past and present) of the *Triplicate* in Crescent City for their help, information, and courtesies, and access to past issues and information contained in their newspaper's stories. I also appreciated the help of the staff at the facilities of the Pacific Tsunami Warning Center in Ewa Beach, Hawaii, and the U.S. West Coast/Alaska Tsunami Warning Center in Palmer, Alaska.

My special thanks to the Editor-in-Chief at Kensington Publishing, Michaela Hamilton, for her unwaveringly positive attitude and professional suggestions. As always, I must thank my agent, Jeanne Fredericks. Jeanne, we have worked together for years, and it has always been such a pleasure to know you, your husband Wes, and your family.

Last, but never least, I so appreciate the help and support of my wife, Judy, who accompanied me on countless trips to Crescent City, who loved talking with Wally and Lillian, but afterwards never ran out of books to read, whether it was inside during a cold rain or outside in the warm sunshine. In fact, by the time this project was completed, we had traveled in three different cars—and we generally keep a car for at least five years. She is the best!

THE RAGING SEA

PROLOGUE

IN THE EARLY EVENING on March 27, 1964, at 7:36 P.M., an 8.4 Richter magnitude earthquake—one of the largest shocks ever recorded on the North American Continent—struck near the Gulf of Alaska, 75 miles east of Anchorage and 55 miles west of the coastal port of Valdez. In a matter of minutes, the earthquake destroyed the downtown section of Anchorage, severely damaging or destroying blocks of residential and commercial buildings, and causing numbers of tract homes to slide into a nearby frigid bay. The quake's motion under unstable ground caused local landslide-created sea waves to crash into nearby coastal towns from Valdez to Seward on the Prince William Sound side and from Homer to Kodiak Island in the Gulf of Alaska.

The savage shifting of tectonic plates forced billions of tons of seawater to quickly surge away, creating the main transpacific tidal wave that traveled west across the Pacific Ocean basin and steamed down toward the North American continent. This southbound tsunami express raced past the Alaskan Peninsula, lashing at some towns while surprisingly sparing others, then hit deep water and sped away at speeds close to 600 miles per hour. (Tsunami is the internationally accepted word for a seismic sea wave and is pronounced "su-nam′-ee"; it comes from the Japanese words meaning "harbor wave." Tsunami and tidal wave are used interchangeably, since the word "tidal wave" is generally understood as the equivalent to "tsunami.")

The transoceanic waves quickly left Alaska and hustled down the coastlines of British Columbia and the U.S. West Coast, including the states of Washington and Oregon, slamming with their worst effects into Crescent City, California, a Northern California coastal town of three thousand people, located close to the Oregon border. In this town alone, the disaster exceeded the combined effects of all previous death and destruction totals caused by tsunamis on the United States mainland and the greatest fatalities, injuries, and destruction ever reported on the West Coast. Insurance executives reported later that the tidal waves that pummeled Crescent City caused more damage per block than in Alaska, the site of much closer, local landslide-induced tsunamis.

Many coastal residents had no idea of the tidal wave's danger until sometime later, even after the tsunami surged down their coastlines and steamed onto land. The sea waves sped nearly as fast as the news of the earthquake, arriving off the shores of the state of Washington a scant three hours after the earthquake first shook. It swept into Crescent City at midnight, seizing countless unsuspecting individuals—whether asleep in their homes or camping on the beach, fishing in rivers, cleaning up their businesses after an earlier flooding, or partying in bars—hurtling through two thousand miles of ocean like a jetliner through cloudless skies in a scant 4½ hours, then circling the globe, again and again. Whether warned or not, asleep inside their homes or awake watching television, people suddenly found themselves pummeled by chilling, monstrous storms of seawater in the middle of the night, as large objects hammered at them, illuminated in surrealistic black and white by the moonlight. They were caught whether they could swim for their life or not.

After the ocean receded for the last time, the reports of courage began to reach a country shocked at the thought that tidal waves could wreak such havoc. The U.S. Air Force later awarded its Airman's Medal, its highest award for bravery under peacetime condition, for the acts of one man. The media ran stories about those who saved the lives of others, while losing loved ones in the maelstrom. The public read how the tsunami trapped others, spinning one woman away in the wreck of her home into the darkness of foam, as she held onto life through sheer will. After the destruction, the city had to rebuild, starting with the numbers of people who magically appeared at morning light with their power saws, trucks, crowbars, and hands to start the process, although authorities had not yet made any official call for help. This is a story about common people who reached uncommon heights.

PART I

The Very Beginnings

1

Simplicity of Life

THE BRILLIANT California sun was a bright red ball, nestling toward the horizon with reddish-yellow streaks painted over the ocean's light blues. Seagulls sailed over the beach, shrieking with sharp cries. Squat boats dotted the waters, securely tethered to buoys and seemingly motionless in the low tide. On board a few of the large commercial fishing boats, fishermen still tended their nets or equipment. Close to calling it quits for another day, they were ready to join the rest who had already headed home to start the weekend or now sat with drink in hand at their customary places in their favorite bars. It was Friday, March 27, 1964, and this day had been like any other one—except that today was Good Friday and it had been a particularly fine spring day.

From shore, Gary Clawson stared at a lonely figure rowing his skiff from the moored boats toward land. Another fisherman from a distance called faintly to the man, but the rower paid no heed. His motion appeared effortless, as the strokes continued rhythmically and the small waves gently lapped against the smaller boat. Spotted with driftwood, logs, and debris, the beaches fanned away on both sides. Thrown against the land by the fierce winter storms that had pounded onto land from the northwest, huge redwood logs littered the scrub brush and sand. A few blocks past the sandy, mottled land stretched the main part of town with its weather-beaten, rustic structures.

The beach curved for twelve miles, its boundaries marked by two doglegged breakwaters. These rock-filled steel and concrete aprons protected the docks within, filled with moored sailboats, speedboats, skiffs, fishing boats, a huge lumber barge, and an occasional thirty-foot trawler. Gorged with runoff from the heavy spring rains, the Elk River pounded into the ocean and split the bay in half. The noise of passing cars from Highway 101 echoed behind Gary and mingled with the sounds of the birds and sea, as the vibrant green shrubs and ocean blues contrasted sharply against the bleakness of the adjacent one-story, worn-wooden buildings and multicolored houses. The smell of the ocean blended with that of the city and its passing cars.

After following the bay's contours, the inland highway turned abruptly toward the mountains, splitting the area between houses and buildings on one side and open fields spotted with trees, structures, and lumberyards on the other. Motorists sped by in both directions, on their way to their homes or motels, or just passing through.

Gary Clawson had grown up in Crescent City, and like most long-term residents he knew many of those in town. A small Northern California coastal city of three thousand, Crescent City was located fifteen miles south of the Oregon border in a rugged, wooded area surrounded by redwood, spruce, and pine trees. Highway 101 connected it with other California and Oregon coastal communities, as mountain ranges paralleled the cities, beaches, and the broad Pacific Ocean.

Clawson studied the rowing man as he neared a dock, and then looked back towards the horizon. Both men gazed out as the sun disappeared into the sea, and as if by magic, the ocean swallowed the daylight to leave a stark gray sky that would soon fade into darkness. Overhead, the moon cut a strong outline with two evening stars already out, barely visible but twinkling.

Gary Clawson knew that a bright full moon would be out tonight. The air would soon become chilly, and the temperatures on this March night would again be in the high 40s, maybe low 50s—not bad for this time of the year. From the clearness of the sky, he knew that there wouldn't be a blanket fog rolling in later this evening to envelop the town and its people. The groves of trees that lined the surrounding mountains were motionless from the lack of a breeze. Yes, it would be another quiet night.

The fisherman worked his way to the wharf and tied his skiff to it. He slowly climbed up the ladder to the dock and walked past a huge lumber barge. Large, rectangular, strapped piles by its side waited to be loaded and join the mass of lumber stacks already onboard. Lumbering and fishing, that's what this town's always been about, Clawson reflected. That and earning your way.

After watching the man walk with quick steps to his car, Gary turned back to his new Pontiac Grand Prix. He had closed his grocery store to start the weekend and was on his way to picking up his fiancée, Joanie Fields. Gary planned to stop by and wish his father a happy fifty-fourth birthday, then continue on with an evening of fun. Clawson liked having a good time and being with his buddies. His friend Jim Burris and others would be joining him and Joanie later at the Tides, a local bar. Life was good for this enterprising twenty-seven-year-old. He owned his own home, a part interest in a tavern with his father and a relative, and his own business, Gary's Grocery, in a town that always seemed to be down on its luck for others.

Good Friday marked the beginning of Easter weekend, redemption and salvation for many serious-minded church-goers, sumptuous feasts on Sunday for most, and a weekend off for nearly all. As the residents went about their lives, the college kids were returning home to spend Easter with their parents, and local residents from shopkeepers to lumbermen were now at home or planning to get there. Some tourists and a few job seekers were settling quietly into their motel units, young mothers fed their babies in beach homes, and families camped out on secluded beaches in the state parks. From the young to the very old, all expected that this uneventful day would become a similar night.

CRESCENT CITY was a folksy, down-home town, where everyone seemed to know everybody else, and the latest "news" about anyone circulated by word of mouth long before it could ever appear in print. These folks grew up together and attended the same high school. Families knew one another and set up businesses together.

Couples went steady with their high-school sweethearts, married young, and stayed married through thick or thin. They knew who drank too much and which drunk needed help to get home at night. They knew who lived where and why, including who lived in the backs of the old wooden buildings and who lived upstairs. Crescent City residents bought from one another and traded services. They had their favorite bars, restaurants, and wooden benches to meet and catch up on what was happening, and the unspoken rule was to "live and let live."

These were independent people with a strong sense of community. The town was small and always seemed to have to overcome hard times, including the present. A slowdown in homebuilding, especially in Southern California, had softened the local economy, and the mills didn't need as many lumber workers—meaning there was less money to go around. The tourist season hadn't started yet, and the fishing industry hadn't been able to take up the slack. But these people could turn to their neighbors for help when they fell on personal hard times, just as they would extend a helping hand when it was their turn to be asked.

The town was a mixture of quaint curio shops, small museums, fishing tackle-and-bait shops, bars, and restaurants that catered to the summer tourist trade, along with welding services, lumber equipment, hardware, and appliance stores, car and truck repair, drugstores, and family-owned department stores that serviced the locals. Blessed with a seemingly endless supply of pine, redwood, and spruce trees, the area had long been a center for logging, milling, and manufacturing plywood and lumber. However, the timber industry fluctuated as the national or regional economies dictated—sometimes even more—and the residents of Crescent City felt those changes. Living on the coast, locals also weren't strangers to the hurricane-force winter storms, high tides, and even minor tidal waves that surged over their beaches. Life simply was to be lived and enjoyed, regardless of whether the times were economically good or not.

People in these small logging and fishing towns had developed a strong sense of community, due in part to their isolation and dependence on one another, as well as simply living in a small town and coming in contact with each other as frequently as they did. When Crescent City had needed a pier to handle its increasing catch of fish and numbers of fishing boats, as well as transporting the area's milled lumber for Southern California's needy housing subdivisions, the residents joined together in 1950 to build Citizen's Dock with their own hands, pier by pier. They donated cash, materials, and labor, then the town officially opened the wharf on March 18th, complete with a parade, fish boat race, crab feed, basketball games, and a dance. Later, the citizens worked together to rebuild and expand the community-owned dock in the same harbor. In 1964, they passed a bond issue to build a municipal swimming pool that could be enjoyed by all.

Crescent City was a conglomeration of old structures with mainly wooden, clapboard houses and one- and two-story buildings. Farmers could still ride their horses down Front Street, a main street of town and closest to the beach, then stop and tether the animals to posts and streetlights—although city officials were quick to add that "no one ever did." The town dated back to 1853 when settlers first pitched their tents on the beach. One year later, four hundred buildings and one thousand pioneers had settled into the area, drawn by the pristine forests, bountiful fishing, ample room to live and breathe—and the prospects of gold in the mountainous California interior.

A number of the city's buildings and houses dated back to the late 1800s. These structures had high-pitched, dark-colored shingled roofs with cut angles and attached garages. Some were Victorian-style homes with high attics, lofts, crow's nests, widow's walks, dormers, and unique roofed apartments that overlooked the harbor, still used by families worried over their seafaring husband's or father's safe return from long days of commercial trawling for fish in the high seas. Most of the structures had peeling paint and dark wood, abraded by the salty ocean spray from the lashings of wintry Nor'westers and ocean storms. The people's main concern for safety, however, was whether their wooden buildings would catch fire, as whole sections of their town before had burned entirely down to layers of smoldering ashes. Accordingly, residents built their homes apart from one another with distinct gaps, not on top of one another as seen in larger cities—and there always was more than enough land to go around.

Situated in a relatively isolated area, the city's prime connection with the outside world is Highway 101 and its north and southbound coastal arteries. The small Oregon beach town of Brookings is some twenty miles to the north, while the tiny towns of Requa and Klamath are twenty miles to the south. The closest major town to the south is Eureka—a 1½ hour drive or ninety miles away—while San Francisco is 375 miles distant. Inland mountain ranges form a natural barricade sealing the coast from any other real highway access. Medford, Oregon, a 2½ hour drive to the northeast, can be reached by driving a curving, mountainous road that cuts through these forests.

National and state parks with towering groves of forests, slashed by ancient rivers and gorges, surround the city and general area. The Redwood National and State Parks, Smith River National Recreation Area and Scenic Byway, and other wilderness areas neighbor the city on its inland side. Jedediah Smith State Park with its massive trunks of old-growth redwood trees is scant minutes by car from the city's downtown section. Crescent City itself is built on a level portion of the lowlands by the sea, a topography that gradually increases its slope to disappear into the mountains. The city was rugged but quaint—attractive in its way but not considered beautiful or attacked by the "cutes," as one resident commented about the luxurious California coastal cities of Carmel, Big Sur, and Santa Barbara.

The sea has always been a part of the lore and life of its residents. Crescent City Harbor is one of the oldest on the Pacific coast, and the crescent-shaped bay is what gives the city its name. Its Battery Point Lighthouse was built at the northern tip of the harbor and became operational in December 1856, only two years after the town of Crescent City was incorporated. Constructed in the same Cape Cod style as the eight original West Coast lighthouses, it was decommissioned in 1953 when deemed unnecessary. Peggy and Roxey Coon were the curators of the lighthouse in 1964, operating it for the benefit of the Del Norte County Historical Society, and this rocky point is accessible by foot only during low tide, completely surrounded by the sea when the tides sweep in.

St. George Reef Lighthouse, the tallest and most expensive American lighthouse ever constructed, stands high on craggy reefs located several miles offshore, and is visible from shore on clear days. A tragic wreck occurred on July 30, 1865, three months after Abraham Lincoln's assassination, when the *Brother Jonathan* ran aground on an uncharted reef scant miles from the harbor. This side-wheel paddle ship was headed to Portland, Oregon, from San Francisco, California, when a savage storm overtook it with foaming, seething waves and howling, whipping winds outside Crescent City. The captain turned the ship back for the safety of the harbor, but the pounding ocean drove the vessel onto the hidden rocks.

This wreck became one of this country's worst maritime disasters, as only one lifeboat with 19 people survived out of the 244 passengers and crew who were onboard. For weeks, bodies and debris washed back to litter over one hundred miles of the California and Oregon coastline. The *Brother Jonathan* disaster provided the impetus to enact federal legislation to safeguard ships' passengers as well as to build a nearby lighthouse. Under the most difficult construction circumstances imaginable, where stormy seas could sweep over the bleak rocks without any warning, it took nine years to build the 134-foot lighthouse on top of a 60-foot cut-rock and concrete base, six miles offshore on St. George Reef. Becoming operational in 1882, the lighthouse was still working in 1964. Geologists believe that an underwater ridge off Point St. George bears some responsibility for the way tidal waves seem to funnel directly into Crescent City and its harbor—and with renewed energy.

The area's history is replete with stories about the wrecks that clutter its ocean bottom. In 1855, the steamship *America* caught fire, and the captain ran it aground in the harbor; a later windstorm off Point Reyes sank the burned-out hull as it was being towed to San Francisco for repairs. Another violent storm in 1911 overtook the vessel *Mandalay*, then steaming from San Francisco to Crescent City. A huge wave crashed over the vessel and washed one man overboard with his two dogs. Five minutes later, another towering wave washed the man back onto the ship, complete with the two dogs still gripping his trousers tight by their jaws. The captain then purposely ran the ship aground to avoid sinking in the violent coastal waters.

In 1924, another storm caught the 122-ton steamship *Shark* while men tried to unload its cargo in Crescent City Harbor. The winds and waves pounded it mercilessly until the vessel broke apart. Two weeks after the Japanese attacked Pearl Harbor, one of Japan's submarines torpedoed the oil tanker *Emidio* twenty miles north of Eureka. The surviving members of the crew abandoned the ship, and the vessel drifted onto Steamboat Rock at the entrance to the harbor. Another winter storm howled in and broke the ship in two, washing one part ashore while sinking the other. The Crescent City Chamber of Commerce found the bow of the sunken ship when it drifted onto land and built a monument with this piece on Front Street in memory of the lost crewmembers.

Over one hundred commercial fishing craft called Crescent City Harbor their home at this time, as well as an equal number of pleasure and sport-fishing boats. Ancillary businesses such as boat repair and maintenance, marine supply, and equipment repair grew up around this industry. The commercial boats caught shrimp, Dungeness crab, salmon, swordfish, and bottom fish such as flounder, sole, rockfish, and albacore. Crescent City was then and still is a leading port for crab and shrimp tonnage in California. Commercial fishing is cold, grueling, dangerous work as raging winds and pounding seas can swiftly rear up to engulf any boat when seamen aren't cautious enough, and fishing vessels capsize with men drowning every year.

Over one-third of the jobs then depended on the local timber industry, the rest from commercial fishing, tourism, and the local shops and services. Due to the richness of the surrounding forests and timberland, lumbering and lumber products had been the area's prime industry since 1853. In the early 1960s, area mills shipped out around 200 million board feet of lumber each year. Some seventy-five lumber mills and seven plywood and veneer plants then operated in and around Del Norte County, and most of them employed Crescent City people. Since those times, this industry has dramatically declined. Oil and petroleum products were the greatest commodities then imported, most passing through bulk-oil tank farms, including those located on Highway 101, south of the business district.

In the news that night, Russia had released two American pilots, captured 17 days before when Soviet jet fighters had shot down their RB66 spy plane in the beginning of the Cold War. U.S. military "advisers" were already in South Vietnam at this time, but U.S. troops had not yet been shipped there to support these consultants, and most Americans didn't pay much attention then to that part of the world. Lyndon B. Johnson was President and had held office for less than four months after the tragic assassination of President John F. Kennedy. The nation and Congress was galvanized now over the issue of civil rights, and the newspapers carried the stories about the latest arrests of civil rights demonstrators in St. Augustine, Florida, among other cities.

Brand new Ford Mustangs sold in 1964 for $2,400. And try these costs for size: men's dress slacks, $6.95; men's flannel shirt, $2.98; bras, $3.00; eggs, 3 dozen for $1; Cheerios, 29 cents per box; and pork roast, 39 cents per pound. A one-bedroom house off Elk Valley Road in Crescent City sold for $5,300 that year, and a three-bedroom home on the river with a fireplace sold for $14,000.

The newspapers that Friday detailed the available church services for Sunday's Easter celebrations. Other stories described the religious activities to be held, ranging from Billy Graham's services in America to those in European cathedrals and pilgrims bearing heavy crosses over the twisted, stone-paved streets of Old Jerusalem.

That Friday evening, Bill and Gay Clawson were happily celebrating Bill's birthday with beer and toasts at their tiny bar, the Long Branch Tavern, south of Crescent City's downtown on Highway 101, with friends such as Nita and Earl Edwards, who also tended bar that night. Gary and Joanie planned to catch up with Bill and Gay and give their congratulations. Later, Mervyn ("Mac") McGuire would also end up at the Long Branch Tavern to visit with his friends. Bill Whippo and LaVelle Torgenson, who lived in a trailer across from the Long Branch Tavern, were watching television, and also just blocks away from the beach.

Born and reared in Crescent City, Mabel Martin had come down with the flu that day and she "wasn't feeling very spry." A seventy-five-year-old widow, she rented a small cottage located downtown behind the G & G Liquor Store at Third and J Streets. After her husband died in a logging accident, Mabel lived by herself in that small bungalow. Bernie McClendon, the commander of the California National Guard Reserve in Crescent City and her landlord, visited her around 6:00 P.M. He had given her a box of chocolate candies as an Easter gift and then left for home, leaving Mabel to nibble on the candies. She then smoked a cigarette, took a sleeping pill, and headed to bed.

James Parks was getting ready for dinner in his trailer by Seaside Hospital. The sixty-three-year-old African American shoe repairman lived in and operated his business from that trailer. A couple of blocks away, Adolph Arrigoni had settled in for the evening in his ground-level apartment. A retired carpenter, Adolph was in his mid-sixties and also a fixture in town.

Betty and Ernie Pyke had closed their Ben Franklin department store after preparing for the anticipated Easter weekend sales. They were at home now with their twin sons, Doug and Steve, who were getting ready to head downtown and enjoy a weekend night on the town with their teenage friends. Bob and Mary Jean Ames were also at home, after Bob Jr. had closed their family's appliance store for the night. Their teenage sons, Guy and Brad, planned to head downtown to "knock around with their buddies."

Peggy Sullivan and her two children had settled into their cottage by the beach at Van's Hotel in Crescent City. Joyce London was at her home on U.S. Highway 101 South, while her best friend, Lavella Hillsbery, was planning a night out with her boyfriend.

Roy Magnuson and his wife, Marilyn, were visiting her parents in Ferndale, California—a two-hour drive south on Highway 101 from the city. Joseph and Eleanor McKay were driving north on Highway 101 towards Crescent City. They were tired from their nonstop drive from Los Angeles, but the couple looked forward to finding restaurant work there and starting a new life.

Staff Sergeants Stuart Harrington and Donald McClure, both based at the U.S. Air Force's 777th Radar Squad facility by the Klamath River in Requa, California, had decided to fish that evening on the river, located fifteen miles south of Crescent City. While walking off base, they talked about the news that day of Russia's release of the two captured U.S. pilots, as well as what they hoped to catch that night. McClure was particularly happy about the latest addition to his family, three weeks ago, of a baby daughter, Jackie.

Three sixth-graders were playing on the beach and planning to camp out near their homes in Coos Bay, Oregon. The McKenzie family had arrived to stay the weekend at Beverly Beach State Park further up the coast. Visitors and locals alike, from Crescent City, both north and southward up the coastline, were simply going about their lives.

2

Earthquakes, Tsunamis, and Good Friday

THE OCEANS and continents of the world rest on huge stone plates; each plate is a massive slab of rock, from a few hundred miles to thousands of miles wide. Seven large plates and many smaller ones cover the earth. These plates fit together like a giant jigsaw puzzle, floating over a softer middle layer, or mantle, that encloses the earth's fiery, molten core. If this planet were the size of an egg, its outermost plate layer would be about the thickness of an eggshell, broken into these fragments. Each plate or fragment is twenty miles thick on average (although some reach eighty miles in thickness) and is composed of hard granite or heavier basalt.

These underground plates have been moving very slowly over the earth's surface for hundreds of millions of years, driven by the boiling, bubbling pressure and movement from its mantle and core. Although geologists debate the reasons why these plates move, the fact is that they do move, and in different directions. Although this movement measures merely inches or fractions of inches each year, over time the distance adds up and shapes the earth's geography with its mountains, valleys, ocean trenches, and plateaus. The constant pressure between the plates builds up tension, causing earthquakes when the moving plates grind and scrape against one another. The powerful vertical displacements can cause tidal waves by creating huge movements of ocean water, whether due to the land shaking, sliding, or volcanic explosions.

Continual collisions between the Pacific and North American Plates cause the great majority of the earthquakes on this continent. These plates basically follow the coastline of North America: they sweep alongside the Aleutian Islands, Alaska, and British Columbia, then down the coastal states of Washington, Oregon, and California, to end at the Mexican Baja Peninsula.

Geologists call the Pacific Basin the "Ring of Fire," because it's rimmed by most of the world's active volcanoes—which evidence the basic instability of the earth's molten core, constantly seething and moving within. Consequently, most of the world's earthquakes and ensuing tidal waves occur in areas bordering the Pacific Ocean. Within this zone and over time, the combination of tremors and tsunamis has destroyed property valued in the multi-billions of dollars and killed over half a million people.

The Pacific Plate and its "Ring of Fire" zone runs in an irregular line from the southern tip of Chile in South America, up the Pacific coasts of Central and North America to Alaska, west along the Aleutian Island arc, south through Japan and the Philippines, then branching west through New Guinea, its southern island groups, and New Zealand. The North American Plate comprises the entire North American continent, sweeping eastward to beneath the Atlantic Ocean.

These two plates clash in a continual battle for territory. At a number of places, stress builds up over time at fault lines. When the pressure becomes intolerable, either the North American Plate or Pacific Plate jerks free and thrusts up to relieve the pressure in an up-and-down strike. This swift upward thrust causes the earthquakes and ensuing tidal waves with explosive releases of energy; however, a thrust from side to side, or a horizontal movement, will cause similar destructive energy releases, but cannot form an ocean-going tsunami since no water is displaced. With the 1964 Alaskan earthquake, the U.S. Naval Civil Engineering Laboratory calculated later that its savage shifting had a force equivalent to the total energy released by 12,000 Hiroshima-equivalent atomic bomb explosions.

Geophysicists measure an earthquake's force by what mathematicians call an exponential relationship, whereby each succeeding number has a much greater effect or higher power. For example, an earthquake of 7.0 on the Richter scale is over ten times more powerful than one measuring 6.0. A magnitude of 8.0 is between twenty-five and thirty times more powerful than one that's 7.0. The 8.4 magnitude of this earthquake was as powerful as the earthquake that leveled San Francisco in 1906 and many times more powerful than the 6.7 earthquake in 1971 that struck Sylmar and Los Angeles.

In 1964, the pressure became intolerable along the Pacific and North American Plates on the northeast/southeastern axis in Alaska. This line, or axis, pointed the energy and the thrust of displaced water directly at the heart of the U.S. West Coast. Although the earthquake was centered under land, it was close enough to the ocean to cause a severe uplifting and subsidence of the earth's layers. The northeast-southwest trend line started from the southeast coast of Kodiak Island, then seaward off Chugiak; it turned north across the eastern portion of the Kenai Peninsula and the western part of Prince William Sound, passing just south of Valdez. Basically, an almost circular area of 11,700 square miles off Alaska's southern coast heaved up with a nearly rectangular area of 20,800 square miles plunging violently down, setting almost 20,000 cubic miles of seawater in motion.

At precisely 7:36 P.M., U.S. Pacific Standard and Crescent City time (5:36 P.M., Alaskan time), on March 27, 1964, this 8.4 magnitude earthquake struck near the Gulf of Alaska about one-third the way up the Alaskan coastline. The epicenter of the quake centered between Crescent Glacier and Unakwik Inlet in the North Prince William Sound, 75 miles east of Anchorage and some 55 miles west of the coastal port of Valdez. The point of the rupture was fourteen miles inside the earth's crust under the Great Columbia Glacier and the rugged Chugach Mountains. It was one of the largest shocks recorded on the North American Continent and the most destructive in Alaskan history.

The Alaskan quake rumbled for over three minutes, punishing hundreds of square miles of mountainous, glacier terrain with severe cracking, slipping, and devastation. In a matter of minutes, the earthquake destroyed the downtown section of Anchorage, severely damaging or destroying thirty blocks of residences and commercial buildings. Landslides caused severe damage in the Government Hill area by Elmendorf Air Force Base. The city's most exclusive residential suburb of Turnagain Heights slid into the frigid arctic waters when the underlying cliff bluffs liquefied and fractured, causing the destruction of seventy-five homes in that slide. The quake destroyed or severely damaged numerous highways, railroad tracks, bridges, utility lines, and airports with landslides, cracking, and slippage. The aftershocks continued for days after the main earthquake struck.

The earthquake's motion and ensuing slides caused damage to smaller towns, close to Anchorage and on the Prince William Sound side, including the coastal towns of Portage, Valdez, Whittier, and Seward. Toward the southwest and Gulf of Alaska, the rumblings caused major slippage at other coastal locations such as Afgonak, Homer, Seldovia, and Kodiak Island. The peculiar aspects of the geology underlying Alaska's mountainous landscape brought about liquefaction and slippage at these places, and large portions of land quickly separated or slid into the sea. When these landmasses crashed down into the ocean, the resulting water displacement created local sea waves that caused extensive damage and fatalities in nearly all of these localities.

The violent upward and/or downward movement of land masses that displaces massive volumes of water, which may or may not be directly above the grating land gyrations, is what causes tidal waves—quite distinct from any created landslides that cause local sea waves. The savage shifting of the tectonic plates suddenly thrusts billions and billions of tons of seawater upwards over hundreds, even thousands of square miles of ocean, and, in this case, hurtles this water mass towards the North American continent as a tidal wave. The entire ocean was now moving from its surface to miles below at its bottom.

At the same time, nearly two thousand miles to the south, Al Smith, his wife, and two grandchildren were planning to stay the night in a beach cottage in Pacific Beach, Washington, two-thirds of the way down the coast from British Columbia. Al was driving to the neighboring town of Copalis on an errand.

Further down the coast, Rita and Monte McKenzie with their

four small children were hiking at Beverly Beach State Park in Oregon. In the throes of marital difficulties, the McKenzies had decided to take their family for a weekend outing, away from their home in neighboring Washington. The family was attracted to the secluded, beautiful setting of sandy beaches, towering rocks, and surrounding cliffs. As they searched for a camping spot, their children played happily on the beach.

Miles down the Oregon coast from the McKenzie family, three sixth-grade boys were also playing on the beach, but near the small-boat basin in Coos Bay. Rick Lillienthal, Rick Cardwell, and Floyd Stewart would spend the night on the beach and had brought along their sleeping bags, camping equipment, and tent. The kids had even taken a black cocker spaniel puppy to keep them company. Their parents had given them permission, as they were only a short distance from the Lillienthals' home. This area was relatively undeveloped and rustic, and the boys had camped out before.

In Crescent City, teenager Mick Miller was going to borrow the family's Lincoln Continental that evening to take his girlfriend out. He was looking forward to parking at the beach as part of their Friday night date. Ray Schach was thinking he might have to do the books that evening at his Crescent City Lumber Company and get caught up with the financial numbers. Don Mather was planning on meeting friends at a downtown bar.

Friday evening found forty-year-old Bill Parker driving from Crescent City to nearby Brookings, Oregon, on business. One of two morticians in town, Bill was also the Civil Defense Director for Crescent City and Del Norte County, its city-equivalent, and a disaster volunteer like others in town. The community simply couldn't afford to pay for positions devoted to disasters that might never occur. Bill had already overseen emergencies involving floods and ocean storms, along with past tidal wave warnings that had not materialized into major problems. As was his habit, Parker had left his whereabouts in Brookings with the Sheriff's Office in Crescent City, just in case he was needed in an emergency.

In Klamath, Sergeants Stuart Harrington and Donald McClure had finished eating dinner with their families. Although the radar station at Requa was self-sufficient, most of the servicemen and women lived in Klamath, ten miles away from the base. After dinner, the two men inspected their fishing gear and readied for their trip into the canyon and mouth where the Klamath River flows into the Pacific Ocean.

TIDAL WAVES have been part of the folklore of the world for ages. A volcanic eruption tore apart the island of Thera, southeast of Greece in 1450 B.C. The vanishing of Thera is believed by some to have formed the basis for the biblical story of the parting of the Red Sea, as well as Plato's fabled city of Atlantis. The destruction of Thera and its Minoan civilization has cultural significance, as the devastation opened the gate for the rise of the Grecian empire.

The most common cause of tsunamis are underwater earthquakes, which can suddenly lift up square blocks of the ocean floor, plummet other huge sections, or fracture away portions as a massive underwater landslide. Any of these events causes a large disturbance in the ocean mass. Such movement forms a bulge or a depression change in the ocean's surface. As water always seeks to find and maintain its equilibrium, the entire ocean surface sways from a tidal wave's disturbance until it can finally return to normal levels.

Not all earthquakes create tidal waves. A sideways motion won't create a tsunami because there is little displacement of water. For example, if you dip your hand in a bowl of water and quickly remove it, ripples race away on the water's surface. However, moving the edge of that hand underwater, back and forth, won't have the same effect. Although the earthquake that leveled San Francisco in 1906 was the worst in U.S. history, that quake's sideways motion dropped the water level in the Bay by only six inches. The 1964 Alaskan earthquake with its "up and down" movement caused an eight-foot difference in San Francisco Bay's level. In order for an earthquake to create a tsunami, the tremor must occur underneath or be near large water masses, be of high intensity, and create an up-and-down or vertical movement to that water. Earthquakes with less than a 7.0 rating on the Richter scale have a very low probability of causing tidal waves, regardless of whether the movement is vertical or not, as their force is limited in pushing away massive amounts of ocean.

The Pacific Ocean commands more than its share of tidal waves. In fact, two destructive tsunamis on average are created each year in the Pacific Basin. When a main or non-local tsunami is created, the energy in the seawater feels the entire bottom of the ocean's floor. The first wave radiating out grows to where it eventually can encompass the entire Pacific Ocean, from the ocean's surface down thousands of feet to its very bottom, eventually touching from Asia to North and South America. The entire ocean is in motion. This wave travels faster than six hundred miles per hour in the deepest waters of the ocean, but at the ocean's surface, the wave's height will be only six inches to one foot, at best, and will be undetectable to any ship passing over it.

Contrary to public opinion, a tidal wave is not just one massive wave. It is a series of wave surges or energy traveling through the medium of water, each following one another through the sea until encountering land. The first surge is not usually the largest movement. In a rippling effect, up to ten or more waves may be heading away in concentric circles at the same time, one behind the other. The more powerful waves usually travel close to one another at an average thirty to forty minutes apart.

The deeper the water, the faster the tidal waves travel. In water 30,000 feet deep, they can rocket along at 670 miles per hour, faster than a jetliner. Where the ocean's depth is 12,000 feet, the tsunami travels at 424 miles per hour. As portions of the wave enter shallower water, the wave becomes higher, but slows down to compensate for its energy being boxed into a smaller area due to the lower depth. At a depth of six hundred feet, the wave's speed decreases to ninety-four miles per hour, then ratchets down to thirty miles per hour when the depth is only sixty feet. However, the surface or wave height of the water continues to rise, as its speed slows down, rising from inches to feet, then ten feet high or more, depending on the particular underwater topography. As the same ocean water volume moves into a smaller space, the wave slows down and rises more in height due to the constrictions placed on its mass.

A tidal wave "feels" the ocean's bottom, gaining a foothold in shallower water. Although the surge is far slower than when in deep waters, it still travels much faster than normal ocean waves, tide changes, or wind waves. The force of the water behind it, its high speed, and the piling up of the ocean on itself combine to give the tremendous power carried by tsunamis. For these reasons, a five-foot tsunami can hammer with considerably more force and damage than a ten-foot storm wave and its typical shore erosion.

The same tidal wave can travel at different speeds and surface wave heights in different places, depending on the ocean's depth, shape of the coastal lands or bays, varying ocean levels, and the sunken terrain in its way. Shallow areas of jutting shoreline points, river heads, and other coastal anomalies extending out to sea further than surrounding offshore deeper bottoms attract tsunamis. While the sea wave slows down at these shallower points, the wave extension on either sides does not. The wave sides actually wrap around that shallow point, swinging with one or both sides as the surge concentrates its energy where the land juts out or shallower areas exist. As the ocean bottom becomes shallower, the wave energy builds at its top into a higher surface wave, the smaller space squeezing the energy upwards. At the same time, the wave length decreases on both sides owing to the different speeds, adding to the wave height and energy concentration. The power of the ocean when in such movement is awesome.

Underwater canyons also can channel the energy towards a particular landmass, while steep cliffs underneath the ocean's surface can act as a reflector, bouncing the tsunami away in an entirely different direction. Islands of coral or offshore reefs can absorb the wave's energy, causing it not only to slow down but also to lose some height. Owing to these factors, the same wave motion can cause gentle flooding in one harbor, but devastating another scant miles away.

The displaced water can take any variety of forms, depending on its overall mass, the contours of the ocean's bottom, any obstacles in its path such as islands, the tide, and a coastline's particular geography. It rarely becomes the TV-pictured "towering" wave that's racing over land. Tidal waves can be a quickly rising series of rumbling ocean flows, like a flooding river, that reach a maximum runup (how high the tsunami "runs" up on land over the usual tide level) and inundation area (its maximum area of flooding). They can also become a gradual rising of the sea over a fifteen-to-twenty-minute period, causing no damage at all. Tsunamis can become a tidal bore, or tumbling wall of seawater, as when churning waters with no crest or bottom pour out from a ruptured dam. Seismic sea waves are higher at high tide than at low, because there's more water for the waves to build on.

However, at any given time or location, scientists still can't accurately predict after an earthquake what form a tidal wave will take or how devastating it might be. Although researchers continually create and experiment with shore models, the size and types of ocean movement still defy accurate prediction.

A sudden dramatic ebbing or draining of the ocean away from shore is the typical sign of an approaching tsunami. As the trough of the wave approaches, rather than its crest, the incoming movement sucks the ocean away from the shoreline before it arrives. The offshore bottom may lie exposed, littered with flopping fish and other sea life. Although this is the time to leave immediately for higher ground—and not explore what's on the exposed bottom—curiosity continues to attract sightseers to these sights. The crest then quickly approaches with the first waves, and the sea surges onto land with its accumulated ocean mass. Being unaware of this basic fact has cost tens of thousands of people their lives.

A tidal wave causes damage not only by its initial height, but also by its runup, or how far inland it surges. People on hills above the height of a tidal wave can be just as much at risk as those down at the beach. The wave may be ten feet high at the beach, but it can be six feet high with the same power two-hundred feet up that hill. It is dangerous to try and see a tsunami, because if you can see one, it's usually too late to get out of its way.

People and dwellings close to the epicenter of an earthquake generally have the greatest risk from tidal waves. In a matter of minutes and before any warnings can be issued, these massive waters can rush over populated areas. This is the great danger when any earthquake occurs offshore, no matter where it's located. In this case, the local submarine landslides—both underwater and from on land—caused most of the fatalities in Alaska from the 1964 series of tremors.

Tidal waves can reach immense sizes on rare occasions. In fact, a tidal wave with a height of 350 feet was recorded on the coast of Ambon Island, Indonesia, in 1674. However, a tsunami doesn't have to be high to create death and destruction. Five-foot-high surges can easily drown people, especially if the victims are young or elderly. If someone can't swim, then a wave only has to knock that person off his or her feet.

Tidal waves can span continents and circle the globe. There's very little loss of energy as the ocean moves, and a tsunami can hit Japan, Hawaii, Chile, and the United States, one by one, each wave stretching for hundreds of miles. The 1964 tidal wave reached the shores of all of them and caused damage in every one. The energy can keep traveling until hitting land, islands, or some natural barrier, then reflect off at another angle, circling the globe until something else gets in the way. The tidal wave from the 1883 volcanic explosion of Krakatoa in the Indonesian islands, for example, circled the globe seven times.

Although the 1964 earthquake destroyed large parts of Anchorage, the city didn't receive any damage from the local and main tidal waves that were generated. The earthquake's epicenter was on the opposite side of the city, and the huge Kenai Peninsula blocked any waves from surging into Anchorage. However, this didn't help other coastal towns that flanked Prince William Sound, were in the southern areas of the Kenai Peninsula, or were located on the east side of Kodiak Island.

The earthquake directly caused more than a dozen local landslide tsunamis in these coastal areas, which in turn brought about most of the deaths. Of the 115 people who died in the Alaska earthquake, nine fatalities were due to the quake's destruction of structures on land with 106 deaths being attributed to the earthquake-created tsunamis. Local underwater or "submarine" landslide-induced surges around Alaska created four-fifths (or eighty-two) of these fatalities, while the uplifting of the sea floor and main tidal waves caused twenty-four Alaskan deaths at Chenega. This factor causes concern for those West Coast coastal communities that are located close to similar earthquake-prone zones.

The underwater slides and coastal landslides occurred within minutes after the shaking began in harbors and bays along the south and east coast of the Kenai Peninsula and the northern shores of Prince William Sound. They generated highly destructive local tidal waves—or tsunamis whose effect was limited primarily to that local area and weren't involved in the destruction and deaths in the Continental United States. The major ones occurred at Valdez, Seward, Whittier, and Kodiak.

The town of Valdez, built on Prince William Sound on the edge of an outwash consisting of silty sand and gravel, lies at the head of the deep, steep-sided fjord of Port Valdez. (Later, this location became the end terminal for the Alaskan Pipeline and transshipment point for loading oil tankers.) The earthquake's rumblings caused a large, unstable slice of water-saturated ground, three-quarters of a mile long and one tenth of a mile wide—including the dock area and part of the town—to rupture and slide into the sea. This massive local landslide quickly generated an initial thirty-foot wave within two to three minutes of the beginning of the quake.

The surge of water shot into Valdez, rolling through the harbor and into the town, destroying what was left of the waterfront, demolishing the fishing fleet, and penetrating two blocks into the city of 1,200 people. Thirty-two persons lost their lives in that slide and the subsequent waves. The initial wave killed twenty-eight men, women, and children outright who were standing on a pier, as they watched the crewmembers and stevedores of the freighter S.S. *Chena* unload cargo. Falling cargo killed two crewmen on board the ship and a third died from a heart attack. After striking the north shore of Port Valdez, the local tidal wave reflected back against the southeast shore, then spent itself along the head of the Port Valdez glacier.

A second landslide at Valdez occurred near the mouth of Shoup Bay. Large underwater chunks of land sliced off the Shoup Glacier near the mouth of the bay and caused more waves to rise. These surges were responsible for the death of one person. This local tidal wave splashed sand to the extraordinary height of sixty-seven meters (or 220 feet) above sea level. These occurrences are akin to what happens when large blocks of ice split from a glacier and crash into the ocean, causing the water to be displaced and huge waves to radiate away. Although those created waves don't have the energy or staying power of an ocean-going tsunami, they can be deadly within a localized area.

Seward at the time was a small town of 2,300 people on the Prince William Sound. The Good Friday earthquake caused a narrow swatch of waterfront, measuring two-thirds of a mile long, to crash underneath Resurrection Bay. This loss of land included all of the waterfront facilities of the Standard Oil Company's dock north to the San Juan dock. The ground that slid into the bay had an approximate offshore slope of thirty to thirty-five degrees, and the ensuing wave spread out in different directions. The slide-generated waves, followed by the main tsunami, were responsible for twelve fatalities, primarily at the low-lying dock, railroad yard, and cannery facilities.

In Whittier, slides of unstable, water-soaked land at the top of the Passage Canal generated waves that destroyed most of the waterfronts, including saw mills, the Union Oil Company tank farm, houses, buildings, and boats. These local landslide waves caused twelve deaths, including that of an infant who was found alive in a snow bank, but unfortunately died later.

Due to the numerous passages, inlets, and islands in the Prince William Sound, the main tidal wave caused devastation and deaths in Alaska before speeding south to the U.S. West Coast. Chenega was a tiny coastal village of seventy-six people and twenty-three persons died there. The main tsunami, traveling toward British Columbia, destroyed the small town except for a small school and one house located on a high bluff. Preceded by a smaller wave and a noticeable withdrawal of water, the sea waves hit Chenega within three minutes after the earthquake ended. Geologists believe that the focusing effects of the unique underwater geography of a small group of islands four miles to the southeast of Chenega caused the force and severity of those waves.

The Kodiak Islands shielded the Alaska Peninsula and Aleutian Islands from the direct action of the main tidal waves; however, coastal towns on its east coast were in the direct path of the tsunami. Making this situation much worse, the earthquake's tremblings caused the entire island to collapse five-and-a-half feet, inducing landslides, which caused, in turn, local waves that killed and injured people. The city of Kodiak and Kodiak Naval Station were the only places in Alaska that received any warnings, as the U.S. Fleet Weather Central maintained a tide station there and issued a local tsunami warning.

This half-hour warning allowed for a complete evacuation of the Kodiak Naval Station, but the people in the city were slow to respond—a typical but unfortunate reaction with tsunami warnings—and many were caught by the first wave. However, they were lucky in that the first surge caused only gentle flooding with a subsequent gradual ebbing of the sea. Some people took this warning seriously and ran to higher ground, but others thought the first surge ended the matter. They were dead wrong. Cresting in at a height of thirty feet, the second wave caught people still loitering about the town. Five blocks of Kodiak were destroyed, all the docks in the area broken up, and eight people died in the city. Four others died in other areas of the island.

The surges continued through Port William Sound and down the Alaskan coastline. More cabins, homes, boats, and buildings were destroyed or damaged, but only one more fatality occurred at Whitshed. Although the tsunami was nearly circular when it left Alaska, radiating away in concentric circles, the wave height was much greater as the tidal wave headed south toward North America than the wave traveling north along the Aleutian arc.

Owing to the direction that the underground land shifts took, the largest tidal waves outside of Alaska were now directed towards the U.S. and Canadian West Coasts. The main tidal wave sped south unnoticed—until it suddenly rose to crest over land—and arrived alongside the Washington coast a scant three hours later. Located two thousand miles away from Anchorage, no one on the U.S. West Coast felt the earthquake that had rocked Alaska that evening. And no one, even if on an ocean-going boat, could feel the ocean's mass then rushing down underneath them.

3

Tragedy Strikes Without Warning

NOTICEABLE DISCREPANCIES appear in accounts as to when the Alaskan earthquake occurred relative to Crescent City time and how long it took for the tsunami to travel there. Some accounts confuse the daylight savings time issue, as well as the time changes between Alaska and the U.S. West Coast. Daylight savings time did not start until the first Sunday of April, which was two days away, and the time change between zones was two hours. With the earthquake striking just after 7:30 P.M., West Coast time, the tidal wave would arrive four-and-a-half hours later in Southern Oregon and Northern California at midnight. This doesn't leave much time, even today, not to mention the warning delays that took place then.

The alarm bell sounded sharply at the Coast and Geodetic Survey's magnetic observatory in Fairbanks, Alaska, when the earthquake's rumblings started at 5:36 P.M., local time (7:36 P.M., PST)—the seismograph had registered an earthquake large enough to start a tsunami. Seismographs are instruments that detect earth shocks, regardless how far away the earthquake is centered. Suspended above the ground, their pendulums detect the slightest of earth's ground motions and track them by recording needles that ink the movement fluctuations on slowly revolving paper drums.

Seven minutes later, at 7:43 P.M. PST, another seismograph alarm sounded at the U.S. Coast and Geodetic Survey's Honolulu

Observatory at Ewa Beach. (All times hereafter are translated to U.S. West Coast time, rather than the local observatory time.) The earthquake's first shock wave traveled through the earth and arrived in seven minutes, triggering the tsunami alarm at the center. The Honolulu Observatory was the nerve center of the Seismic Sea Wave Warning System (SSWWS) operated by the Geodetic Society, the only one covering Pacific Ocean tsunami disturbances from Hawaii to Alaska and the U.S. West Coast. In response, the observatory requested immediate readings from seismograph stations located in Fairbanks and Sitka, Alaska; Pasadena and Berkeley, California; Tucson, Arizona; and Guam and Tokyo.

The problem with seismographs, however, is that although these instruments can determine an earthquake's epicenter, magnitude, and time of occurrence, they cannot tell whether that quake's strike is "up and down" or sideways—a key element in determining whether an ocean-cruising tsunami has been born. Simply stated, both vertical and horizontal shifting look the same to a seismograph, a problem that continues today.

Additionally, since a tidal wave's speed, direction, and even height is directly influenced by its strike path, the ocean's depth, and underwater geographical contours at any particular place, it is very difficult to determine whether a tsunami will be destructive or not, once it is underway. Predicting how tidal waves will react on land is an art, not a science. Since most earthquakes don't cause tidal waves, the monitoring agencies have to wait until confirming data becomes available indicating that a tidal wave has even been formed. This basic problem continues even now, but in 1964, no tide gauges operated off Alaska's coast that could quickly monitor ocean-level fluctuations in this tsunami's path.

Various centers, including Hong Kong and Manila, wired earthquake readings to Honolulu. Using triangulation, a world-wide globe, and data from these reports, seismologists were able to pinpoint the exact location of the earthquake's origination. However, they still had no idea whether a tidal wave had been generated. At 8:36 P.M., PST, the U.S. Federal Aviation Agency informed Honolulu that it could not contact Alaska through its cables. This information, however, was discounted because other causes could have been present. Investigators later discovered that the earthquake had ruptured the underwater communication cables and was responsible for the severance.

One hour and nineteen minutes after its tsunami alarm sounded, the SSWWS's Honolulu Observatory issued its first advisory at 9:02 P.M., PST:

> THIS IS A TIDAL WAVE (SEISMIC SEA WAVE) ADVISORY. A SEVERE EARTHQUAKE HAS OCCURRED AT LAT. 61 N., LONG. 147.5 W., VICINITY OF SEWARD, ALASKA, AT 0336Z, 27 MARCH. IT IS NOT KNOWN, REPEAT NOT KNOWN AT THIS TIME THAT A SEA WAVE HAS BEEN GENERATED. YOU WILL BE KEPT INFORMED AS FURTHER INFORMATION BECOMES AVAILABLE. IF A WAVE HAS BEEN GENERATED, ITS ETA FOR THE HAWAIIAN ISLANDS (HONOLULU) IS 0900Z, 27 MARCH.

The system was in the dark, even though the tidal wave was well underway, causing death and destruction down the Alaskan coast toward British Columbia and heading directly toward the U.S. West Coast. The Honolulu Observatory's use of a different time (although precisely the same time when translated) is due to its use of Greenwich Mean Time as its standard, and the "Z" in the message stands for "ZULU" time, which is another word for the Greenwich standard. One hour before this warning was sent, locally caused landslide tsunamis had already devastated Valdez, Seward, Whittier, Kodiak, and smaller towns. By this time, the main tsunami had covered one-third of the distance to the U.S. coastline, surging against numbers of coastal communities along the way.

The information slowly kept trickling in. The U.S. Navy's Fleet Weather Control Station reported tremors in Kodiak and damage to its tide gauge. The F.A.A. reported that the International Airport tower at Anchorage had been destroyed. The Honolulu Observatory issued its Bulletin No. 2 at 9:30 P.M. This one stated:

THIS IS A TIDAL WAVE (SEISMIC SEA WAVE) INFORMATION BULLETIN. DAMAGE TO COMMUNICATIONS TO ALASKA MAKES IT IMPOSSIBLE TO CONTACT TIDE OBSERVERS. IF A WAVE HAS BEEN GENERATED THE ETA'S ARE ATTU 07457Z . . .

The estimated arrival times (ETAs) then followed for Adak, Dutch Harbor, Kodiak, Samoa, Canton, Johnston, Midway, Wake, Kwajalein, Guam, Tokyo, Sitka, San Pedro (Los Angeles), La Jolla (near San Diego), Balboa, Acapulco, Christmas, *Crescent City*, Legaspi, Neah Bay, San Francisco, Tahiti, Tofino (British Columbia), Valparaiso (Peru), Honolulu, Hualein (Taiwan), La Punta (Peru), Marcus, Hong Kong, Shimizu, and Hachinohe (Japan). These locations were reporting stations in the then-warning system chain with tide, tsunami and tide, or seismograph-monitoring equipment. The ETA of the first tidal waves was set at midnight for Crescent City—which proved to be accurate.

At 9:55 P.M., PST, Kodiak confirmed finally that a tsunami had hit there. The station reported that it had experienced a seismic sea wave with ocean surges from ten to twelve feet high over mean sea levels. At 10:37 P.M., PST, the Pacific Tsunami Warning Center in Honolulu sent out a definite warning in Bulletin No. 3:

THIS IS A TIDAL WAVE (SEISMIC SEA WAVE) WARNING. A SEVERE EARTHQUAKE HAS OCCURRED AT LAT. 61 N., LONG. 147.5 W., VICINITY OF SEWARD, ALASKA, AT 0336Z, 27 MARCH. A SEA WAVE HAS BEEN GENERATED WHICH IS SPREADING OVER THE PACIFIC OCEAN. THE ETA OF THE FIRST WAVE AT OAHU IS 0900Z 27 MARCH. THE INTENSITY CAN NOT BE PREDICTED. HOWEVER THIS WAVE COULD CAUSE GREAT DAMAGE IN THE HAWAIIAN ISLANDS AND ELSEWHERE IN THE PACIFIC AREA. THE DANGER MAY LAST FOR SEVERAL HOURS . . .

The message stated the differing location-arrival times. California's Disaster Office (its civil defense agency) received this warning advisory at 10:44 P.M., but as Crescent City wasn't then connected to this system, the warning didn't continue on directly to the city. The obvious slant of the bulletins toward Hawaii and its vulnerability was owing to the SSWWS's location in Honolulu and its equipment oriented toward that area's tsunami risks. Death and destruction had already occurred on the Alaskan and U.S. West Coasts hours before the Ewa Center knew it. To correct this deadly deficiency, the Alaska Tsunami Warning Center in Palmer, Alaska, was created in 1967, to monitor tidal waves for Alaska and the U.S. West Coast.

Many U.S. West Coast residents, in fact, had no real idea about the tidal wave danger until the tidal wave had surged over their shores and past their coastlines. Radio and television reports had quickly filled the air with initial stories of the earthquake, but no connection had yet been made about the danger of a tsunami. Crescent City locals who were watching the Johnny Carson show received their first televised tsunami warnings around midnight—just as the first waves were arriving—although the news about the Alaskan quake had been out for two hours.

A local radio station in Crescent City, KPLY, didn't know about the earthquake and ensuing tidal waves until it began receiving telephone calls after 10:30 P.M. from around the United States asking if the tsunami had affected them. Some residents made the connection between the Alaskan earthquake and an incoming tidal wave. The curious had just enough time to leave their houses to go to the harbor or downtown to "watch the wave"—no different than in other places or times in years past—and be entrapped when the main waves surged onto land. This incredible power of tsunamis has surprised and trapped countless numbers of people over time.

AFTER DEVASTATING small cities and towns in the Prince William Sound and Gulf of Alaska, the southbound tsunami express passed the Alaskan Peninsula, lashing at some towns and surprisingly sparing others. At 11:00 P.M., the main tidal wave cruised into Tofino, Port Alberni, and other coastal locations in British Columbia. Tossing aside cars and buildings in its path at Port Alberni, the waves surged forty miles through the Alberni Canal, causing extensive damage, but no deaths occurred. Authorities on Vancouver Island reported numbers of houses damaged or destroyed by the waves, but, again, no fatalities and limited injuries were reported. Since most of these Canadian towns are sheltered from ocean-generated storms by being inland on protective waterways, they didn't experience the extensive damage as did those further south.

The tidal wave first hit the northern shores of Washington at 11:15 P.M., surging into other coastal towns in this state as late as 11:55 P.M., depending on how the energy was reflected or slowed at a particular location. As the sea waves reached towards towns on Washingon's coast, flooding occurred and surges headed up rivers. At Moclips, located in the middle of Washington's coast, the second and highest wave occurred around 1:30 A.M. (about the time of the fourth and largest one that speared Crescent City) and was reportedly eleven feet high. Eight beach houses were damaged, but no injuries were reported. Lower down, the second wave was also the highest when it hit the south bank of Joe Creek; the wave deflected to the northwest and inundated dwellings on the north bank. A bridge lost three pilings and two twenty-foot concrete spans.

The first wave arrived at Copalis, Washington, about 11:30 P.M., spinning trailers over and trapping Al Smith in his car while he was speeding toward Pacific Beach to reach his grandchildren. The ocean washed his car into the Copalis River, and as a deputy sheriff wrenched open the car door to rescue him, the waters also inundated the sheriff's vehicle. Both men, however, reached higher ground and safety. At the same time, the ocean lifted the beach cottage with Mr. Smith's grandchildren and wife, tearing it partly apart, and carried it inland. When Al Smith finally arrived, he happily discovered that his family had safely survived their ordeal.

Later surges washed out the bridge over the Copalis River, dropping one car and its driver, Len Hulbert, into the surging waters. He had stopped on the bridge to watch the tsunami run up the river and pile logs against the bridge's footings. When the bridge collapsed, he and his car plunged into the river. Although the car door pinned his leg in, Hulbert was finally able to pull loose, force the door open against the current, and make his escape.

Just before sweeping down the Oregon coast, a four-foot wave hit the dock at a tiny place called Ilwaco and caused minor damage. However, four teenagers were camping at nearby Beards Hollow on the beach when the first wave hit at 11:35 P.M. The tidal surge filled their car with water, shoving it back sixty feet until underwater objects caught the vehicle. The youths escaped unharmed when they jumped out and waded to higher land, before the ocean receded. Later surges completely inundated the area that they had used for their safety.

The surges left Washington relatively untouched: two people were injured and two more suffered heart attacks, although the waves destroyed one fishing boat and several skiffs were lost. The sea waves barely touched Seattle, with the off-lying islands in the Juan de Fuca Straits providing protection. Miraculously, no fatalities had been directly linked to the inundations and destruction brought about in Canada and Washington. Unfortunately, as the tidal wave steamed into Oregon and California, the impact would be greater due to their offshore geography, lack of protecting landmasses, and strike direction.

AS THE TIDAL WAVE ripped down the West Coast toward Crescent City, most residents were either watching television or already asleep. Had the tsunami occurred during a busy afternoon or a rush hour, heavy debris washing over the highways and into the downtown congested areas would have greatly increased the death toll. Even so, how close you were to the sea and what you were doing at the time made a difference between life and death.

Gary Clawson, his friends, and fiancée were having a "gay old time" at the Tides on Front Street. The Tides was a ground-level bar and restaurant in the middle of the downtown section, half a block from Front Street on I Street but still close to the sandy stretch of land leading to the beach. Gary was playing his guitar for the crowd, Joanie Fields and Jim Burris joining in the singing. Before then, Clawson had stopped by and wished his dad a happy birthday at the Long Branch, then driven to the Tides to meet his friends. He was as intent at having a good time as he was in being successful with his life, whether it was business, scuba diving, or fishing. Gary's parents, Bill and Gay Clawson, had left their Long Branch Tavern for home and were now watching television. Their friends and employees, Nita and Earl Edwards, had stayed behind to tend the bar.

Living close to "B" and Battery Streets by the Dutton Dock, Adolph Arrigoni was sleeping in his apartment. James Parks, who operated the shoe repair shop from his trailer on Front and Battery Streets, was also asleep; he lived about two blocks from Adolph and each knew the other. Having taken a sleeping pill for her flu, Mrs. Mabel Martin was deeply asleep in her home at Third and J Streets.

Living near Highway 101 South, Joyce London at the time was reading with her family. Her television wasn't working, so she had no idea that there had even been an earthquake in Alaska, let alone that there was the possibility of a tidal wave. Her friend Lavella Hillsbery and her boyfriend were out on the town.

Another friend, Irene Wright, and her three small children were in their small cottage located a few blocks from Joyce London's place. Irene's husband, Billy "Irish" Wright, wasn't with her at the time. He currently was serving a six-month sentence in county jail for public disorder and drunkenness, among other charges.

Roy Magnuson and his wife, Marilyn, now were driving back from Ferndale, California, after having visited with her parents. They had heard about the possible tsunami, and Roy was worried about his fishing boat that was moored in the bay. He wanted to return quickly, so that he could "ride the wave out" in his fishing trawler and save it.

Mac McGuire was watching television when he heard the news of the impending tidal wave. He ambled down to the docks to see how his boat was doing. Bob Ames, Jr., was at home, while his sons, Guy and Brad, were out seeing a movie with their friends. And Ernie Pyke was also home with his wife while their twin sons, Doug and Steve, were downtown with the younger crowd.

Del Edwards, however, was at the U.S. Navy Training Center in San Diego. His mother was the director of the local Red Cross chapter, and he heard later on a San Diego radio station that a small Northern California town had been wiped off the map, but the announcer didn't give the city's name. He learned which city it was only when his mother called the next day to tell him that their family was fine.

Teenager Bob Cochran had been at Enderts Beach on South 101 where the tidal waves that night were their fiercest. However, he and his girlfriend had had a fight that evening, and he had taken her home earlier. Bob then returned to his family's home. "I guess I was lucky we weren't there," he wrote later, "as we both would have been swept away." Cochran later became a lawyer in town.

Gene Shach, who also became an attorney in Crescent City, fortunately had driven that night to a basketball game in Eureka—a three-hour drive away. He heard later that the town had been savagely hit by the tsunami.

U.S. Air Force Sergeants Stuart Harrington and Donald McClure were fishing in the night at the mouth of the Klamath River in California, just south of Crescent City. The two men stood on top of a driftwood mound on a sandbar, where the ocean meets the river's flow to the sea.

AT 11:08 P.M., three and a half hours after the earthquake struck, the California Disaster Office in Sacramento issued its first emergency, all-points bulletin to the California Highway Patrol, all police, and all civil defense officials of coastal counties and cities, stating that a tidal wave was "probable but unconfirmed." At 11:50 P.M., the state's Civil Defense Office issued a similar bulletin, removing the "unconfirmed" notation and giving the estimated arrival time for the tidal wave in Crescent City as midnight—a scant ten minutes away.

Located within a few blocks of downtown Crescent City, the disaster-communication and emergency center at the Del Norte County Sheriff's Office received the bulletins. When the dispatcher read the first bulletin at 11:08 P.M., he immediately called the sheriff, Civil Defense (C.D.) head, Crescent City chief of police, California Highway Patrol, and others on the "Emergency Control Team." The sheriff, the C.D. director's alternate, the C.D. communications chief, and various team members were at the sheriff's office by 11:20 P.M. Sheriff O. E. Hovgaard quickly placed all of his deputies on alert, and the staff monitored short-wave frequencies for further news. The C.D. communications chief alerted all of the radio and ham operators in the area about the potential emergency.

Bill Parker, the Civil Defense director for Crescent City and Del Norte County, needed more time before he could be at the emergency control post. Bill was still in Brookings, Oregon, when he received the dispatcher's telephone call. His first task was to find a ride back. The friend who had given Parker the car ride up didn't want to return then, feeling that these tidal wave warnings seemed to just "come and go without anything else happening." Bill felt fortunate, however, when he found someone who was driving back then to Crescent City.

However, once Parker was inside the car, it quickly became evident that there was something wrong with the driver. As soon as he drove off, the man had trouble with his steering. The car began to weave from lane to lane, and Bill Parker realized that his driver was a "well-concealed, but well-oiled drunk." Bill asked solicitously, "Are you tired?" He hoped the man would answer back that he wouldn't mind if Bill drove.

"No," said the driver. "Don't you like my driving?"

"Oh, yes," Bill said, smiling back. "I like your driving," he said, trying not to offend the erratic driver. He wasn't interested in trying to thumb down another ride on that desolate road in the middle of the night.

"Where did you say you wanted to be dropped off?" said the drunk. Bill didn't want to tell the man his actual destination—the Sheriff's Office.

"To my mortuary," he instead answered. The drunk seemed to become a little more under control as he slowly drove through Crescent City. When Bill Parker stepped out of the car, he thanked the driver. As Parker stepped quickly over to the Sheriff's Office, the drunk gave a nervous glance at Bill and then the police station, floored the accelerator, and drove hastily away.

Civil Defense, Crescent City, and Del Norte County officials already had agreed on the emergency plans in case of a tidal wave. This city was no stranger to flooding, tsunami warnings, and emergencies. The Emergency Control Team planned to quickly mobilize police volunteers, the County Sheriff's Department, California Highway Patrol, Crescent City Fire Department, and other agencies. These authorities would fan out, in turn, and warn the residents in the low-lying areas.

The Coast Guard's emergency network at this time was already operating. From its connection to the SSWWS network, the Coast Guard already had alerted its Crescent City station. Their local personnel were now warning those down at the harbor, including advising fishermen to sail their boats quickly out to sea before the waves could catch any tied-down vessels in shallow water.

The emergency team discussed whether or not a tsunami alert should be issued or an emergency evacuation declared. Crescent City had already endured numerous standby alerts and warnings stating the probability of a tsunami cruising down—and nothing had happened. The warnings received so far did not indicate how destructive this tsunami was. The authorities knew that receiving the initial warnings of the ETA, or estimated time of arrival, for any tidal wave could become an all-night wait before receiving an "all clear" or a confirmation of destruction potentialities. Bill Parker noted later:

> Our problem that night was the first warning we received didn't confirm the tidal wave. The second message confirming its arrival then came nearly at the same time the first wave did. The state was having problems, as well, in that it couldn't confirm the degree of the threat with the lack of information from tide stations. Although we knew the ETA for the tidal waves, no one knows how bad they might be or where they might strike hardest, if at all, once it comes on shore. This was a difficult decision, and it still is today.
>
> This is always a judgment call on whether you authorize an all-out evacuation or not. You don't make any friends, but that isn't the point. You know that most evacuations don't make any difference, and people really get upset with you because of the inconvenience, expense, and lost money. It's always the "big one" that you're trying to prepare for and to minimize loss of

life. You want to keep property loss down, but it's saving lives that you're shooting for.

So far there had been nothing unusual to indicate that this situation would be any different from past tsunami warnings, and the emergency team had worked together before in assessing the dangers of previous emergencies. When the second warning was received, the authorities decided on a full-scale alert, rather than an all-out evacuation. With ten minutes to go before the first inundation would begin building, and after receiving their instructions from the dispatcher, police began knocking on darkened doors with people asleep, warning radios and televisions turned off, while others were driving around in their cars, drinking in bars and restaurants, or simply walking around town that Friday night.

It didn't help when Neah Bay in Washington, one of the seismic sea-wave monitoring installations, reported around midnight that it had not observed any abnormal wave actions. The deputies in Crescent City didn't have a chance to complete their door-to-door knocking when the first wave arrived at midnight. They couldn't have come close to completing their task.

Local radio stations KPOD and KPLY were on the air when the first waves hit. However, since neither a full-scale evacuation nor news about the alert had been received, the stations didn't give much play to the possibility of another tidal wave hitting their area. In fact, KPLY didn't even know about the impending calamity until people from out-of-town places such as Denver, Houston, San Francisco, and Seattle began calling around 10:30 P.M. to ask if the seismic sea wave had hit Crescent City.

The television broadcasts earlier that evening had interrupted their programming with news about the Alaskan earthquake, but none indicated that anyone on the U.S. West Coast, including Crescent City, should expect a tidal wave onslaught as severe as what was then surging south. One man was on business in Medford, Oregon, a two-and-a-half hour drive from the area. When he heard about the oncoming tidal wave from a San Francisco radio station, he quickly called up his wife in Crescent City. When he asked her about the tsunami, she replied, "I don't know what you're talking about."

No general alarm had been issued for the U.S. West Coast; no general system then existed. However, as tidal waves move faster than any warnings, it is doubtful that this made a great difference. And night presents other problems as it hides pre-tidal movements, communicating to masses of individuals is more difficult, and people are asleep. This tsunami was closing fast on Crescent City.

The city's authorities can't be faulted for the lack of warnings. Tidal waves move as fast as a jet airplane, and entire national and regional systems can't keep up with this speed, let alone a small municipality. Even today, there is a very real question whether adequate warnings can get out, be received in time, and seriously relied on by people in today's high density, coastal areas.

As Crescent City's officials were deciding on their plan of action, the tsunami crashed down the coast of Oregon, now less than thirty minutes from Northern California. Oregon wasn't as lucky as its neighboring state of Washington. Four people drowned, a number were injured, and one woman suffered a fatal heart attack. All of the beach towns in Oregon suffered damage, much of it extensive. Its coastal communities discovered the next morning that their bridges, trailers, cars, motel units, and breakwaters had been destroyed or severely damaged. After the tsunami and its several surges passed, logs and debris choked most of the river mouths. Most of these communities again received no warning, but even if they had, it's quite likely under these nighttime circumstances that they would have suffered the same losses.

The town of Seaside is tucked just inside the Oregon border. The Necanicum River flows north towards Washington and parallel to the beach in Seaside until it swings into a bay that opens to the Pacific. The first wave powered into the open bay at 11:30 P.M. Following the bay's contours, the surge dramatically surged north in the opposite direction of the main tsunami, at the same time swinging around into the river and heading down parallel to the initial direction—all on top of the river's contrary flow into the sea. The surging wall of water was ten feet high, sweeping away two bridges while damaging six others some distance inland. Families needed to retreat to second-story levels when the ocean poured into their living rooms. As with all other rivers and streams, the tsunami gained momentum and size when these channels crammed its energy into their narrower confines.

The ocean pushed tons of tree stumps, fish, logs, cars, furniture, and silt up rivers and deposited them along the way. Mrs. Mary Eva Deis died of a heart attack at the age of fifty when the wave and debris slammed into her home by the Necanicum River. It is not difficult to imagine the heart-stopping fear and racing anxiety when the ocean thunders into your home unexpectedly in the dead of night, ripping at the structure with debris. The heaviest damage occurred along Neawanna Creek, normally a placid tributary that flows two to three blocks north but parallel to the Necanicum River. Homes were flooded far up along the creek or ripped from their foundations, and the ocean awoke some residents who found themselves surrounded by it.

After the largest surges, the railroad tracks of the Spokane, Seattle & Portland Railway were still spiked firmly to their ties, but were now swaying across Neawanna Creek. There were no pilings under the bridge trestle; the wall of water had swept all of them cleanly away. The wave slammed trailers around at the nearby Venice Trailer Court, and then continued on its way up the creek, dumping cars and trailers along the way.

The town of Cannon Beach lies south of Seaside, and the tidal wave also gave it a rude awakening. As with their California counterparts, Oregon disaster officials received the warning that a possible, but unconfirmed, tidal wave was on the move. No alarms were sounded here either, and few precautions taken before the sea wave flooded parts of the city. The first wave struck at 11:34 P.M., penetrating up Elk Creek as it flows into the sea at Cannon Beach. The tsunami whooshed up this tributary, ripping out a bridge and everything in its path. Estimated at nine to ten feet in height, the surge struck first at high tide, "spewing a wall of water and foam twenty-five feet high," observers later reported.

The wave swept the two-hundred-foot long bridge one-quarter mile upstream, leaving sightseers clustered on the sides where the bridge once had been. The ocean deposited two pieces of the bridge in a mudflat, the parts cleanly severed as if sliced by a sharp kitchen knife and looking like ordinary bridges—except for the fact that they led to nowhere and a house was sandwiched in between. The house originally had been a two-family residence located two hundred yards below the bridge, and the tsunami had ripped the structure from its foundation at the same time. A third piece of the bridge was left high among four massive trees, as if a playful giant had tossed it there.

The waves swept numbers of boats moored to a Cannon Beach wharf into the ocean after the pier gave way from the pounding. The tidal wave raced past Depoe Bay and pounded into Beverly Beach State Park, all on its way south towards Crescent City and past.

RITA AND MONTE MCKENZIE bedded down inside a lean-to with their four small children at Beverly Beach State Park. Nestled between Depoe Bay State Park and the small town of Newport one-third of the way down the Oregon coast, Beverly Beach has beautiful sweeping vistas of beaches, sand dunes, sunsets, and bleak offshore rocks. After a seven-hour drive from their hometown of Tacoma, Washington, the McKenzies had started their Easter weekend camping trip on the beach.

Monte McKenzie was thirty-five years old and worked as an engineer at the Boeing Company in Seattle, Washington, while his twenty-nine-year-old wife was a homemaker devoted to their children. The couple had been experiencing marital difficulties, and Rita had filed for divorce that previous October. However, she later withdrew the divorce petition just before the matter was set for trial. Family was important to both of them, and Rita and Monte saw this outing as a way to bring themselves and their family more closely together. They weren't worried about the ocean or the safety of their young children (ages three, six, seven, and eight), since Rita was a trained Red Cross senior lifesaver and had taught all of her children how to swim.

They arrived at the park late, and the family was unable to find the path above the beach that would take them to a nearby campground. As nightfall was approaching, they stopped the park ranger and asked if they could camp on the beach for that night. He gave his approval, provided they couldn't find anything else closer on higher ground. The McKenzies searched around, not finding anything above the beach, but they eventually discovered a cozy area below that opened to the sea. They found a makeshift, driftwood shelter on the beach, claimed it, and unpacked. After eating dinner outside, the McKenzies watched the peaceful waves lap onto the shore and enjoyed the serenity of their tranquil spot as their children played in the sand.

Soon, the ocean shimmered under the light of the warming full moon. It was a beautiful night, as the family nestled close together in their sleeping bags inside the shelter. They listened to the gentle waves lapping on the beach and soon fell asleep, unaware of what had happened in Alaska hours before. Meanwhile, the ranger continued going about his duties that night. When he received the tsunami warning, the ranger could not find where the family was sleeping.

The McKenzies' first recognition of danger was a dousing by the first wave that crested in. Rita McKenzie said later, "We were awakened shortly after eleven o'clock by a small wave. The water woke us up. We grabbed the kids. But then came huge waves, one after another—battering waves—nothing like ordinary tides. We were completely helpless. I had two of the kids by the hands, but I have no idea what happened. Nobody had a chance."

Monte McKenzie told his pastor later that the first wave swept over the children and that everyone began screaming. Then a second wave crested in, higher than the first. "There was only a foot of air at the top of the lean-to we were in and we had to struggle to get to that space. Logs were being thrown at us like matchsticks," he said.

Another large wave inundated the terrified family, and it swept away the two children that Rita had in her grasp. The salty mass of ocean water pummeled her into the sand and grit, and then pulled her back into the sea when the waters eddied away. She continually called for her children, but there was no answer. Rita was soon rolled back onto the beach by another tidal surge. Battered by logs and debris, she was knocked unconscious as the tides raced once more over land.

Meanwhile, Monte McKenzie was fighting for his life. He observed later, "The first thing I knew was that the roof was off the shelter. The next thing I remember was that I was standing on a bank and the wave had receded. My son was screaming about thirty or forty feet away from me. But before I could move, the next wave hit and I was pitched over a bank."

This surge carried McKenzie over the beach and slammed him against a cliff some distance away. He couldn't see anyone, and he couldn't hear any further cries for help. The force of the ocean pinned him against the cliff, but he was able to hold to the rocks when the waters began swirling away and down its sides. Monte finally was able to pull himself onto the rocks, then scramble up the cliff and look down. The moonlight silhouetted the grotesque shapes of logs, driftwood, and debris, now floating over a beach completely covered by the foaming ocean and surging sounds—but there was no sign of his family.

McKenzie ran for help to Highway 101 that passed close by the bluff. He tried to wave down passing motorists, but no one stopped for the frantically waving man. It was late at night and this was an emergency for everyone. Monte raced back to the park ranger's house and told him what had happened. The ranger quickly called the police. By now, the ocean had receded and left behind a litter of logs, driftwood, swollen lumber, and other flotsam.

Ever mindful of the thundering seas, the two men searched for some sign of the missing children and Rita McKenzie. They found none. The police quickly arrived and joined them in the search. Lincoln County Sheriff's deputies shortly thereafter discovered Rita's unconscious, severely injured body. She had been washed over four hundred yards (about a quarter of a mile) south of the campsite from where the family had been sleeping before so peacefully. The police sped her and her husband immediately to Pacific Community Hospital in Newport, Oregon, ten miles away to the south.

Their four children were still missing.

Nearby Newport sustained minimal damage, after the sea crested into Beverly Beach State Park. At the coastal town of Waldport fifteen miles south, however, the surge forced large logs across Highway 101 and severed any further travel over this vital artery. One car later smashed into a huge log, but the driver lived despite being injured and the car totaled. The sea demolished a boat service house and reduced an adjacent float to kindling, strewing the pieces over the bay.

Further south, the surges reached heights of twelve feet as they raced up the Suislaw River in Florence. The ocean battered trailers, felled power and telephone poles, and damaged boats. The first tidal responses were insignificant: the first high wave of eight feet didn't materialize until 12:25 A.M., and the largest at twelve feet didn't arrive until 1:22 A.M., according to the Coast Guard station's gauges at the river's mouth. The last surge washed out significant portions of the bulkhead at the marina, tore apart the boathouse, knocked over pilings, and twisted the loading ramp into an unrecognizable shape.

The tsunami raced up the Umpqua River at Reedsport, creating an eleven-foot wave at its height, and ripping two boats from their moorings. At nearby Coos Bay, the waves tore boats from their moorings, ripped out forty-foot floats, yanked away dock pilings, and sank a large charter boat by flipping it over and rolling it into the channel. The first wave cruised in at 11:40 P.M. and reached nine feet; subsequent waves were even higher. One group of people escaped injury when a man looked up and noticed the first wave building up. The people were able to run to higher ground just before the ocean swept over where they had just been.

Mrs. Leland Stanley was asleep in a panel truck parked on a Coos Bay beach parking lot. The tide picked up the vehicle with its sleeping passenger and carried it one hundred feet inland. The sea swept the truck over a picnic table where its wheels caught one edge. When the ocean receded, it left the vehicle with the front end deposited on the table's top and rear dug into the sand. The woman was unharmed, but her husband couldn't be found. The Coast

Guard searched for him throughout the night. They called off the search when he was finally located the next morning in Gold Beach. It turned out that the couple, who had driven from the San Francisco Bay area, had a bad argument that evening. He had stormed off into the night, leaving her in the vehicle. Both were fortunate that the stormy seas didn't catch them outside their truck.

Sixth-graders Rick Lillienthal, Rick Cardwell, and Floyd Stewart were camping at the beach by Rick Lillienthal's home near the Charleston Small Boat Basin in Coos Bay. The boys had played hard that evening, and each was sound asleep in his sleeping bag inside their tent. The night sky was clear, and the moonlight illuminated everything outside. Their black cocker spaniel, Feather, slept outside the tent.

Not yet one year old, Feather awoke when he sensed the tidal wave's approach. He began howling loudly, then ran inside the tent and continued barking at the sleeping boys. Feather nipped at the boys' feet and licked their faces. The tidal surge by now was nearly upon the unsuspecting boys and their dog. The dog's persistent antics finally awoke them, and they heard the roaring sounds of the rushing ocean becoming louder and louder.

They had just managed to scamper outside their tent when they spotted the mass of seawater barreling down on them, pummeling a ten-foot skiff in front. The big wash swept over the boys, but they were awake and able to catch their breath in time. The tide then swept over them, pounding the large skiff over their heads. The boys struggled under water as the churning currents thrashed them about. They were able to fight their way to the surface and stay on top of the moving sea. The ocean swell surged with them in its grasp and steamed over land.

When they spotted the first opportunity, the boys grabbed onto floating debris and held on until the first-wave action quieted down. The threesome quickly swam and waded through the ocean to higher ground before the waters swept back to rush in again with an even larger surge. They were completely soaked from head to toe when they finally returned to Lillienthal's home. Feather followed the boys into the house, his tail wagging and yelping excitedly. They had survived and Feather deserved a good part of the credit. One newspaper account carried the headline "Dog Senses Tidal Wave, Boys Saved."

By this time, the tidal waves were sweeping debris down the coast toward California. At Bandon, the surges broke a one-hundred-log boom apart and destroyed numerous other piles, as it did at other places. Although the tsunami swept numbers of these and other logs inland or onto the beach, it carried the rest down the coast to join the debris in transit. Succeeding waves carried this amalgamation of driftwood, lumber, large logs, furniture, cars, and other flotsam on their southward journey, and parts of this dangerous flotsam were hurled into Crescent City when the tsunami focused its attention there.

The first surge approached the town of Gold Beach sixty miles farther south at 11:43 P.M., when the ocean began noticeably withdrawing from the beach. This was about the same time when the tidal wave began withdrawing the sea to build up outside Crescent City, even though Gold Beach is a good ninety-minute drive away. Additional surges occurred at Gold Beach for three to four hours afterwards, tearing apart four hundred feet of the Rogue River Boat Service dock, destroying every piling, and scattering the pieces along the Rogue River. As the ocean ebbed and flowed in massive surges, boats tore loose from the dock and made wide circles around a large island in front of the broken landing. The wave actions destroyed boat ramps, docks, and sank or damaged twenty boats. This destruction included one jet boat, used for pleasure cruises up the Rogue River to Grants Pass (near Medford). Fortunately, the dwellings in this area were built well above the river on adjacent bluffs, so these wave movements didn't destroy homes.

A scant fifteen miles from Crescent City, Brookings experienced only minor flooding and very little damage. One of the ironies of tidal waves is that different coastal areas can be hit much harder than others, at different times, or not at all. This pattern can then reverse itself with a different tidal wave, as tsunamis are very capricious.

The water did rise to within a foot of its dock and other facilities. The south bank of the Chetco River overflowed to partially flood a field and cover the low end of the boat basin dike, but when the water receded, there was no damage. In the Winchuck River area, water pushed into three houses; however, the water level was only six inches inside the home closest to the sea.

More damage was averted when a coast guard cutter towed the large cargo barge *Chetco* out to sea before the tidal wave arrived. With a length of 215 feet and beam of 55 feet, the barge drew fifteen feet of water. It was towed back one week later, pushed into the dock stern first, and then loaded with one million board feet of lumber bound for Southern California. A similar, fully loaded barge with more than one million board feet of lumber was moored that Friday night to Citizen's Dock in Crescent City. A disaster was waiting to happen there—and it did.

Observers at Brookings reported that the water didn't flow there in a big wave, but just kept rising quickly up the sides of the dock. It stopped just below ground level at the port, and the stacks of lumber, residences, construction equipment, Coast Guard installation, and everything else on land escaped damage by the slim margin of twelve inches.

A few months later, the thirty-two-foot long salmon troller *Titan* struck an uncharted rock formation in the channel entrance to the Brookings port. The obstruction ripped two gaping holes through the craft, which quickly took on water. The Coast Guard, spectators on land, and another boat towed it to shallower water upriver and beached it. Divers later discovered that the tsunami's powerful undersea currents had moved the huge underwater rocks to their new, unanticipated location.

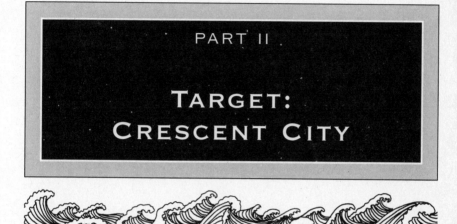

PART II

TARGET: CRESCENT CITY

4

The Crescent's Allure

CRESCENT CITY is located in Del Norte County, the northernmost county on the California coast. Consisting mainly of state and federal forest reserves, Del Norte County abuts Humboldt County to the south with its principal lumbering coastal town of Eureka. The Klamath River curves northwest through Humboldt County and flows into the ocean at the southern border of Del Norte County, passing the small river towns of Requa and Klamath.

Edging beside Del Norte Coast Redwoods Park and the Redwood National and State Parks, U.S. Highway 101 northbound cuts around Requa and Klamath and passes over mountainous cliffs that overlook the ocean on its twenty-mile path from those towns into Crescent City. The highway then plunges down from these dense mountain forest preserves into Enderts Beach and the beginning of what becomes the city. The towering redwoods of Jedediah Smith Redwoods State Park begin on that mountain range and continue northward to the Smith River, which empties into the ocean north of Crescent City. These forest reserves and mountains prohibit any access to inland California except for Highway 199, which winds its way through the forests, canyons, and mountains to inland Medford, Oregon. This is basically undeveloped and wild country—even today.

Crescent City's harbor and shoreline sweep in a crescent-circle to the west before rounding Point St. George. There are twelve miles of beach and harbor, protected by two breakwaters. In between the breakwaters were the Dutton and Sause piers to the west, privately owned by lumber companies, and Citizen's Dock to the east, with its over one hundred commercial and pleasure craft docked in a protected leeway.

Once down from the mountains, Highway 101 becomes a five-mile straight shot northward over near sea-level beaches into the business district of town. This thoroughfare is two to three blocks from the ocean with the first breakwater starting midway on the level run from Enderts Beach into the city. Curio shops, motels, restaurants, the Long Branch Tavern, a trailer park, gasoline service stations, and a Texaco Oil bulk transfer station were located on both sides of this straightaway. This initial area, called Highway 101 South, was inundated by the tidal waves to where the lands turn up to the mountains.

The business district of town starts where U.S. Highway 101 turns northwest up M Street and to the right, bordering a thirteen-block section of Crescent City that continued around the harbor and away from the warehouses, lumberyards, mills, and mixed residential/light business areas. From this point on, Highway 101 heads inland for a stretch, past the turnoff for Highway 199 and on to Brookings, Oregon, some twenty miles away.

A map of the city, included in the photo insert, indicates the areas that were flooded. The business and residential districts are laid out in a simple grid: the first street intersection where the harbor meets the Pacific Ocean is at A and First Streets. The street closest to the Harbor is First Street (or as aptly called, Front Street), then one block inland is Second, continuing this way to Ninth Street. The alphabet streets parallel each other and intersect the numerical streets. A Street is closest to the Pacific Ocean and the protective cliffs with M Street being where U.S. Highway 101 turns inland at First (or Front) Street. When driving northbound into town, the first major intersection is M and First Street; continuing up M Street, or even A, led to houses and buildings on higher levels of land.

From Front Street and its protective two-foot high seawall, a two- to three-block walk over sage brush, sand, and debris led to the Pacific Ocean. This swath of sandy land was wider farther west of town at Citizen's Dock and down toward Enderts Beach. In 1964,

Front Street was a charming, rustic, and frontier-looking conglomeration of one- and two-story wood curio shops, souvenirs and gift-stores, redwood carving shops, restaurants, bars, coffee shops, and service stations. It targeted the heavy tourist trade that would begin in two months. The businesses geared to the locals were concentrated from E through M streets with most residential housing located on the somewhat higher land located from A to D Streets at Third Street and going farther inland.

Once past the tourist area of First and Second Streets, the business district became a mixture of camera, drug, restaurant, cleaners, clothing, appliance, department, and other retail stores. Although commercial uses occupied much of First, Second, and Third Streets, residences and apartments were located throughout this area. Newer residential housing tracts were being built above Ninth Street. However, the land was still relatively undeveloped—except for a scattering of lumber yards, mills, and an industrial area—once inland from M Street towards Elk Creek.

Moving away from the ocean, the land gradually gains elevation. Thus, Fifth Street is higher than First or Front Street. However, the land tilts downward to sea level from the protective cliffs in front of the lighthouse and beginning alphabet streets of A and B Streets to the higher alphabet street intersections, starting from D Street to M.

Thus, the highest points of the central city are located at Fifth and A Streets, and the lowest from First and D Streets sweeping around the harbor to Citizen's Dock and Highway 101 south to the mountain pass. The higher land contours protected some sections of structures and people from worse impacts by the surges.

Completing the city's layout are Elk Creek and the Elk Creek bridge overpass. Roughly bisecting the town between the business district and the Highway 101 South area, Elk Creek sweeps from the south to the ocean under 101 at roughly First and M Streets.

THE 1964 sea wave hit Crescent City hard because it was in a direct line with the ocean approaches from the Alaskan earthquake's strike direction. The path of the tsunami was unimpeded by islands or peninsulas and became a direct shot into the harbor. The city is located in a primarily low-lying area, and rivers flow into the sea from above, its middle, and below the town—all with their magnetic pull for tsunamis. The shoal areas off Crescent City's coastline, such as the Cobb Seamount, contribute to the pull and buildup of wave heights, as well as the ability to redirect tidal waves into the bay.

As the tsunami sweeps more or less parallel to the coast, these shoal areas slow down that portion of the wave that passes over them. The part of the wave that is further offshore isn't impeded and turns inland to fill the gap left behind by the delayed wave. The two waves then can merge in a wave that is now headed towards shore—or in effect being pulled into the bay—with an increased intensity. The wave feels the bottom contours, surging through the underground canyons. Their energies focus into the rivers and bays, both of which low-lying Crescent City has in abundance.

Tsunami hazards vary widely between coastline places. For example, during a 1995 seismic wave runup in Mexico, the tidal waves hit two neighboring villages. At both locations, the maximum height of the surge was twelve-feet high. Although the towns were one mile apart, the damage inflicted was strikingly different. At Boca de Iguanas, houses were spun around and even stone walls were knocked from their foundation. At nearby La Manzanilla, the ocean simply rose slowly, flooded some portions, and receded as quietly with much less damage. One plausible explanation is that there's a river inet and a fifty-foot deep canyon in front of Boca de Iguanas, pointing straight at its heart—just like Crescent City.

Although all coastal towns and harbors are vulnerable to tsunamis and high-tide storm surges, Crescent City has a history of being unusually susceptible from both the north (Alaska) and south (the 1960 Chilean tidal wave), more so than any other West Coast community. This characteristic has been attributed in part to the effects of the Cobb Seamount, located four hundred miles to the northwest at its farthest point. This is a crescent-shaped embankment with its southern boundaries from northern Point St. George to Patrick's Point, located forty miles to the south of the harbor. This shallower underwater ridge has the apparent ability to redirect tsunamis there by its contours, and it vibrates when hit with this energy, reflecting the waters away then with even more power. Researchers credit the Cobb Seamount as a factor in focusing the 1964 tidal wave and causing it to approach the crescent-shaped bay from below it.

Experts also point to Crescent City's geographic anomalies of its underwater terrain, jutting shore points, and land-cutting rivers that create shallower areas offshore from deeper bottom levels, as well as a long gradual slope of the ocean floor that leads up to its harbor. With its crescent bay protruding away from the surrounding coastline and shallower waters miles offshore, tidal waves can slow down offshore of the city. Still moving faster than that point, the long sides of a tsunami actually wrap around these slowing areas, swinging towards the bay with one or both sides bent inward, concentrating energy towards that coast. The wave is pulled from below or south of the crescent and rides the long gradual slope of the ocean floor up into its harbor and adjacent areas. The tsunami then surges in from below the bay, even though the crescent faces a southerly direction. This is what happened in 1964—and the ocean then surged through the downtown area, up Elk Creek, curling southeasterly into the 101 Highway South area, which was also hit by waves coming in directly from the sea.

To an extent, every coastal town has a flooding problem, given high tide and heavy storm conditions. However, Crescent City experienced this flooding every few years, even when a particular storm wasn't necessarily that severe. As one resident observed, "Any time you had a heavy storm and tide, we had some flooding on Front Street." The city had had these problems from its founding. For example, a high tide in 1866 washed several buildings away from the beach, including part of a large brick warehouse.

The winter of 1861–62 was especially fierce with heavy rains and huge ocean waves. According to published accounts, water washed ashore at high tide as far inland as Second Street. The currents carried in huge logs, swept into Front Street buildings, and caused damage. The tide pushed driftwood forward, splintering the Crescent City Wharf, which the receding sea then carried away.

In 1882, the storm runup from an unusually heavy gale, according to the *Del Norte Record*, on a "most fearful" day tore six hundred feet off the seaward end of the rebuilt wharf, then owned by the Crescent City Wharf and Lumber Company. Lumber stacked on the deck floated out onto the bay. The damage to the wharf was especially severe, and the local economy suffered, since lumber couldn't be shipped out or goods received until the dock had been rebuilt. The local newspaper reported, "Rocks and logs and gravel were buried against the fronts of buildings, breaking in the doors and sometimes carried through to the yards at the rear. The water splashed up the inside of rooms and over the bars and counters therein."

The Smith River to the north experiences the same tide flows as does the Klamath River to the south. As to the Smith River and an especially fierce high tide and storm, the *Del North Record* observed in 1882, "A number of the boats used in salmon catching were carried away, the houses of employees of the cannery were floated out, the breakwater was destroyed, and various other losses sustained in the immediate vicinity of the fishery."

A similar high tide occurred in 1915 in Crescent City. Old black-and-white pictures memorialized the hundreds of logs and mounds of debris deposited in front of the stark, wooden buildings and structures crowding Front Street. The waterfront and ocean then came to the very edge of the street. To remedy this problem, the town built its two-foot seawall on the oceanside of Front Street, pushed the beach back over two blocks, and built up the area's height to a few feet over sea level to act as a natural barrier.

LOCAL INDIAN LORE in Crescent City relates that five hundred years ago the "sky became dark and the earth rocked to and fro like a cradle." Indians fled in all directions to their huts and to the protecting woods. After the earth stopped rocking, the Indians began to emerge from their hiding places. Then the sea swept up from the ocean, covering the entire valley but for a few of the highest places. Only a few natives survived, as the ocean carried everyone else away. Many residents, especially the settlers on the crescent-shaped bay, believe the legend to be true. As yet, however, there have been no geologic excavations to substantiate this story.

In the twentieth century, several notable earthquakes shook and tidal waves rose prior to 1964 to damage U.S. West Coast towns. The April 1, 1946, Alaskan earthquake with a 7.3 Richter magnitude occurred south of Unimak Island, creating another destructive worldwide tsunami that killed 159 people on the Hawaiian Islands (primarily in Hilo, Hawaii). The April Fool's Day tidal waves raced around the world, creating damage to boats and property in nearly every coastal community from Alaska down to the states of Washington, Oregon, and California.

A ten-foot-high wave surged into Coos Bay in Oregon and Half Moon Bay in Northern California, causing flooding but no reported injuries. A seventy-three-year-old man drowned when the ocean plowed into Santa Cruz, California. However, Crescent City experienced only minor flooding when a relatively small three-foot wave crested in, followed by smaller surges. This tidal wave caused little reported damage, no deaths, and no injuries in the town.

Crescent City residents later experienced run-ups of one foot from a 1946 Japanese earthquake and six inches from another such quake in 1952. Both of these caused extensive damage and deaths in Japanese coastal towns. Later in November 1952, a tidal wave of 7½ feet crested in from a quake off the Kuril Islands of the Soviet Union. This action caught fishing boats still tied to their moorings, sinking four vessels and capsizing another in Crescent City Harbor. An 8.3 earthquake in the Aleutian Islands on March 9, 1957, caused extensive damage in Hawaii, but it was barely noticed in Crescent City with a tidal surge of 1¼ feet.

A May 22, 1960, Chilean tidal wave, however, affected Crescent City and the Pacific Basin. Generated by an 8.6 earthquake off the coast of central Chile, these tidal waves cruised into the Aleutians and Alaskan waters. This tsunami caused no damage or fatalities in these waters, however, and the highest recorded wave was 5½ feet high at Massacre Bay in Alaska. As no local landslide or submarine earthquakes were involved as in 1964, Alaska was spared. The earthquake, however, generated waves that were murderous on the Chilean coast (drowning 1,500 people), the Hawaiian Islands (sixty-one fatalities), and Japan (nearly two hundred killed).

The tsunami raced northward across the Pacific Ocean, pummeling boats and harbors from the Baja Peninsula to Washington. It traveled fourteen hours across the Pacific Ocean to get to California, cresting into all of the state's coastal towns and causing damage from Crescent City and Santa Barbara to Los Angeles and San Diego. Los Angeles Harbor alone suffered in excess of one million dollars damage with forty boats sunk, and the harbor was closed for one day; San Diego experienced the destruction of barges, docks, and boats. Although the coastal towns of Washington were generally spared, the waves swamped boats and caused damage in Oregon coastal towns from Seaside to Newport and Gold Beach.

The first surge powered into Crescent City at 8:10 A.M. at an initial height of 8½ feet, which rose to eleven feet in forty minutes. Around noon, a thirteen-foot wave surged over the beachfront and up Elk Creek, causing flooding of two to three feet from Front to Third Street. The wave action sunk three fishing boats, including a fifty-foot trawler, and damaged others. The surging waters caused damage at the Dock Café, located just off Citizen's Dock, and deposited tons of logs and debris for two blocks up from Front Street. This action fortunately didn't kill anyone and injured only three people. City workmen quickly cleaned up, as the police re-routed traffic and kept order.

An 8.1 earthquake north of Japan in the Kuril Islands created a three-foot wave on October 12, 1963, just six months before the 1964 Good Friday tsunami. This resulted in heavy surges through the harbor but no major damage.

Past tidal waves had caused little extensive damage, few injuries, and rare deaths in U.S. coastal towns, including Crescent City, and false alarms have repeatedly occurred. In some instances, residents had evacuated the entire city, as on March 9, 1957, when the false-alarm scare of a fifty-foot wave traveling at five hundred miles per hour was reported. However, nothing happened or came in from the sea other than the one-foot "burp" of ocean. When the angry residents returned to their homes, they forced the resignation of the sheriff who had ordered the evacuation. And the tsunami of 1960, while not a false alarm, had incurred only minor damage and injuries. The city's residents remembered those experiences.

This time was different. Although Good Friday had turned into a beautiful moonlit night, the ocean at midnight would be at high tide, just when the first tidal waves were arriving in Northern California.

5

The Ride from Hell

FIFTEEN MILES SOUTH of Crescent City, U.S. Air Force Sergeants Stuart Harrington and Donald McClure were fishing during the night at the mouth of the Klamath River in California. A full moon sharpened their silhouettes, as weird shapes and shadows surrounded them. The two men stood on top of a high driftwood mound on an expansive sandbar that stretched for two hundred feet. The river's sparkling currents flowed gently around its defined edges to the sea, and then disappeared into the quiet waves lapping back into the debris.

Years before, a freak "perfect" storm had helped to form the sand spit. The ocean's thunderous waves carried tons of sand toward land, as the river surged from behind and kept this buildup packed into a low tight bank. The narrow sandbar then sloped quickly down into the Pacific Ocean. Carved out by centuries of crashing surf from the sea with cutting freshwater flowing from its back, the river's mouth was now nearly one-half mile wide. The channel was much wider where they fished, as the Klamath quickly narrowed behind the men eventually to a three-hundred-foot width. Further upstream, the river compressed even further.

Millenniums ago, the current's constant downward sweep had carved a deep canyon offshore into the ocean's floor, continually eroded by the strong underwater rivers. The tidal wave now rapidly approached this tranquil area, these deep cuts waiting like a magnet to pull it toward and up the land.

Speeding first through the 25,000-foot depths of the ocean at 550 miles per hour on its transcontinental run from Alaska, the tidal wave braked abruptly when the water levels became shallower. In deeper water, the tsunami had been indistinguishable from any other surface wave as countless ships steamed overhead.

This movement translated into the concentric series of waves that were rolling down the coastline in intervals and dragging at the ends of their two-hundred- to three-hundred-mile lengths. As the first wavelength tightened five to ten miles from the Klamath River's mouth, its height started to rise when the huge volume of mega-million tons of water scraped the relatively shallow bottom. The tsunami slowed down to ninety miles per hour when the ocean's depth narrowed to six hundred feet, its mass and energy pushing the surface up more. As the sea became shallower, the tidal wave's front kept slowing down, squeezing the moving mountains of water ever higher. The back of the tsunami, however, moved in oceans still over one thousand feet deep and kept barreling along at the much higher speeds.

This massive, surging energy bounced off underwater mountains and bent towards these submerged valleys. Feeling the shape of the canyon directly in front of it, the tidal wave funneled into the underwater channels and charged directly for the mouth of the Klamath River. Reaching north of Crescent City and south towards San Francisco, the rest of the sweeping wave searched for more deep canyons in the ocean's bottom that could pull it further inland.

At the same time, the tidal wave was drawn back toward the mouth of Crescent City's harbor. The offshore topography, bends, and contours of this shoreline, however, pulled the tsunami to strike these close-by areas sooner, even though they were south of the buildup now in progress just miles offshore from Crescent City. This condition was a variable of the ocean's depth, offshore canyons and islands, underwater terrain, and how far the tidal wave's energy had to bend at this particular location.

One mile out from the unsuspecting fishermen, the ocean already had increased to two feet above normal high tide. The tsunami sped towards the men at fifty miles per hour. In larger tsunamis, the crest of the wave can roll forward to form a turbulent wall of water, savagely pushed from behind by even higher waves. With tens of miles of seawater pushing from behind, the force of the surge is extremely powerful. This one was as well.

Both Stuart Harrington and Donald McClure were stationed with the U.S. Air Force's 777th Radar Squad in Requa, California. The military had constructed the Requa radar installation a few miles from where they now fished, high on the bluffs overlooking the Pacific Ocean by the river's mouth. Most of the servicemen and women lived in the city of Klamath, ten miles away from the base, as did these two. Both men had spent that evening with their families, then inspected their fishing gear and driven together over Highway 101 to the Klamath River exit. The asphalt turnoff eventually led into a dirt road that wound its way on the downward side of the river.

After parking the vehicle on a rim, the two men walked to the remote trail that led down to the river. The annual ritual of spring budding and flowering already had started. Wild flowers bloomed in vibrant colors during the day, but all were now muted in the night air. Their walk from high ground to the lower mouth of the Klamath would be long and arduous. The rugged countryside was thick with towering conifers of white and Douglas fir, ponderosa and sugar pine, mixed with an occasional broad-leaved black oak and chinquapin, the sloped clearings rocky with scrub brush of manzanita and bitter cherry. Closer to the water, red and thin-leaf alders, birch, aspen, and blackberry vines flourished.

The men had to be careful when walking down the narrow, winding path. Their footing became treacherous at times due to the path's sharp decline and loose sandy gravel. They stayed their course, looking forward to fishing and being in the wilderness again.

Once down on the shoreline, they waded in their hip boots through the currents to the sandbar. It wasn't long before fishing lines were in the water, and time flowed by easily. Don and Stuart enjoyed their time together, joking around and having time off. Both looked forward to this start of Easter weekend. They soon caught several eels, using an old lantern to cast down flickering light, while they unhooked their catch or baited hooks. Lines cast out, they waited patiently for more action, as the ocean rippled gently against their driftwood fort.

The time approached midnight. Bantering back and forth, they didn't pay attention to the slight hissing sound slowly building up that heralded the tidal wave's initial approach. They were out in the ocean's throat late at night, and the unusual sounds of nature blend with the usual in a primeval sort of way. Suddenly, a loud crash that sounded "like a cannon shot" cracked through the night air.

Jerking their heads toward the sound, they froze at the sight of the twelve-foot wall of water bearing down on them in the moonlight. It then stood poised overhead, as if a film had stopped midshow. The bulging wave's white crest held captive huge logs and driftwood that protruded from it like a crown of thorns. The solid mound they stood on was thrust upwards, as they stared with mouths gaping at the tons of debris that now swept overhead.

The churning ocean crashed over the two men, as the wave pounded into them and up the river. The rampaging currents buffeted their bodies, twisting them savagely sideways, head over heels. They reached instinctively for anything to grab onto, desperately trying to work their way back to the surface.

Arms and legs thrashing about, Stuart Harrington fought his way through the washing-machine actions of the tidal wave and kicked toward the ocean's surface. Although he strove mightily and grabbed for anything with which to pull himself up, Stuart stayed weighted down. He couldn't get to the surface. The filtered moonlight above gave him a murky glimpse of large overhead objects in the raging waters. They barred his way to gulps of precious air. Still struggling upwards, Stuart grabbed at a massive log as the currents smacked his head against it. The collision stunned him momentarily, but he didn't hurt from the inpact.

He clawed his way around the large log. Grabbing a thick underwater branch, he propelled himself to the surface, gasping for air and coughing up brackish water. His lungs hurt, then the pain disappeared. Stuart searched through the frothing saltwater for his friend, but couldn't find him. Caught in the white-capped surge of ocean rushing upstream over the river's opposite flow, Harrington found himself surrounded by debris and grotesque shapes. He then spotted Don McClure ten feet away, illuminated by the strong moonlight over the shadows. McClure was clutching another large log in the swollen currents.

"Are you all right?" he heard Don yell. "Get your hip boots off, grab a log, and ride with the waves." Damn! He had forgotten about his hip boots. No wonder it was so hard to stay afloat, his mind raced. Harrington grabbed a small log under each arm for buoyancy. Even weighted down as he was, Stuart didn't want to try and work the boots off. He didn't want to let go of the precious logs that kept his head somewhat above the surging sea.

Currents pushed over currents, and driftwood and logs continually veered toward the men to pummel them. This was logging country, and it was expected to find some in the rivers. The amount of this debris, however, was much greater than either had ever seen. They didn't know that the tsunami had already smashed into coastal logging camps as far away as Washington. The massive ocean movement was carrying this and other trophy wreckage down as it swept south towards Southern California and struck at land. The tidal wave hurtled the refuse and two men up the river at over thirty miles per hour. It was a ride from the very depths of Hell.

In a panic, Stuart knew that he had to get his hip boots off. Filled with seawater, their weight dragged his head down into the currents even while holding onto the logs. Frantically, he tried to strip them away. He locked an arm over one log, then unsuccessfully ripped at his waders with the other. When he let go of one to reach for the bootstraps tied to his belt, the lifesaving log under his other arm slipped away. Stuart's heavy jacket and clothing pulled him straight down under the water. He fought his way again to the surface and grabbed at more debris. Getting out of the soggy, heavy-leaded weights of boots and clothing seemed impossible in the fast-moving, bucking water. This was a life or death problem, and he knew it.

Fate seemed to intervene, however, just before he went down for what "was getting close to being my last time." After two or three tries at ripping away the dragging weights, the waders slid off his legs without further effort. They had ripped from his belt, dragged down by their own heavy bulk and the strong currents. Meanwhile, the churning sea continued racing upriver, leaving behind gray images of the riverbank, surrounding hills, and towering conifers.

A short time later, the currents carried both men by a monstrously large log. Its stark outline clearly visible, the object was six feet wide and over forty feet long. "Would we be better off on the log?" Stuart yelled over the current's raging sounds.

"Yes!" McClure shouted back.

Both men kicked towards the log, but it was difficult to make headway. Swimming against swirling currents while wearing heavy, soaked clothing is an incredibly difficult feat, even when knowing that failure means certain death. By their frantic movements, the two eventually reached their target. Don McClure got there first. Grabbing a broken limb, he kicked with his legs and scrambled up the log's sides. McClure motioned for Stuart to come closer.

Legs bicycling through the sandy seawater, Harrington made little progress against the churning, debris filled water. His waterlogged clothing dragged him under the ocean once more, and Stuart gagged more from gulping in the salty, suffocating sea. He reached again for the log and tried to pull himself up. Harrington desperately raked at the log's sides with numbed fingers, clawing at its bark for a grip. The harder he tried to climb up, the weaker he became.

Stuart started to slip slowly underneath the currents. He was giving up. Looking up, he stared as McClure raced down the floating log and grabbed at his hand. Stuart's head now was completely underwater. He felt one arm jerked up, as his neck pulled out of the water. McClure tugged mightily up again with near superhuman strength and yanked him over the log's sides.

Harrington fell gasping on his stomach, his body spread-eagled over the tree trunk with arms outstretched. As Stuart straddled the felled tree, he realized that he had no feeling in his hands or feet. His limbs were completely numb from the cold seawater, the night air, and the pounding by debris.

Stuart sensed next that the water seemed to have stopped flowing. That was odd, he thought. It was as if they were now floating off the coast in a fishing boat on easy ocean swells. As he looked around from the safety of his perch, Harrington realized the ocean had completely stopped moving.

In his panicked attempts to get on the log, he hadn't picked up that the sea had stopped rushing inland. Before the two men could decide what next to do, however, a noticeable surge of rushing seawater caught them once more from behind. Their necks snapped back, and the acceleration nearly threw both back into the ocean. The log and its accompanying mass of floating rubble and driftwood shot back up the river in a second wave thrust.

Their log punched up and around the various curves and bends of the Klamath River. After several minutes of this travel, the log, its passengers, and the floating jetsam then began slowing down again. Harrington estimated they had traveled another two hundred yards or so with the second wave surge.

The moonlight painted a strange white-streaked pale over the surrounding hillsides and overhead mountains. It outlined the bobbing log with its grim occupants, as well as a strange clutter of discernible and indiscernible shapes that bounced about. The movement seemed to lessen, then finally stop. The sea gently lapped at the obstacles trapped inside its grasp, just as it did at the river's mouth. Stuart was stunned when he realized where they were. The tidal wave had pushed them two miles inland from their fishing spot.

The two men began shouting for help, but they heard only their pleas echo back. As they listened in the night's stillness, there were no other sounds than that of objects slapping up and down. They watched the surrounding waters silently become smooth and flat. There were then no ripples, no sounds, nothing.

The men started yelling again whether anybody was out there. The shouts and silent answers alternated. Shortly, they heard a voice bounce back, "We hear you. . . . Where are you?"

Stuart and Don shouted where they thought they were. The voices from somewhere seemingly onshore yelled, "Hang on, we're coming." The sound of these voices reassured Stuart. Help was on its way, and the water was calm enough for them to paddle from one log to another. The Klamath River was some one hundred feet wide at this point, narrower than it had been before.

As they searched for a route to shore, the men noticed the surrounding driftwood began again to thrash about. The smaller objects started bobbing and dancing in the ocean in crazy ways. Larger branches and wood objects now randomly circled around their log. Harrington next felt their log move slightly backwards, back towards the Pacific Ocean.

"The wave has crested," McClure yelled down. "It's going back out to sea. We'll have to swim for it." He quickly ripped off his jacket and shirt, and then waited for Harrington to do the same. However, Stuart couldn't get his off. Raking at it with numbed and bloodied hands, the sticky jacket stayed in place. He tore at the zipper, but couldn't get it to work. The zipper instead ripped into sections. Stuart stared down incomprehensibly at his jacket.

"I can't get it off," he finally shouted. "I can't do it. My hands . . ."

McClure edged his way down quickly from the other side. He grabbed the jacket and ripped it off Stuart's back. McClure next seized Harrington's shirt with both hands, tearing the buttons off with a fast pull in two different directions, then yanked that off his back. Don darted back to the other end.

"Don't go till the log starts to go downstream," he warned. "We're getting closer to shore!"

The receding currents angled the log closer towards the river's right-hand side or its northern bank. Stuart watched the shadowy shapes of the overhanging trees and limbs by the banks. They began to pass faster. The huge log picked up speed, as the torrent accelerated everything back to the ocean. They soon were heading down the Klamath River at thirty-five miles per hour, faster than they had been thrown inland. The underlying currents now flowed in the direction of the tidal surge. Stuart shook his head, not believing this turn of events. He felt a surge of fear.

"Can you make it all right?" McClure shouted.

"I'll try," he answered back.

"Don't dive in," McClure warned. "Save your strength."

Both men slid back into the cold, salty water, leaving what once had been their shelter of safety. They swam together towards the shoreline. Don swam about twenty feet from Stuart, as the fast-moving currents made the two work harder this time to angle against the currents towards shore.

The waters tossed and turned the debris, as the mess accelerated back to the ocean. They had survived the massive wave first cresting over them, the pummeling underneath the bore, and then the second ripping surge, only to be caught in as bad a situation as ever. The ocean seemed determined not to be denied.

Dead tired, arms and feet moving with little energy or motion left, the two men pushed themselves beyond their limits. Hypothermia and the beating they already received had exacted their toll. Harrington plodded with excruciating effort slowly through the waves towards the cliffs, about midway from where the tsunami had stopped to turn back. Realizing he was closer to shore, Stuart turned around and asked roughly if McClure was "all right."

"I'm coming," Harrington heard his friend reply. Stuart didn't know whether Don was staying back to ensure that he safely found land, or was as spent and worn out as he was. With that in mind, he mentally pushed onward, not knowing what his arms and legs were really doing. Sheer instinct drove him forward.

Shortly, Harrington was about ten feet from a soaring cliff and just below what he knew to be the Requa boat docks. Stuart realized he had to keep going; he was at the mouth of the river and the ocean. He couldn't give up this close, as the alternative was to be swept out to sea and a certain death. Still angling against the current, he labored ahead. One hand hit a boulder, and the current swept him into a huge rock. The swift currents swept his body around, as his feet slid off more slippery rocks. Stuart grabbed in desperation with both arms and clung to the large rock. He tried, but couldn't stand upright in the shallow, rushing water.

Harrington could tell that he was close to land. He felt a surge of fear at the thought he was so close, but might not make it. Thick with large objects and a frothing ocean, the river seemed to flow by even faster. Stuart tried to steady his spent body against the rock, as he peered into the water for his friend. He saw no one. He became annoyed with himself at the now constant retching of saltwater spewing from his throat and lungs.

Stuart called out, but Don didn't answer back. He yelled out as strong as he could again, but only heard the rush of the sea going by him in answer. He didn't feel cold, as hypothermia was already shutting down his body, and he clung desperately to his perilous perch.

6

A Sea of Destruction

THE TSUNAMI crested up the Smith River when it surged over the Oregon border into California just above Crescent City. Joe Sierka of Ship Ashore had a hard time trying to save his dock when the bore hit it. The series of waves washed the dock to the river's mouth, then back beyond its original pilings when the ocean receded. Joe and others finally chained the dock to the shore, but thirty pilings had completely washed away.

The California Highway Patrol, Coast Guard and Sheriff's Office deputies were busy warning people in Crescent City when the first wave arrived just before midnight, catching the high tide at its zenith. The first rise exceeded the tidal gauge, as did the third and fourth waves, and it measured out at fourteen feet above MLLW (mean lower low water), or about nine feet over low tide. As the high tide was then five feet over the MLLW measure, the first wave was fourteen feet over normal low tide levels.

The first ocean surge easily mounted the two-foot high seawall between the beach and Front Street, flooding the lower parts of town at Front Street. Just before midnight, Gary Clawson, Joanie Fields, Jim Burris, and other friends were enjoying themselves down at the Tides on Front Street. A ground-floor-level, bricked bar and restaurant/coffee shop, the Tides was located on I street—about midway in the downtown section—between Front and Second Street, or about three blocks from where the ocean met the beach.

Gary's group was singing as he played the guitar. A six-foot tall, handsome man with a hawk nose and piercing blue eyes, Gary had always wanted to play the guitar professionally but felt he wasn't good enough. Most thought he was. He also was a very good businessman even from the start, creating his first business when he was eighteen years old. This business, Clawson Distributing Company, bought Mother's Cookies, Bluebell Potato Chips, and Dolly Madison pastries from Oakland, California, distributors, then sold the products to supermarkets and retailers in Del Norte County. While doing this, he decided that owning his own grocery stores would give him an extra part of the markup. One year later, he opened his first grocery store in 1956, selling that one when he got divorced in 1960.

Clawson then sold life, health, and accident insurance for one-and-a-half years, before deciding that he wanted to get his dad out of the forest. By then, he had bought another grocery store, calling it "Gary's Grocery." As Gary's father was a "timber faller," a logger, a fifty-four-year-old man who kept coming home "hurt all the time," Gary told him, "Let's do a little bar." His father didn't need any further encouragement, since he wanted the change and was also a "two-fisted" drinker, according to his son. Gary then brought him in as a partner (along with a relative, Amos Brown or "Brownie") in the Long Branch Tavern on Highway 101 South.

Others had joined in the sing-along, when a sheriff's deputy suddenly burst through the doors and yelled, "A tidal wave's coming." Everyone piled out of the Tides, onto the street and initial darkness, only to run into rivulets of seawater. Followed by the others, Gary stepped down toward Front Street, through running seawater that covered his ankles.

Illuminated by the overhead streetlights and interior lighting of several closed shops, people watched dumbfoundedly as the "greenish-looking" first wave kept flowing over the seawall into the city, pushing logs and debris along. The ocean rose rapidly with smaller waves seemingly riding on top of the crest. Saltwater quickly covered Front Street and logs now blocked traffic. Since the height of the town increased towards the cliffs on the western side, the run-up was uneven with "fingers" of flooding past Second Street.

Staring at the scene almost clinically, Gary viewed this with little emotion, appraising the cut redwood logs that slowly drifted past, the sea now about one foot high. A few people stared down at the sea, then hopped up towards higher ground to get away from the wetness. Most didn't. The ocean was acting up again, and people around this area had become used to that.

Clawson, however, wondered what had happened to his small bar, the Long Branch Tavern, which he and his parents owned south of the downtown section and about as close to the beach as they were now. This was his and his father's night off, and Earl and Nita Edwards were in charge tonight. Understanding the sea and its fickle currents from his diving experiences, Gary knew that different parts of the city would be affected differently by the ocean's flows.

He decided first to tell his parents, Bill and Gay Clawson, about the flooding at Front Street and see what they wanted to do. Since it was late, Gary was sure that they would be home now, not still celebrating at the Long Branch Tavern. He and Joanie drove to their house, located on higher ground and away from the city. Jim Burris headed off to be with his friend, Juanita Wright, who lived by the beach in the Highway 101 South area.

Mac McGuire heard about the tidal wave on television, but like many others, this didn't mean that much to him. Listening to a tidal wave warning doesn't really register unless you've seen a serious one. After the first wave came and went, he drove down to the dock to check on his boat. Although its battery was dead and couldn't get to sea, he just wanted to see how it had fared.

Once down by the dock, Mac found that he couldn't get near his boat. The sea already was two feet over the dock, and the forklifts, loose lumber, and logs "were dancing on top of the ocean." However, McGuire just didn't feel right as he watched the waters dance. Since he was still "smoking real good," McGuire decided to buy some cigarettes. He walked back to his old 1940 Ford pickup, driftwood piled high in the back, waiting for Mac to carve it into small wooden animals and fish that he'd sell to the tourists. He drove south down Highway 101 to the Long Branch Tavern.

When the first wave action brought seawater near knee-deep to their trailer, Bill Whippo and LaVelle Torgenson in the Highway 101 South area considered leaving for higher ground. Although their trailer was on the ocean side of Highway 101 and opposite the Long Branch Tavern, they and others unfortunately would change their minds.

Bob Ames, Jr., was then watching television when he heard the news about the tidal wave, and his sons were still out on the town. Ernie Pyke was at home, while his twin sons were also still out. After hearing the news, both men decided to drive downtown to their respective businesses and see what had happened.

Other residents were still asleep. Adolph Arrigoni, James Parks, and Mrs. Mabel Martin were asleep in their beds, totally unaware of the tsunami or the shouts of police from the streets, who didn't know who was home or not. Mrs. Clara McIndoe was listening to the radio in her home at 636 Second Street, unaware yet of any flooding.

Roy Magnuson and his wife, Marilyn, were driving closer to Crescent City and at this time were about one hour's drive from town. Joyce London, who lived behind the Del Norte Ice Company in the Highway 101 South area, was at home with her husband. Mrs. Macy Franco and her two small children were sitting uneasily in their trailer in the Gypsy Court a few blocks down. Tired from their nonstop drive from Los Angeles to Crescent City, Joseph and Eleanor McKay had eaten dinner and were already asleep at the Surfside Motel.

Even as the first wave began subsiding, the second one started building up. The second major rise was three feet smaller than the first and started about 12:15 A.M. At eleven feet over the low-tide line, this tidal surge flooded beachfront motels and parts of the downtown city, littering the area with more debris, logs, merchandise, lumber, and now floating cars. Observers reported that the waves again surged in "with smaller waves again riding on top of each crest." Then it receded.

Thankfully, the first two waves weren't fatal ones. Although the surges caused flood damage—in fact, more than any other previous tidal waves had done—there were no reports of deaths or injuries from them in Crescent City. The first flooding reached from the Pacific Ocean to past Second Street. Aside from leaving debris scattered on the streets, the first wave caused only limited damage. This allowed the Crescent City police and county Sheriff's Office deputies time to move in, start sealing off the area, and begin moving people out. When the second surge was smaller than the first, many people concluded that the real danger from this one had passed.

The first wave actions, however, did cause some damage and closed down one of the town's two radio stations. Bill Stamps operated radio station KPOD from a building on Second Street. A friend telephoned him at 11:30 P.M. at home with the news about the tidal wave, just as it was starting to build outside the harbor. As his son was then camping by the beach in a driftwood shelter, Bill ran down there and quickly got him back home. He then drove over to his station and began operating. He was soon cut off the air when the ocean's movements damaged lower portions of the building, severing the ground electrical cables, and cutting off the structure's electricity at 12:35 A.M. With station KPOD unable to operate, Bill grabbed the cash and books from his office in the dark and walked to higher ground.

A *Triplicate* newsman reported that one foot of water had collected in numbers of buildings and offices after the first two waves. The ocean pushed several cars crazily around on Front Street, but they were still upright. Water was running across the approach to the dock, but the timber pilings now were leaning in different directions. Citizen's Dock was in a shambles, as the surge had been highest there. According to one observer, it looked like "the Pacific had come in, picked up the buildings, debris, and water, then put them in a huge dice cup, shook everything up well, and deposited it all willy-nilly." The reporter covering the story passed several of the pubs in which the "people were still sitting, laughing, and talking with the juke boxes blaring."

Having been alerted by television, radio, and friends, and believing that the worst was over—as had been the case in the past—merchants and sightseers converged onto the area. To prevent looting and sightseers from getting in the way, the police completely sealed off the low-lying areas, but allowed local businessmen and residents to pass.

One account written later by Helen Williams indicated how the first waves failed to greatly alarm numerous people:

Our family was one of the group of sightseers, because one daughter heard a news bulletin on the television and awakened us. As was our custom, we piled into our car, not bothering to change from our nightclothes, and set out to see how high the water had come.

We drove down Pebble Beach Drive (the street closest to the protecting cliffs and A Street), noting that the ocean water lay curiously still, but very high against the bluffs on the side of the road. [*Note*: These bluffs are thirty to forty feet high and protect the city from tidal surges coming from this direction. The waves surged through the bay below the bluffs and into the city's middle.]

We drove down A Street in front of Seaside Hospital and onto Front Street. A few puddles lay on the street and the gutters had water, while some small driftwood was scattered about. We waved to a National Guardsman standing near the Surf Hotel on H and Front Streets, but we decided to return home and to our beds.

Little did we know that another wave already had been heading into the harbor area. This wave did little more damage, but the third and fourth swept into the city with terrific violence, tearing up buildings, carrying them to other areas, knocking down power poles, and floating hundreds of cars about as though they were corks. The familiar driftwood rode in the water and battered every obstruction as it entered town.

One half-hour after the second wave receded, the larger third wave moved through town around 1:00 A.M., just as people were cleaning up. Estimated at sixteen feet above MLLW (average low tide level), its height was clearly higher than the first two and surged easily over the four-foot parking meters on Second Street, which was a long four blocks from the ocean.

This ocean thrust rushed over the outer breakwater barrier by Seaside Hospital and the sand-and-rock breakwater to the south, which was designed to protect Citizen's Dock. Its currents swept between the two barriers with even more strength, then steamed up

Elk Creek and spilled over land. This spillage surged in a quite surprisingly near-complete circle to head in the opposite direction between the barrier and Citizen's Dock, then rage against the fishing fleet moored in those supposedly "protected" waters.

The tsunami cut power lines, knocked down telephone poles, and pushed two miles inland before eddying to sweep southward to the sea. Its surges trapped people inside their homes and businesses. Cars with people still inside danced around like toys, and fires erupted at gasoline stations and a bulk-oil plant in the Highway 101 South area. The ocean raged over the land, racing up and over Elk Creek, and joined with more flows from the sea in various cross-currents. The sea moved deepest in its thrusts up that waterway, nearing 2½ miles inland at its greatest penetration.

These major surges were not just high waves that swelled through a bay. They were huge, stepped-up jumps in the ocean's level that crashed in, limited only by the geography of low-lying areas. Later, experts would classify the wave actions as tidal bores: a "terrifying mass of water that rises up and comes in like the churning waters from a broken dam," as one reported. The ocean flooded a twelve-mile long area of the city with all four surges, pummeling nearly two miles inland with the last wave—and these waters were deep. Over one mile inland, the fourth wave and its mass were well over a man's head, at times more than fifteen feet in the low depressions closer towards the beach.

Breakwaters, docks, city, and land were completely covered by the ocean. A boat could have motored over the ocean from that far inland and cruised straight to Hawaii or Japan. The sea would recede with tremendous force and drain everything away, only to return again with more force and accumulated debris. Only the higher hills to the north and northwest protected parts of the city.

A building on Citizen's Dock enclosed an automatic tide gauge that indicated these violent tidal flows. The gauge recorded fluctuations on drums of graph paper, including the first tidal-wave bore, the second, and then the third. The first time recorded by the tide sheet was 12:42 P.M., just after noon that day when the tide was falling. The tide reached its ebb and quickly climbed back up in height when the first of four waves began to surge past the tide gauge at 11:39 P.M., or eleven hours later, at high tide.

Even though the first wave caused limited damage, this one exceeded the gauge's limits and caused a flat line at the graph's top. Similarly, the water level again exceeded the limits with the third wave, as all of the recorded "tide" changes peaked and subsided quickly. The fourth and largest wave arrived at approximately 1:40 A.M., but its duration could never be determined. When it surged over the gauge building, the tide record became badly torn, waterlogged, and barely legible—because this wave destroyed the building. Scientists later reconstructed the tide-gauge record by supplementing it with hand leveling of high-water marks and interviews with residents.

This fourth great surge was a "black mass," estimated to be twenty-one feet high when it crashed up Elk Creek after surging well over the breakwater barriers. The ocean swept along huge mountains of debris with more cars, trucks, huge logs, and splintered houses that became battering rams against what remained of the city's interior. After the third surge had receded, some people were able to get to higher ground before this one arose. Others didn't. Fires raged in the night from ruptured oil tanks and gasoline stations, shorted electrical wires quickly sparking the flammable liquids into towering flames and making this into a true inferno.

The flows arrived in two ways: direct ocean thrusts between and over the breakwaters, including directly over 101 South, and the tidal surges up Elk Creek that leapt over each bank and then backwashed to flood an additional thirty-two square-block area. In total, the ocean inundated over fifty-nine square blocks of the town. (See the inundation map in the photo insert for the details.)

Elk Creek was a magnet for the tsunami, as tidal bores roared up and down that channel several times, spilling over its banks, then surging back over the heart of town. These back-and-forth ocean torrents hit people from all different directions—after midnight on a cold spring night—including one strong flow that curved south behind Highway 101 for several miles before eventually heading back out to sea.

Carrying tons and tons of debris, currents eddied in different but distinct paths throughout the city and area, until hitting high land or mountains and eventually curling around to steam back to the sea. Due to their higher inland location at the eastern end of town past Fifth Street, the McNamara and Peepe Lumber Company and Hamilton Brothers Mill became two different "elephant's graveyards" for cars, houses, boats, and all types of flotsam.

As the topography of Crescent City is uneven—slowly becoming higher as you walk inland, but with a gentle westerly sloping up towards Seaside Hospital and the bluff's side—the inundation area was also uneven. Even though at Fifth Street, there is a nearly one-hundred-foot decline down to the beach area, the tidal waves surged up those inclines to Fifth Street with six-foot depths being the norm at Third Street. The inundation line undulated from west to east, depending on the topography, but clearly doubled inland at the mid-section of the city where Elk Creek ran to the sea.

The fates played with people's lives, as the tsunami surged back and forth. One businessman slept through a friend's continual telephoning; otherwise, he would have been downtown cleaning up when the fourth wave hit. A woman went to warn her girlfriend about the tsunami, but she was instead caught by the surge. One young man now realized how lucky he had been when he had fought with his girlfriend. They were down at the beach and left before the seas rose.

THE FIRST WAVE caught the police authorities and U.S. Coast Guard by surprise, before they could warn most of the people about what was coming. Even then, residents still slept through warnings with their radios and televisions turned off. It's easier, of course, to see people and warn them during the day. According to Bill Parker, "The warnings spread like wildfire by word of mouth during the day."

The first surge helped the authorities, but put another problem in motion. When people saw that the oceans were rising and coming on land, some decided that it was time to leave. But when the second wave crested in smaller, it motivated others to return who then were caught by the larger, final waves. As one major inundation section involved the downtown businesses, various owners were at home outside this area and didn't experience the first dousing. Thinking that these ocean actions were the last, they came down to clean up and were caught by the next one.

The nighttime also turned out to be a blessing and a curse. At night, the downtown area clearly had fewer people outside. However, it's more difficult to survive then when people can't see as well as they can during the day. Regardless of the conditions, Del Norte County's civil defense plan seemed adequate, but it couldn't be fully implemented.

Bill Parker's concern was that the people in Crescent City had endured false alarms before over past tsunami warnings. In fact, the residents forced one local Chief of Police to resign in 1957 due to a false alarm that came in the middle of the night. Another problem was that "people are people." Regardless of what tidal-wave warnings are made, they'll still go about their lives, risking them for any number of reasons, regardless of what evacuation orders are in place. When deputies warned people to leave, some just didn't. You couldn't arrest them, unless martial law had been declared, and even then this wasn't a real alternative. As Parker said, "You're trying to warn people and get them out of the area, not waste precious time arresting, transporting, booking, and confining them in jail."

Regardless of the warnings or how they're being enforced, people are usually asleep in the middle of the night. Even when awake, some wouldn't get up to answer the strange knocks at their door. There is a natural reluctance to letting a stranger into your house in the night. Even during the daytime, Parker's experience was that people would stay glued to their television sets and ignore the door knocks or doorbell ringing. Some don't take tsunamis seriously enough, no matter what the authorities say, while others become curious, again don't listen, and drive into the area. Tidal waves then hit suddenly with full force and as quickly are gone.

People also don't like to be inconvenienced. One asphalt contractor became angry during a previous tsunami warning, because the authorities wouldn't let him into the area with his load of blacktop. He immediately stormed over to the disaster headquarters and located Bill Parker. The man was so angry that Parker finally wrote up a statement that warned him about the dangers and that any entry would be totally against the city's advice. The man signed it, but at the last moment decided not to go into the quarantined area. Since the asphalt couldn't be used when it cooled down and hardened, the contractor never let Parker forget about that lost load of blacktop.

"We couldn't even spell tsunami at first, let alone know what one was really about when I first took on the job," said Bill. "And we didn't know how to convert Zulu time (the Greenwich Mean Time used as a time standard) to our conventional time. When we first had a tidal wave warning in 1953, my office tracked me down and said that they had received a 'tsunami' warning. No one then knew what this term meant or what to do about it."

That first time, Bill Parker called up the state and federal-level disaster offices, and their response basically was that "a tsunami wasn't part of the emergency plan." Finally, one office directed him to a U.S. Navy office in Oakland. He called them up and asked about the tsunami warning. The man told him to "wait a minute." Bill could hear the man apparently rifling through some papers. The Navy officer soon was back on the telephone line and said, "You must be all right. The tidal wave passed through your area ten minutes ago."

Afterwards, the overall emergency plans and procedures became better. Bill Parker's crew was prepared, but the residents, waves, and their timing didn't cooperate. When the Governor's office first called him up to ask what was going on, the first two waves had just come and gone with minor flooding. Everyone thought that was the end of the matter, as had always been the case. He told them that there had been only minor flooding and "that was it."

The time delays, however, and intensity between the initial and final waves had been a mixed blessing. Although the delays fooled people into thinking that everything was over and they could start cleaning up, the fatalities would have been considerably higher had the first wave been as powerful and high as the last one. When the first waves came onto land, police were able to move in, survey the damage, and deal with sightseers and possible looters; they also began moving the public out immediately when they saw the second wave building up. They finished the job after the second, smaller wave pushed through.

Thus, by the time of the fourth "great" wave, County Sheriff O. E. Hovgaard, his men, and the other authorities had been able to warn nearly all of the people and close off the entire waterfront district. They had sealed off a two-and-a-half block by eleven-block area within the city, which basically covered the area between the breakwaters on both ends of town, then up Front Street and past Third Street. This "quarantined area" further extended half a mile south along Highway 101.

Remembering that past tsunamis resulted in simple flooding, however, the Sheriff's deputies, CHP, and police volunteers allowed residents and businesspeople back into the area. At times, other residents simply ignored the roadblocks and drove past the startled or preoccupied authorities.

It was difficult for even the authorities and disaster officers to believe that something could really be that dangerous. Nothing else seemed to be happening any place else on the coast. At least, they hadn't received that word. The officials wondered out loud, "Why would this happen in just this one small section of the coast?" Others wondered the same thing.

A deputy sheriff at one roadblock at the Elk Valley Road detour said: "We couldn't get the people to move out. We tried to evacuate the entire area, and people just sat there. Some even said we'd moved them out twice before and nothing had happened then. Some thought we were calling 'wolf' too often. I don't know how many lives were lost or people injured because our evacuation was ineffective due to this disbelief."

When the areas were blocked off, most people didn't know what had happened, and everything appeared normal. During and after the fourth wave's arrival, the deputies were busy escaping themselves or trying to rescue others. Simply surviving became the rule. Police Officer Johann Jochimsen wrote: "After the second wave hit, we all thought that it was over. I was inspecting the damage when I got caught downtown by another wave. I scrambled onto the roof of the Thunderbird Motel, but not before getting soaked to the skin. I had plenty of company. Twenty-five to thirty people from the motel also climbed up on the roof. We watched cars float up L Street, their horns blaring."

The authorities were also handicapped by not being able to contact their personnel or issue warnings, since the tsunami had already severed the primary telephone cables into the area. Although neither of the city's commercial radio stations was on the air when the largest waves hit, one station later returned. The first surges forced Bill Stamps of KPOD from his radio station at the harbor and damaged the building. Radio station KPLY, owned by Virginia and Mason Deaver and located outside the affected area, was able to continue broadcasting. However, KPLY and large portions of the town soon lost their telephone connections.

As the police, deputies, highway patrolmen, firemen, and U.S. Coast Guard personnel worked in these confusing circumstances, ordinary citizens were out and about that late night.

GARY CLAWSON stepped away from his car and scanned the grounds in front of the Long Branch Tavern. The area was soaking wet, like Highway 101 directly in front, with small driftwood and flotsam scattered about crazily. A sprinkling of sand shimmered under the light of the moon. The parking lot and surrounding scrub brush looked no different than if a heavy dose of winter rain had fallen, but the air smelled strikingly salty. He knew that smell, especially from where he stood, but this one was of pungent saltwater and lots of it. The time neared 1:00 A.M.

Gary heard the whispers of the sea against the rocks, a few blocks away. A lonely car cruised by with wet tire sounds. More cars usually passed by at this time of night, since 101 was the main thoroughfare through town and the only way to drive north to Oregon. The Highway Patrol's warnings about the tidal wave must be working, he thought, along with the ocean's flooding that had come and gone.

The sky was clear and cloudless, with sparkling stars. No enveloping, chilling fog had formed to blanket sight and dampen sound. The air was cool and in the low 50s, typical for this time of the year. Like others that Good Friday evening, Gary at first had been downtown. The small tidal waves that crested in one hour before and washed up Front Street with their foot of saltwater and debris were still fresh in his mind.

Leaving that behind, Gary and Joanie had soon reached his parents' home. Upon arriving there, Gary discovered that Nita and Earl Edwards were with them in their living room, having run from the bar when the sea approached. As he listened to their description of the ocean "spreading inward," it seemed to him that the overflow at the tavern had to be more of a "hiccup" and measured in inches.

Since Front Street was closer to the beach than the Long Branch, he concluded that any flooding this time at the tavern had to be less. The Edwards, however, couldn't swim. The ocean's threatened advance was more than enough for them and their customers to flee for higher ground. Earl and Nita raced in their cars back to the Clawson home on high ground, leaving the cash box behind and the doors to the bar unlocked.

Everyone soon decided to drive back down and look around. They planned to retrieve the cash and lock up the place. If more flooding was in process at the tavern, they could just as easily come back home. As Gary and Joanie drove to the Long Branch, they saw no signs of the ocean's flow until they pulled onto Highway 101. The car's headlights illuminated the haphazard driftwood and noticeable dampness on the road. Pulling into the parking lot, Gary heard his father and mother's car crunch behind over the sand and debris. They parked next to his car.

The Long Branch Tavern was an old, weather-beaten, one-story house that had been converted into a bar. Two large bay windows and the front door opened towards Highway 101, with parking places both in front and back. The Long Branch set thirty feet back from 101 on the mountainside, and a normally busy Shell service station operated next to it. Heading on Highway 101 toward the downtown section was the Shell station, a car repair shop, Texaco and Union Oil stations, a bulk oil plant, and the Nichols' Pontiac auto dealership. The highway crossed Elk Creek at a bridge one-half mile up from the Long Branch. A redwood curio shop was on the tavern's left side, south towards the small Wayside Market and eventually where Elk Valley Road intercepted 101.

Across from the Long Branch and 101 on the ocean side was a trailer park and the Frontier Chuckwagon Bar and Grill, a much larger steakhouse and bar. Beach motels, including the Breakers, lined the highway south towards Elk Valley Road. An access road paralleled 101 one block west towards the ocean; strips of sand, driftwood, and scrub brush stretched two blocks further until reaching the beach and expansive Pacific Ocean.

Elk Creek flowed four hundred feet behind the tavern on the inland side, paralleling Highway 101 and winding its way down in a serpentine course to the sea. The tributary eventually made a left-hand turn to cross under the highway at the Elk Creek Bridge. The river was full now with the winter's rains and runoff, and its width reached forty feet in places. The rush of Elk Creek to the ocean could be easily heard in the night's stillness.

The Edwards quickly pulled up, and Gary led the group to the tavern. Although nothing seemed out of the ordinary, he had a "strange" feeling inside about all of this. Gary shook the concern away, deciding that this was probably due to the moonlight, weird hues and shapes, and the ocean's recent deposit of sand and debris. He opened the door and flicked on the lights, as the rest huddled behind him in the doorway.

The floors were wet. The markings and spots on the wall showed that only several inches of the ocean had passed through, just as Gary had suspected. The strong smell of salt air continued on inside. He and his father walked around the premises, inspecting for damage and looking for anything out of the ordinary.

The Long Branch was a small tavern and obviously not watertight. When the group walked in, a large shuffleboard table was to the left, a dance floor immediately in front of a long polished bar, and ten barstools with five booths on the sides. The front part of the bar once had been a shop selling and repairing chain saws. To the right, the owner's living quarters with its bedroom, old kitchen, and living room had been converted into a lounge. The bar area stepped up to the lounge.

The group speculated on what the ocean might do next. Would there be more flooding or was this it? Yes, they finally concurred, any more worry about tidal waves would be like the other times.

Another false alarm, and the danger had passed. Bill Clawson remembered out loud the tidal wave warnings given out four years ago. That "ocean belch" had caused only minor flooding on the docks, and it really hadn't been serious enough to worry about. "The damn fools never get it right!" Bill emphasized. Year after year and despite the warnings given, no serious damage had ever occurred.

Everyone decided to "let the party begin, again." They were already down there, no damage had occurred, this was the weekend, and it was still Bill Clawson's birthday. Bill grabbed a beer, hopped on the bar, and lifted his bottle in a toast, yelling, "Let the tidal waves come." The rest eagerly followed Bill's lead, grabbing more beer bottles or pouring drinks. It was time once more to enjoy life.

BILL CLAWSON was a hard-working man who had worked lumber his whole life, enduring more than his share of injuries. This fact of timber life had sold him on the idea of working the tavern with his son. If anything, this would be a fun way to earn a living. Bill was a slim man, nearly six feet tall, while his wife was heavyset.

Slightly shorter and more muscular, Gary was exactly half his dad's age and had a strong desire "to do something with his life." Although relatively young at the time, Gary didn't want to follow the logging life of his father, as other sons in the area did. He put in long hours at his mini-grocery store during the day, then watched over the Long Branch in the evening, to ensure that he wouldn't have to work on the mountains or haul those logs.

Joanie Fields was 5′4″, petite, and in her mid-twenties. Although the word had been out in town for a few months that she and Gary were engaged, both now knew they were more likely to stay friends than be married to one another. Gary was a busy man, and to meet his goals and ambitions took time away from their relationship. However, they enjoyed being together when they could, and tonight was no exception.

Nita and Earl Edwards had relocated recently to Crescent City from "down south" in California. Earl was a short, stocky man in his mid-fifties, while Nita was about the same height and in her early forties. They first met the Clawsons at the Long Branch as customers. Earl had started working for Timber Transport, a local log and lumber hauling company. Soon they became good friends, and Nita began working full-time as a waitress at the tavern while Earl would help out at times as the bartender.

Rounding out the group was Bruce Garden, who within minutes joined everyone at the bar. Bruce was Gary's uncle, having married his mother's youngest sister. He was in his mid-forties, and as Gary described, "Was built lanky like a baboon." Gary and Bruce were good friends, and Bruce had wandered in when he saw the lights on again at the Long Branch. The party was now well underway, and the tsunami could wait.

As the celebration grew at the Long Branch, Bill Whippo and LaVelle Torgenson were across the street in their trailer a block down from the tavern. They were drinking coffee and watching the television reports on the tsunami's progress as it headed down from Alaska. Bill Whippo had left Anchorage, Alaska, in 1952 to run the Tyson chrome mine for the J. W. Mining Company in Del Norte County. He and his "girl," LaVelle Torgenson, lived in a trailer located between the Del Norte Ice Company and the Frontier Chuckwagon on the ocean side of U.S. Highway 101 South. Although Whippo was fifty-five years old, he was lean and athletic-looking.

They heard the reports of the Alaskan earthquake from their television. Having lived in Anchorage for a long time, Bill followed the reports with keen interest. He had mined for gold one year on Resurrection Creek by the city of Hope, on the Kenai Peninsula of Alaska, and he pondered what it would be like if a tsunami hit this coastal place, as one did there some years ago.

Bill was also concerned because their trailer was located on land only a foot or so over the high tide level. When the first wave brought in the sea almost knee-deep at his place, Whippo decided it was time to get out fast in his pickup. However, LaVelle wanted to take all of her things from the lower drawers of a chest and put them on top of their bed, so the articles wouldn't get wet. After the ocean overflowed the highway again, but this time lower and with less seawater, Bill and LaVelle decided that the danger had passed, and they turned the television set back on.

[illegible]

as the Gold [illegible]

heights, as well as the [illegible]

As the [illegible]

should areas [illegible]

[illegible]. The part [illegible]

and turns [illegible]

[illegible]

one mile along the [illegible]

[illegible]

PART III

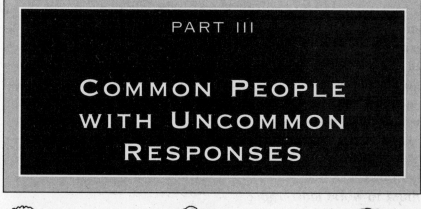

Common People with Uncommon Responses

7

The Heart of the City

The night was sharply clear and starlit. Some people saw the moon as being so full that the skies were "near daylight," although others don't remember anything except black darkness. One fact is clear: the ocean water and the night air were cold, "damnably cold" as one survivor said. The high during the day's afternoon sun had been over 60 degrees; by midnight, the temperatures were around 50 and dropping. The moonlight's illumination made it easier to see, and this fact allowed some to survive, including one newspaper publisher.

Wally Griffin, who owned the *Crescent City American* and Crescent City Printing Company, attributed that full moon to his being able to live to a "ripe old age." Thinking like others that the worst was over, Wally stopped at the Elk Creek Bridge to shoot more pictures of the extensive damage for his newspaper. His back was turned, at first, from the ocean. Turning around towards the sea, he saw flickering movements in the distance. From the moonlight, he then picked out the black mass of the fourth, large wave building up and surging at the creek's mouth. Wally ran to his car, gunned its accelerator, and sped away, just beating the monster wave in their race towards higher ground.

The downtown section of Crescent City contained curio shops, dry cleaners, flower shops, bakeries, cafes, supermarkets, and hardware stores. There were furniture stores, department stores, appliance retailers, photo studios, a newspaper, coffee shops, service stations, clothing stores, and a health food store. Believing that the worst was over, several owners drove down to their stores after the first reported incidents to inspect the damage—and quite a few couldn't swim.

Storeowners Ernie and Betty Pyke had saved money for years to build and open their Ben Franklin variety store on Third Street. The happy event had taken place a short three months ago. Being Easter weekend, their store was well stocked with merchandise, and they eagerly awaited the holiday sales. The Pykes and other business owners wanted everything to be in good order for their customers, so they headed downtown to inspect and clean up. Ernie, his wife Betty, brother Bud, twin sons (Steve and Doug), and an employee (Mary Lou Vashaw) were mopping up floors and putting stock higher up on counters, when the waves caught them "flat-footed."

Doug was a sixteen-year-old teenager at the time and had been driving around town with his twin brother, Steve. When friends told them that a tidal wave had rolled in, they headed to the family store, as well. "The water was only up to the curb, so you didn't even necessarily get your feet wet," Doug said later. "Then, the next flow went over the sidewalk and into the store."

The third wave caught people generally inside their stores. This water didn't come in as a big wave, but as a continual "rising, rising, rising, where you didn't know if it would ever stop," observed Doug. They had started to stack merchandise higher on the counter and display tops, when the ocean currents again rushed into the building. When the water was about half a foot deep inside, the brothers locked the front and back doors. Then, Doug and Steve pushed a large fortune-telling machine against the two front doors.

They watched outside the plateglass window as a large six-foot by six-foot redwood planter floated silently past in the moonlight. As they continued to hold the fortune-telling device against the doors, they stared incredulously as the green water rose outside the large bay windows. The white neon lights were still working inside, so everyone could see the ocean levels rise. The colored waters quickly rose past their waist, shoulders, over their heads, then above the window to where all that anyone could see was dark-green water completely covering the bay windows.

"I couldn't believe that the glass could hold underneath that much pressure—but it did," said Doug. "If it had given way when all of us were just staring at it, all of us would have been instantly killed."

When the ocean rose outside, its level surged well above people's heads. But for the sounds of the sea against the building, it was quiet inside as water slowly rose on the floors. Without further word, everyone made a mad scramble towards the second-floor stockroom. Mary Lou and Bud made it first to that higher room, but as Ernie, his sons, and wife reached the stairway leading up, the ocean ripped through the back door with a loud crash. Ocean rapids and boxes smacked first into Betty, then into the rest of the group caught below. Doug and Steve grabbed quickly at their mother's arms and kept her from being swept away.

Merchandise crashed in from the back as the sea swept numbers of large boxes towards them. The tidal wave had eddied backwards from the hill above the store with such force that it buckled the aluminum freight door at the back, rather than bursting through the front. Because of this, the glass storefront had held so far, but boxes and debris filled up the doorway, cutting them off from the stairwell that led to the safety of a second story.

They waded through chest-high water that was constantly rising to a second, mezzanine office that overlooked the floor below. Once the scared and soaked group made it up to that room, Ernie hollered for them to climb on a desk. However, it began to float away. The front windows then blew out below from the water pressure and debris with sounds like shotgun blasts. The lights flashed off into total darkness, when the currents snapped the outside power poles in half. Doug grabbed a nearby flashlight and flicked it on, allowing everyone to see "pretty clearly inside what was going on."

Inside the higher office, the foursome knew that they had gained a half-story above the entire main floor level, but the sea kept quickly rising. Ernie yelled again for people to get on top of the large desk, but his wife loudly replied that she couldn't because it was floating away. People tried holding onto the desk or stood in seawater to their waists, even though the office was located six feet over the main floor below. They worried, of course, as to how much of the ocean would pour in, as they didn't have much "ceiling room to go."

Hearing a strong "hissing" sound to one side, they fearfully saw a large propane tank that had crashed through the front window from the *Triplicate*'s offices across the street. Doug thought the family "had bought it this time," when they heard the metal counters banging into everything, including the tank. The tank continued to slam into the counters and then the office walls, which started cracking and buckling.

The family was trapped. From office windows to one side of their roost, they stared outside at the car headlights driving away, as people tried to speed away from the sea. Then the large "big one" or fourth wave rolled in, and they couldn't see any more headlights, figuring that those "people were now goners." Toward the south end of town they saw the large bulk fuel storage tanks catch fire. Closer to them, electric arcs flashed and sparkled outside, as wires shorted out and power lines fell into the ocean.

An older, large two-story house swept towards them, finally grinding to a stop in the street by their front door. Standing in chilling saltwater to their waist on the second level over the main floor, the ocean had risen now to fifteen feet high. "We could see nearly everything," Doug said. "It was a clear, moonlit night outside, and there wasn't a cloud in the sky."

With the aid of the flashlight, the family not only felt the green water swirling around them, but also clearly saw the merchandise, clothing, countertops, Easter items, and driftwood surging around them. When they next heard hissing sounds from that floating eight-hundred-gallon propane tank, the group became near panicked. Propane spewed out next to them from the leak, and the pungent odor of the gas permeated the air. One spark and no one would have ever known what had happened in that building.

Backs to one wall, the group waded away from the sounds and smells, worrying about their fate. As they waited to see what would happen next, powerless to do anything, the sea seemed to quiet down, then finally began to recede. The family stared silently as the ocean level dropped. As they discussed what they should next do, the sea's rushing pullback became clearly audible. When the ocean sucked down to what seemed to be at waist-level on the main floor, they left their office perch and moved down to the ground floor. Pushing though debris and merchandise, the group waded toward the back door.

Moonlight poured in from the blown-out freight door and illuminated the store's shadowy interior, as counters and merchandise bobbed up and down with weird motions. As the flashlight's beam swept around the destruction and blackish ripples, twisted shapes and smashed counters grotesquely took shape. They were soon outside, where Bud and Mary Lou rejoined the family. As they waded away from the building, the group saw cars stacked up and trashed in the parking lot behind the store. Furniture, logs, trees, fish, and whatever "could be thought of were floating outside in the seawater"—but they had somehow survived.

As Ernie waded outside, the thought coursed through his mind that they had already drowned. He then noticed blood swirling in the water in front of him. Looking down, Ernie realized that the blood was coming from his foot. He wasn't wearing any shoes, and somehow he had stepped on "something sharp." Ernie didn't know what had happened to his shoes, whether he had kicked them off or they had been ripped away by the ocean. It was a severe laceration, so police immediately transported him to Seaside Hospital. Once there, Ernie and everyone else had to wait their turn. "Quite a few people were injured and not many doctors were around at that time of night. The doctors put in many stitches to stop the bleeding. I lost count after a while," Ernie said.

While his father was at the hospital, Doug and his brother were taken to their grandmother's house on Cooper Street, away from the high waters. Doug didn't feel cold at all. "It's like being in an accident: you don't think of the cold air or seawater. You just think about surviving and what's happening around you. It's that adrenaline rush that keeps you from feeling the cold or any pain," he said.

Bob Ames, Jr., was watching the boxing matches on television when a news bulletin interrupted the program. The announcer said the Alaskan earthquake had generated a tidal wave then heading south towards California and that it was best not to travel to any coastal city areas. His mother called afterwards and told him that the tidal wave had already hit, leaving saltwater on their store's floors. "Just like before," he thought. "It's time to clean up."

Bob's mother worried about her two grandsons, Guy and Brad, who were supposed to be at the local drive-in that night. Bob immediately drove to their general appliance store to start cleaning up and to "corral those kids and get them home." He parked behind the Safeway at Fourth and L Streets, pulled on his hipboots, and hiked to his store through seawater.

Guy and Brad Ames had been "kicking around" that night with their four buddies: Jim and Bruce Tosio, Greg Gilcrest, and Jerry Schwiekl. They had seen a drive-in movie that night, then driven back to town, finding more and more debris littering the road from the first two waves. "It was a little wet out," said Guy, "as if we had been in a rainstorm, so we decided to check how the hardware store had done." Once there, they found some seepage of ocean under the front doors, but this wetting hadn't made it up the 1½ foot concrete loading dock at the back. The teenagers were telling jokes and running around, "just fooling around and doing the things that kids do," said Guy.

Bob Jr.'s mother, Fern, father Bob, and brother Bert soon joined the cleanup effort. He tried to get his sons to go home, but when they answered that they weren't in the way, Bob Jr. decided to let them stay. The family began moving inventory to higher places and sweeping the saltwater outdoors. They decided to seal the store doors to keep any more water from coming in.

The last wave hit as they stuffed rags in the cracks around the door. Brad ran inside while his older brother, Guy, and four friends were caught outside by the tidal surge. Bob Jr.'s brother, Bert, ran up and yelled, "We've got to get out of here. The water's up to the windows."

In just seconds, the ocean surged four feet over the sidewalk and kept rising. Bob Jr. said later, "It was like looking into an aquarium." They decided that they couldn't get out, so they ran upstairs to a small storage area. He and his parents, brother, and son, all converged there at the same time in a mad scramble towards the higher level.

Suddenly the lights blacked out, when the fuse boxes blew as the ocean swells crested higher. The sea suddenly crushed the windows and rushed inside with a swooshing sound. The floor level they were standing on shifted downward at an angle. “It sounded like shotguns going off,” said Bob Jr. “We later found glass imbedded in the back walls from the pressure of the exploding windows, and three interior walls had collapsed.”

In the total darkness, the group inside listened to the loud continual crashing downstairs from logs, counters, refrigerators, stoves, debris, and dishwashers smashing into one another. The floor they were standing on suddenly buckled and sagged into the ocean. Frightened, the group ran to a corrugated sheet-metal wall, on which a fiberglass rain roof had been attached and overlooked the outside parking lot—but there was no window.

The men kicked and beat on the sheet metal with their hands and feet. In several minutes, the metal wall finally gave in. They pushed it out, as the ocean surged up through the buckled floor. One by one, each gingerly worked his way through the narrow opening to where the rain roof with its supports had been nailed to the wall. They lined the wall with the ocean scant feet below.

The moonlight illuminated the choppy ocean and floating objects just below. A car with two people inside floated up L Street. The silhouette of a house cruised past as it floated between their building and G&G Liquors. They heard a woman trapped inside the house as she yelled for help, later determined to be Mabel Martin, but there was nothing that anyone could do. “The roof extension gave us a panoramic view of what was happening below,” said Bob Jr. “We clung to the sides of the building. It was dangerous, but that small carport roof was able to hold us.”

Having to deal with one danger after another, Bob Jr. hadn’t had time to worry about his son, Guy, and friends who had disappeared outside. Although their situation was precarious, he and his family now searched below for some sign of his son. What those on the roof didn't know was that the kids had jumped on a 1960 Chevrolet—but with all smiles—when the fourth bore first surged in. "This is fun," they said to one another and grinned. However, the raging waters rushed higher with "waves on top of waves as if a river had burst over its banks."

"One guy we never saw before tried to outrun the surging ocean," said Guy. "But in his confusion, he ran the wrong way toward the beach, not away from the sea." The teens watched in awe as the tidal wave swept him up and carried him soundlessly away into the darkness. They never saw the man again.

Without time to reflect further, they saw the ocean continue to gorge itself to even higher levels. Swelling over the windows of his parents' store, Guy heard the glass shatter as the sea poured in. Like his family, Guy's immediate predicament overshadowed any worries about them that he might normally have had. Cars banged off poles with metallic sounds, and when one vehicle hit a nearby power pole, every overhead and store light around blacked out, plunging the area into darkness. The tidal surge picked up and pummeled their Chevrolet even more, filling the car with brackish water, when the teenagers couldn't roll the windows up fast enough. The sea rolled over its windshields, as the car began to sink.

The kids watched the outline of another car spin towards them, then veer away and pass quickly out of sight. Guy next spotted his grandfather's Suburban delivery van floating towards them. Being older, he coaxed the others onto the van. As he convinced the last boy to jump on the vehicle, Guy discovered he himself was too far away now to leap on it. He was forced to leap from the car's top into the roiling waters and swim for his life towards the larger vehicle, now rolling away from him. With frantic efforts, Guy finally swam close enough to the van, where his friends were able to pull him up.

From their perch, the family watched with horror as the first car began to sink and Guy's friends jumped onto the van. They stared as Guy leapt into the maelstrom and barely caught the larger vehicle in time. Another vehicle surged into view, its interior filled with water, the fearful faces of two people pressed against one window. Their constant cries for help echoed from inside the car. Those on the roof could do nothing, nor those in the sea nearby, as the raging currents swirled cars around so violently that it looked like the rapids at the bottom of Niagara Falls, according to one observer. There was now a feeling of helplessness and terror. As they watched below, the ocean swirled the kids and the trapped couple from their sight.

Away from the view of his parents, Guy saw another boy float by on one of their store's refrigerators. As the large white appliance passed, the boys on the Suburban grabbed the lone kid and pulled him on it. At the time his friends pulled him aboard, the tsunami was forcing him toward the graveyard of debris that was blocks away by the McNamara and Peepe Lumber Mill.

The ocean continued to pour in; the water level rose higher and higher. To Guy, the action seemed to be like a "river in total flood." Cars drifted by and houses spun past them in the darkness. The water created great "circling eddies" in which the Suburban turned endlessly.

As the van bobbed around in the currents, power lines suddenly snapped with sparks like fireworks, and poles with their electric lines sagged into the sea. The flashes from nearby shorted transformers startled them, and the situation now seemed as if a war had been declared and the boys were in the middle of it. As electricity arced into the sea with blue-green glows, they watched the blue flashes silently, a few in horror. Another surge caught the car and the teenagers sailed towards the sparking lines. Guy said, "I kept thinking who unplugged all of the electricity? We were almost goners there." One of the boys said later, "I thought we were five fried kids."

Back and forth, the teenagers shifted their weight on the van's top to move away from the downed lines. At first, nothing happened but they continued. By not panicking, the boys' ingenuity slowly began to work. The delivery van began to drift away from the power lines, then sailed directly towards the Glen's Bakery building, which housed the bakery below and apartments above. The Suburban slammed into one wall, the sea high enough that the teenagers slid off the van onto the building's carport roof.

The near submerged car next drifted into their view, spinning around with the couple's plaintive cries for help sharply echoing out.

As the vehicle moved closer to them, they saw that it was a Volkswagen with an elderly couple trapped inside. The car's dome light illuminated its watery interior and the sheer terror on their faces. The trapped occupants had rolled up the windows to keep the sea out. However, the car was now becoming their tomb, as seawater had totally flooded its insides. The tidal wave slammed the Volkswagen against the same building with a noticeable "thud," and debris pinned the vehicle against the second-story level.

As this was happening, the water level started dropping. It was as if someone had pulled the plug from a bathtub. The ocean swirled in a different direction and lowered, retreating back to the sea. Two boys jumped quickly into the sea and dogpaddled to the car. Although they pulled hard on the doors, then once more, with the currents churning around them, nothing opened. The couple trapped inside kept pounding against the windows and windshield in a futile effort to get out.

The three other kids soon joined in. Swirling in water over their heads, they took gulps of air and pushed themselves down to the bottom to hold the car up from sinking to the bottom. As they pulled the floating hulk against the current, they finally managed to rip open one door. The teenagers pulled the nearly unconscious couple out of the car, then through the sea to the carport roof. Once there, they administered CPR on the elderly couple and revived them.

Meanwhile, the water level swirled down, indicating that the ocean was rushing away again. The teenagers knew they had to get to higher land and away from those currents. By holding onto buildings and grabbing power poles, they worked their way inland against the current. The group was two blocks away in water up to their knees, when the tide sucked away with a "whooshing" sound. Had they delayed getting away by a few minutes, the kids would have been fighting again for their lives.

Back at the Ames building, the group on the rooftop watched as the ocean again receded, and debris, appliances, and logs headed off in different directions. Seeing their chance, Bob Jr.'s group scrambled back down, then waded through the store and its mangled interior. They climbed over the debris and fish to get to the back of the building. Once there, they needed to smash a window to get outside.

They waded out in waist-high water towards the Safeway building, as the moonlight guided their way. Other trapped people began leaving adjacent buildings where they had been hiding or trapped inside. People would say loudly "that was a good one" or "glad we made it" to one another. Bob and his wife looked for their son, Guy, and his friends. They worried when they couldn't find them.

RAY SCHACH was a friendly sort, like many in this town, saying to people, "Come on down to the city, and I'll tell you more over lunch." He is now 90 years old, spry, and "still dancin' and cuttin' wood." Schach was at his Crescent City Lumber Company by Second and N Streets when the tsunami hit. "The later tidal waves caught all of us by surprise," he said. "We basically received an 'all clear' by the first two waves. However, even the Coast Guard ship out in the Bay didn't know a thing when the third and fourth waves began coming in."

Ray was standing near the middle of his long lumberyard building when he heard a "loud roar." He turned around as the third wave "around four feet high" carried away his pickup truck. He quickly jumped into a heavy logging truck as the levels increased. The surge carried him and the truck for two blocks over to the McNamara and Peepe (pronounced "peep") Lumber Mill. He watched as his main building moved, as well. It landed over one hundred feet from its original position toward a scattering of houses.

Numbers of other cars, motel units, furniture, showcases, debris, appliances, and vehicles were being deposited by McNamara and Peepe at the same time. Much more was to follow in these last, great surges. Located at the northern end of Elk Creek, the tidal waves roared up and spilled over the banks, carrying along the wreckage. Debris caught on other debris or dragged on shallow land. When the waters receded, the deposits at the lowest water levels remained. Other waves simply piled up more and more refuse.

At this time, the "garbage dump" for the tidal wave was building up. As Ray's truck bobbed up and down, another truck floated by. He threw a chain over it, and tied both of the huge logging trucks together. "All you think about is survival," he said later. "Just survival. That's all it's about."

The third wave had pushed his logging truck so far up, that when the large fourth wave hit, Ray simply floated further up with the other debris in his chained two-truck raft. "It was a clear, moonlit night, and we could see everything. It was an amazing sight to see the transformers blow, as lines broke, poles snapped, and the ocean caught live electric wires with balls of fire shooting up. Cars were snapped against poles, and then the huge fires just a couple of blocks from me blazed up." However, Ray wasn't injured and the heavy trucks grounded on the higher land when the ocean waters finally withdrew again.

The wave actions scattered huge amounts of lumber and large sawmill-sized logs around the city, area, and in the ocean. Ray Schach's mill carried "a lot of lumber," as did the other yards and mills in the inundation zone, not to mention the barges and docks by the beach. The lumber from these places was simply strewn all over the map. Then, large logs and lumber floated into the bay from both up and down the coast. The tidal waves carried these down south from the Oregon log camps into Crescent City's harbor. They even drifted up from the Klamath River and Happy Camp mills located south of town. After the first waves hit, the "Japanese currents" swirled northward from the Klamath River below. It didn't take long for these logs to come up into the bay and be caught by the last wave heading into town. By then, the ocean's movements had filled the harbor with lumber and huge logs.

The tremendous amount of fish left behind by the tidal waves still stands out in Ray's mind. "In places at my lumberyard, there were several feet of fish," he said. "The stench was overpowering and that fish smell was everywhere."

DON MATHER was drinking at a bar in downtown Crescent City. His wife was out of town, so he took the night off with friends. Warned by a sheriff's deputy, Don watched the first wave wash over Front Street. He was the night manager of Bay City Market, located one-half block up on G Street between First and Second Streets.

Curious as to what happened, he went to see if any real damage had occurred. None had then, nor had the first two waves affected the Safeway at Fourth and L Streets. He drove down Highway 101 South to park above Enders Beach and watch the action. Don was driving his father's old Buick, and it stalled after he put on the brakes.

"It was a moonlit night, the stars were out, and there wasn't a cloud in the sky," Don recalled. Then the larger waves came. He saw the harbor drain, then a "huge black mass" race in. He watched the flashes of light as power poles snapped and the raging fires started at and around Nichol's Pontiac. Fortunately, his stalled car had kept him from coming any closer to the tidal waves.

Once he got his car started again, Don couldn't drive through town due to the debris and high water on Highway 101. Instead, he drove down Elk Valley Road and behind the town. Worried about the cash in Bay City's safe, Don stopped at Jim Howland's house and talked both him and his brother, John, into grabbing their shotguns and coming with him to guard the market.

Once arriving there, he found Bay City Market to be "a total mess," wet with debris churned inside and its food and canned goods destroyed. A large log had sailed through the structure, knocking a huge hole through one wall. Three large, one-hundred-pound cash registers were still on their counters, although the counters were scattered throughout the building. Live flounder flopped on the floor; sand and merchandise from other businesses littered the store. The flooding waters and debris had knocked out all of the windows, leaving the cash and registers vulnerable. The men spent the night guarding the store.

The owners and an employee at Trehearne's Department Store were cleaning up after the first two waves with their backs turned to the ocean. If one worker hadn't yelled, "Another one's coming," the five-foot initial wave that crashed through the store's front door would have smashed directly into them. The people ran to a second floor landing, scant feet ahead of the crashing ocean. Windows exploded downstairs from the water pressure, and the building rolled and shook from the crushing tides, as electrical lines shorted outside and caught fire. When the eight-foot-high currents at their location receded the first time, they decided to act but had to jump into the circling sea, as the stairwell was now too weak to walk over. When the water level finally became more manageable, the people waded through the strong currents, linking their arms together to keep their balance.

The tsunami trapped manager Cozy Collins, Dale Cleveland, and other employees at Daly's Department Store, located at 964 Third Street, as they were cleaning up. When the front glass windows shattered, people found themselves entombed in a swirling mass of debris, counters, and the cold ocean. They grabbed onto support columns, jumped onto counters, and climbed up wall shelving. The ocean pushed them right to the ceiling. They watched in amazement as huge logs powered into the front as large racks of swimsuits "swam out" the back.

Trapped in a closet by a jammed door, Cozy Collins stayed afloat in the rising waters, which he thought stopped when his head touched the ceiling. He had to move his head sideways so that he could breathe from the upper side of his mouth. Later, he discovered the hole in the ceiling where his head had been driven through the drywall. He had been breathing inside the rafters.

What became clear was that if the last wave had been one to two feet higher, the number of deaths downtown would have dramatically increased, given the numbers of people already trapped. As Cozy Collins and the Ames family discovered, there was no further room for error. The difference was measured in inches as to who survived or not, or where chance had taken them.

The six-story Surf Hotel, at Front and H Streets, sustained heavy internal structural damage when the currents receded with all their power. A city policeman noticed a car back into the street near the hotel, as the fourth wave rolled in, and wondered why he couldn't see the driver. The vehicle swung around, moving away on the crest of the incoming seawater. Driven ahead by the surging ocean, other driverless vehicles soon began following that car.

Margaret and Buck Gurney owned the cocktail lounge in the hotel, and their apartment was located twelve steps below the hotel's lobby floor. When the waters first came, the ocean quickly climbed up those steps. It then rose over the floor of the lobby, which is at the higher H Street level. The couple ran to the mezzanine floor as seawater poured in. The ocean climbed towards the mezzanine floor before stopping. When the ocean rushed out, the Gurneys said that this "made a terrible sucking sound, taking furniture and everything out imaginable with it."

A United California Bank (UCB) manager, Bob Quigley, and his Operations Officer, Jim Johnston, were also at the Surf Hotel. The two men were forced to jump to the second story during the big wave and stared down as their cars disappeared into the night. Bob's car was later discovered piled in with merchandise at the rear of Nielsen's Hardware, carried one block before being slammed through a plate-glass window. People wondered how they would get that car out, as it hadn't touched any supporting walls on its way in. Meanwhile, the currents swept Jim's car to the same hardware store.

Quigley discovered later that smashed bank furniture in the UCB building had slammed against the front door and windows, then swept back against the back wall, then surged the other way once more to smash against the front, evidencing the changing currents. Most of the interior looked like it had been cleared out for a dance.

Weighing three tons each, three eighteen-foot by twenty-four-foot steel doors from Buckner's Auto Mart were ripped away. Twenty- to thirty-foot-long logs slammed through the building, smashing one end out. The sea hammered gaping holes through its cement-block walls, smashed out windows, and left the building looking as if a terrorist's car bomb had exploded outside. The tsunami piled cars three deep inside the repair shop, slamming one small car through the office. Numbers of vehicles were missing, having disappeared into the night.

Glenn Smedley owned G&G Liquors and tried to combat each wave that washed into his liquor store. The first wave brought in 1½ inches of seawater, and he swept it out. The next wave brought in a foot of water. As Smedley continued to sweep out water, he decided to lock the door. When he peered out, he quickly changed his mind. A wall of water loomed up in the moonlight, rolling a car over and over towards him.

Quickly running "pell mell" away, Smedley tried to outdistance the wave. Soon hearing a yell from behind, he looked back and saw a Cal-Trans street cleaner driving now in front of the wave. As it passed him, Smedley jumped on the vehicle and hitched a ride. He watched the third wave, well over six feet high, crash through his liquor store. Urging the driver to get that "buggy going," the mass of sea caught up with them and pushed the heavy equipment ahead even faster. The vehicle lifted off the street and skidded, wheels touching now and then onto the street, as it surfed over the water before grabbing ground again. Finally, the street turned upwards on a hill, and the ocean's surge began to subside. The heavy street cleaner lumbered up the hill with the ocean nipping at its back end. It finally groaned up a large incline with the wave's power lessening and reached safety.

Jim Yarborough was at that time the owner and publisher of the *Del Norte Triplicate*. His son, Steve, was a freshman at Del Norte High School. Since this was a Friday night, Steve could stay up and watch a black-and-white, late-night movie on television. About midnight, he watched a TV-news flash about the Alaskan earthquake and the tidal waves now rushing down towards California.

Steve hurriedly woke up his mom and dad and told them the news. They quickly dressed and raced to the *Triplicate*'s offices, then located at Third and J Streets. Once there, they watched one tidal surge send ocean water up to Third Street. His father wondered what had happened at the harbor, so the three of them jumped in his Jeep Wagoneer and headed down toward Citizen's Dock.

As they drove over the Elk Creek Bridge, they saw water gushing over the curb. Jim hung a U-turn in front of a county grader that was working to clear debris off the highway. With the grader in hot pursuit, Jim sped up L Street to just beat the next wave, cutting over to Fifth Street where he parked above the newspaper building.

They were walking down to their facility from the higher ground, but the ocean soon met them. Another surge forced them to run back up J Street. The power lines burst around their building, just as a huge tank at the bulk oil farm exploded. They watched the flashes inside their building, as the 550-degree hot linotype machine, with its molten lead inside, flashed and exploded when cold saltwater surged over it; the ocean tossed 1300-pound rolls of newsprint around like so many toothpicks, destroyed equipment, and gutted the interior. The sea reached a height of nine feet inside, and they later discovered a small flounder in an editor's desk drawer. The building had buckled in the middle, bulging out at both ends. Later, it would be completely torn down.

One man lost his produce van when the ocean captured it. The savage currents washed it from the Bay City Market blocks up and over to Fourth Street. A huge log crashed through the van, but left the truck's front rig undamaged. Redwood logs skewered buildings, including one large log that bashed in the front of a dry-cleaning store. The loud crashing sounds people heard were the sounds from logs and cars smashing against buildings and vehicles.

The surge carried entire buildings for blocks, and most businesses lost all of their stock and inventory. Coins, appliances, clothing, food, canned goods, hardware, pet food, cars, radios, and everything imaginable joined the circus of logs, trees, and other bric-a-brac roiling in the currents sweeping between land, sea, and streets. Back at Glenn Smedley's liquor store, the tidal wave blew out all of the doors and windows, slamming a fourteen-foot by sixteen-foot walk-in box filled with three hundred cases of beer though the back of the building. "All the booze," he wrote later, "except for some on the top shelf, went out the back door. People were finding bottles from the store all the way to McNamara and Peepe's lumber mill."

At the same time, Dale and Ruth Long stayed in their apartment above G&G Liquors. They were there during the night, and as Dale said, "We knew that it was coming, but we were pretty complacent because we had had that type of warning before." When the last wave hit, they never heard the shattering of the plate glass window and doors, nor the hundreds of bottles washing out. "The mass of water absorbed all of the noise from the shattering," he commented.

Gaping holes punctured many buildings, and all of their windows were blown out. Store interiors were shredded, looking as if everything inside had been dumped into a giant blender that went on a drunken wild binge. Far inland, the waves did damage with just small amounts of water. When only two inches of ocean came onto the floor, every accounting machine plug at the Bank of America shorted out.

Downtown motels closer to the beach also were prime targets. The Thunderbird Motel was a thirty-two-unit motel located towards Elk Creek on L Street, between Front and Second. This two-year-old structure fronted the Bob Ames Building and G&G Liquors and took the brunt of the tidal waves, thus allowing other structures to sustain less damage. The ocean movements at this area were also less powerful, as the tidal waves first had to surge over the breakwaters, harbor buildings, and other structures to get here.

Motel owners Walter and Nadine Mehlhoff calmed their upset, nervous guests as the first waves rolled in. When the ocean continued to surge into the motel, they led everyone to the second-story roof. They then had a bird's-eye view of what was going on—and they were safe. The roiling seawater forced thirty people to that roof, including several who weren't even guests. Parents held their children tightly, and couples clutched each other.

The motel took frightening hits from debris, and in the moonlit darkness, some wondered if they would ever get out alive. The slamming noises and sensations, sucking sounds, piercing cries of sirens, and flaming fires on the horizon were unnerving at best. Fortunately, the building had been well built and newly constructed, preventing another large disaster from happening. Although the structure was left barely standing afterwards, the happy survivors clapped their hands applauding its construction when they finally made their way back down to safety.

The violent currents had ripped away one side of the building, rammed cars through rooms, and gutted the office. Cars were stacked up on top of one another, three deep against the motel's sides. Walls bulged from the force of the receding ocean, and nothing was left behind in the washed-out units except ripped-out plumbing lines.

After most people, including Gary Clawson and his friends, had left the Tides Motel, one wave washed a man from its back door down a long alley, depositing him on the stairs of the Central Hotel. Three women climbed on a bar in the coffee shop for safety; the water tossed one end of the bar into a liquor store next door, spilling them back into the sea. The women scrambled onto a toppled jukebox wedged in a doorway for safety as the waters rose. Outside, two men with the group were forced to climb a telephone pole and hold on for survival. Other than some painful bruises, this group escaped relatively unharmed.

The nearby Royal Motel provided sanctuary even for next-door apartment dwellers. Awakened by a friend's telephone call at 1:00 A.M., one man in a second-story apartment decided to ride it out. After an ocean surge in excess of ten feet carried the ocean up to his windowsill, the man broke a window and jumped to the roof of the adjacent Royal Motel. He stayed on the roof with the others, watching the cars and houses disappear below in the maelstrom.

The swirling currents from the sea deposited mounds of fish everywhere. Survivors discovered them in desk drawers, rafters, hanging flower baskets, and heaped in large piles. The washes of the ocean didn't leave large piles of sand behind, due to the force of the sea's powerful pullback. Over time, the normal blues of the coastal seawaters turned into a deep muddy brown due to the powerful turbulence.

The ocean didn't crest in as huge towering waves, but instead was a very rapid rising of the sea, like a "flooding river shooting uphill," according to a policeman by the Surf Hotel. This action was more like the rush of pounding waters when a dam ruptures, crushing and demolishing buildings. Whether built from sturdy redwood timbers or not, the surges ripped some buildings from their foundations and rolled them away, while slamming against other structures that managed to stay upright.

The ocean set upon the quaint, old buildings that once had marked the city's rustic landscape. The currents lifted the Odd Fellows Hall, located at Second and G Streets, completely from its foundation, carried it down the block, and then deposited the remains at a crazy angle. Constructed in 1871 and built of redwood, this two-storied structure joined the other historical structures that the ocean played with like jacks or pitching coins.

The same tides swept up towards Seaside Hospital, which was

located three blocks inland on A Street between Front and Second. The waters dramatically surged up the steps of the hospital but didn't invade the building. In retrospect, what's amazing is that the surges even came that close. Seaside Hospital was built adjacent to the tall cliffs on the northern side of the city which kept the tsunami from breaking in from that direction.

JIM PARKS drowned in his thirty-foot combination home and shoe repair trailer. The trailer was set originally at Battery and Front Streets, Battery being the street closest to the Dutton and Sause piers. The trailer was swept away, crumpled, and nearly broken in half, one end sticking up in the mud two blocks away. His death certificate reads that his body had been discovered in the "Battery Street" area.

Adolph "Frenchy" Arrigoni also died here. His body was found covered with debris on Third Street, his feet sticking out of the mud. He had lived in an apartment at B and Second Streets which had washed away during the night. Harold Rankin had tried to talk Frenchy into leaving his car to come to their house for safety. But Frenchy had refused.

Other than the fact that Arrigoni might have drowned in his car, where Rankin was apparently the last person to see him alive, and not in his apartment, there are no other details about his death. His death certificate simply reads that Arrigoni's body was discovered at "235 Battery Street," his address. One newspaper account mentioned that he was a "well-known Crescent City carpenter," but no one alive remembers much about him. Nor is there anything further about Jim Parks' death. Both men were simply found dead in the mud.

It is an unfortunate fact of life that "dead men tell no tales." Only those who survived were able to paint a picture of the awesome powers that were unleashed that fateful night.

8

Structures on the Loose

THE SAVAGE tidal surges slammed into a house on Highway 101, ripping it away from its secure foundation, and spinning the remains across the highway. A neighboring house was turned around on its foundation with all of the flowerpots still in place on the windowsills. One resident looked out his front door and watched incredulously as five cars floated up the street past him, one by one. None had drivers.

Inundating her home, the cold seawaters caught Mrs. Clara McIndoe, a seventy-six-year-old widow, by surprise. Being treated later for extreme exposure, she said from her hospital bed, "I hung onto something, and I guess that's the reason I'm still here. I lay there for hours and almost froze to death before someone got me. I was born in '18 and 88.' I've lived a long time, but I've never seen anything like this."

The bore surged seven feet high into nearby Helen Boone's house. The ocean's surge that smacked against her home's sides awakened her as the sea picked up her house and carried it away. She began screaming for help in a frightened high-pitched voice. Her house eventually caught on a sunken car and came to a swirling stop, the structure tilting with one end thrust high into the air. Floating at the lower end as more seawater rushed in, Helen continued yelling for help and two boys finally heard her screams. When the waters receded and before another surge could build up, they scrambled into the wreckage through a broken window and one carried her out on his back. Although Helen recovered, she could only talk in a whisper from then on, because her screaming had permanently damaged her vocal cords.

Owing to her flu and having taken a sleeping pill, Mabel Martin had been sound asleep for hours. In fact, Mabel slept through all of the warnings and the first three tidal waves that crested in that night. As Bill Parker observed, "It just wasn't possible to warn everyone in time, because some just slept through it, for one reason or the other." Mabel Martin was one of these people.

The seventy-five-year-old woman awoke only after the third wave had come and gone. Mabel had no idea that anything had happened during her sleep. She lit another cigarette and was smoking it when she noticed that a piece of plywood over a broken window was rattling. The plywood cover soon blew off. When Mabel's house gave a lurch and started to "jerk and wobble," as she said later, she thought it was an earthquake. "God help me," she thought.

Her house was located behind the G&G Liquor Store at Third and J Streets. Although she didn't know it at the time, the tidal wave had picked up her house and was carrying the structure away with others. As the ocean filled her house, Mabel clung to her bed in fear. The raging sea soon tore the overhead roof away from the walls. It collapsed on top of her, smashing down the headboard from her bed. The debris pinned Mabel down, her left arm across her chest. Only able to move her head to one side, the wreckage now completely covered and immobilized her.

Her wooden bed floated on the ocean's surface, pushed up by the flooring, and lodged beneath the eaves of the now free-floating roof. An air pocket allowed the screaming woman to breathe as she and the debris-filled roof floated for blocks. Mabel was completely trapped under the rubble. Bob Ames, Jr., and his family from their rooftop perch heard her cries and watched Mabel's house float past into the night.

Time passed quickly for Mabel, who lapsed back and forth into unconsciousness. After shivering uncontrollably, she became numb from the cold saltwater, but her worries as to whether the ocean would finally engulf her mouth and nostrils never left. Finally, she felt the encapsulating wreckage stop with a sharp shudder. She reached down from her bed and felt the ocean foam still around her. Although she was trapped, Mabel felt glad to still be alive, but worried over how long she could hold out. She screamed again for help, the waters surging back and forth close to her face. Searchers wouldn't discover Mabel Martin until mid-morning.

RUTH LONG, her husband, Dale, and their twenty-two-month-old son, Ted, then lived in an oceanside, rear-corner apartment above G&G Liquors at the corner of Third and L. Dale's mother, Tina, lived one block away in a similar rear-corner apartment above the shop area of their family business located at the corner of Third and K.

Dale worried about the potential saltwater damage to his equipment at their welding shop, called Fashion Blacksmith, so he headed there after the first wave. He put all of his tools and what equipment he could on higher workbenches and then returned. He expected "a bit of minor flooding," but nothing else.

Tina called and said she could see that the garbage cans at their welding shop were now floating away. Dale told her not to worry about this, which turned out in hindsight to be an excellent decision, because the big wave was just arriving. Ruth Long stared outside and saw a Volkswagen floating by with its dome light on and a frightened, elderly couple inside. She worried that the tidal wave's withdrawal would sweep them into the ocean, but there was nothing she could do. These were the people later saved by Guy Ames and his friends.

Ruth watched houses spinning around in the shadows of the moonlight. Some of these houses had been built in the early 1900s. Although built sturdily, some lacked foundations and others had been built partially on sand. The first surges lifted these houses cleanly up and carried them all over the city. Later, the ocean would pound those floating structures with debris and break them up, adding this wreckage to what rammed into other buildings, such as where the Longs lived.

Worried about Tina, Ruth and Dale Long flashed their flashlight at her unit in the Fashion Blacksmith building. Dale's mother finally signed back with a bright light that she was okay. The Longs learned the next day that Hiller's Shell Station had saved her. The last surge had knocked this structure away (as seen by Patrolman Evans), and it smashed into the first floor of the Blacksmith building. With this wedged underneath, the service station became that building's support. Engineers later concluded that the building would otherwise have collapsed.

Meanwhile, the water level kept rising as Dale held their son and Ruth clutched their toy terrier, Koko. The sea rose rapidly to the last step of the stairway that led into their apartment. The air and water smelled heavily of oil; Ruth saw "all of the colors of the rainbow on top of the water," indicating the heavy amount of gasoline and oil that had spread over the ocean's surface. Large logs had smashed through gasoline tanker trucks and cars, spreading this oil and gasoline around. Portions of this would ignite later and set structures on fire.

Seemingly an eternity later and to their relief, the ocean finally began to recede. One step at a time, the sea went back down the stairs. When the water was waist high, a county grader appeared from the shadows below them. Dale ran down the steps and began wading through the ocean toward his mother's place. Ruth, now carrying both Ted and Koko in her arms, and other apartment dwellers quickly followed after Dale. Eight people jumped on top of the heavy grader which soon lumbered off Third Street to head up L. As the grader reached safety, Ruth heard explosions and saw flashes of light—the bulk oil-tank farm had just blown up. Dale later said that the grader and its human cargo looked like a "roost covered with chickens."

The county and city had mobilized every type of equipment on hand to save people. Graders, steam shovels, fire engines, and whatever they had that could move were brought in the search for survivors. The use of this equipment, however, depended on the tsunami's course. When fire engines couldn't make it down to help people because of high-water levels, the firemen were forced to stand on an overlooking hill, lights flashing and sirens sounding, with no way to assist until the ocean finally receded.

Diane Anderson was staying in town with her parents prior to her wedding the following week. Their home was located on A Street, two doors down from Seaside Hospital on the same side of the street. They had stayed up late watching the Johnny Carson Show when a news bulletin about the Alaskan earthquake interrupted the programming. Afterwards, Diane walked upstairs to look out at the ocean for the first time that night.

The moon was full, and visibility from the second-story window was clear. She could make out the outlines of the jetty (the breakwater) and Battery Point Lighthouse below. As she stared out, "some unknown force" seemed to pull the ocean away from the jetty. The water receded beyond the lighthouse, going farther out than any low tide she had ever witnessed before. For a time, the lighthouse was no longer situated on an island, but stood on a huge rock jutting from an endless beach. "Just as the ocean had ended withdrawing," she wrote, "it suddenly came rushing in, passing the lighthouse and rolling up and over the jetty, much the same way as water overflows in a bathtub."

Diane ran to a front window just in time to watch logs float up B Street to Front Street and then disappear from sight. The surges had turned her parents' home and the hospital into "a small island surrounded by water, logs, and debris." Despite this, her brother ran out to help a family on Battery Street. After her brother returned, they heard the receding water tear and rip buildings away from foundations. Electric wires snapped and sparkled, and they noticed a sharp odor of gas in the air.

Running upstairs to a front window and looking out, they saw the bulk plant near Elk Creek explode, sending flames into the sky and illuminating all of Front Street. Water now covered the entire area. "The explosions were continuous as one tank after another went off like firecrackers," she wrote.

Later, they discovered how close the tidal waves had come to their home. Owing simply to where her parents' house had been built years ago, Diane and her family had been fortunate. Whether the tsunami destroyed people's lives or not just depended on where they lived or were at the time. Due to this good fortune, some had no idea what had happened until after the last huge wave receded.

Joan Clark, whose home was on high ground toward the end of town, was watching television at the time. A station out of Eureka was showing a program featuring the pianist Liberace, and the time was "around two o'clock" in the morning. Suddenly a newscaster interrupted the programming and announced: "A tidal wave has flooded Eureka, having passed Crescent City." Next, she heard loud knocks at her front door. She let those friends in and they told Joan and her husband, Bud, about the tsunami's destruction. They had no idea what had happened, since their house was located above the city on Ninth Street.

Bud Clark quickly put on his deputy sheriff's uniform and headed immediately down to the city. Just blocks away from his home, Bud couldn't believe what appeared before his eyes. Houses were in odd places and buildings had been pushed off to different sides. Cars were strewn all over the area, stacked on top of one another and wrapped around power poles. He immediately began searching for people to rescue and help, finding one "old lady in the morning" that was injured and pinned to her bed, but who was not identified.

Bud tried to keep people out who shouldn't be there, letting only those in who had the proper pass issued by the Sheriff's Department under Bill Parker's plan. Knocking late at night on the front doors of houses that had already sailed away from their foundations, Bud Clark said he felt strange when doing this. "I did come across one 'old boy' who was sitting on a table in his living room," he said. "When I shined my light on him, he just smiled at me and said, 'You should have been here. It was one helleuava ride.'"

Getting anywhere took time. Bud needed to drive around debris, then turn around and try another way where the wreckage became too severe. He tried at times to clear away a path so that he could make headway over some streets located away from the damage zone. Others were simply impossible to drive over. He stayed on duty until the next evening.

HEROES WERE BORN that night, and Joe Snow was one. He drove to the Tides Motel between the first and second waves, finding the police urging everyone to get away. The streets were congested, and there was some traffic as people drove around, seemingly trying to decide where they should go. The second wave brought in more flooding and logs, as cars started to float around, and Joe Snow heard screaming from inside some of the vehicles. Joe saw that the headlights of some cars were on, and stayed on, until the larger third wave poured in at 1:00 A.M. Then those lights disappeared.

Joe realized that three children of a friend, Dan Bunting, were staying at home by themselves. As the second tidal wave began to recede, he drove toward Dan's house, located between Second and Third Street on M towards the lumberyards. At times his jeep floated on Highway 101 as he drove, but when Joe reached M Street, his tires caught traction again and he sped towards the house. On the way, police at a roadblock ordered him to come to a stop. He rolled down his window, yelled that there were people inside that needed rescuing, and drove straight through. The police didn't try to stop him and turned to the next car that had been behind him.

Halting his vehicle in front of the dark house, Joe hastily knocked on the door. When at first no one answered, he yelled his name and that it was an emergency. When the door slowly opened, he burst through and told the children that they had to get out. Dixie (age eight), Jimmy (age nine), and Timmy (age fifteen) dressed quickly, and he hustled them into his car just minutes before the third wave struck.

As Joe Snow drove away, Dan Bunting arrived at his house just as this wave surged in. Surrounded by water, Bunting climbed quickly to the roof of his house and jumped to a neighbor's roof. When that house began to disintegrate, Dan jumped to a third, where he was picked up by Paul Green, who was rescuing people with his grader.

The fourth wave blew the house off its foundation and ground it down on one end, destroying the surrounding area. Thanks to Joe Snow's efforts, however, Dan's children survived.

CHARLES LAKLIN had been out on the town with his buddy, Ernie Seaburg. Charles' wife was out of town, so he had accepted Ernie's invitation to stay over at Seaburg's B Street apartment. The two were ready to turn in; the time being "before midnight." There weren't any toilet facilities there, so Laklin "stepped outside for a minute." At that exact moment, the first small wave surged inward.

Its height was less than three feet, but Charles said later, "Small as it was, the wave still made noise." Ernie heard it and hollered at him, wanting to know if it was raining outside. The stars were shining above Charles, so he knew that wasn't the case. As he didn't have the slightest idea what was going on, Laklin quickly finished up what he was doing and hustled indoors.

Once inside, Charles remembers two later waves. "The second one came over my bed," he recalled. "It soaked both of us to the bone, but where else were we to go? The third one picked up the house." Frenchy Arrigoni lived next to Seaburg's apartment, and they later learned that he had died.

Once the seas receded from their neighborhood, Charles recalled that both men were "just plain soaking wet." Seaburg seemed to be calm through all of this and continually kept trying to build a fire in his woodstove and make coffee. For some reason, he couldn't do either. Laklin finally asked Ernie, "What are you doing, you crazy old Swede?" He then realized that Seaburg "was cold, wet, and apparently in shock." Laklin took his friend to Seaside Hospital for treatment and then continued downtown. While seeing entire city blocks destroyed, he heard someone screaming for help on Second Street. Laklin discovered his former landlady crying for assistance from within the boarding house where he had once lived. A log had smashed through her front window, pinning the woman against one wall. He freed the elderly woman and took her to the same hospital. She later recovered from her extensive injuries. Back on the streets again, Charles helped a friend, Turf Club owner Cliff Moore move some belongings to another place on Seventh Street. Charles finally slid into bed that night, but he couldn't sleep long as daylight soon came. Laklin spent the next day with the National Guard on patrol against looters.

Patrolman Harold Evans was another who rose above the call of duty. After the second wave, he commandeered a state road grader to take him into the flooded sections. By the time Evans arrived, the third wave was receding. He came to Mrs. Maude Kincaid's house on Second Street and knocked on the door to get the people out. Maude and her son, Bob, told him they had awakened to find seawater surrounding their beds to their chins. As they talked, the fourth wave surged in.

Looking outside a window, Patrolman Evans watched two cars float by. As the currents began breaking up the floor, he saw Hiller's Shell Station across the street disappear from sight, then all of the lights in the area blacked out. The ocean quickly surged inside, inundating everyone, and the house began moving. The structure completely turned around and traveled backwards.

As the sea rose over a ground-floor bedroom window, the house accelerated and tore off the front part of an adjacent store, shearing off one side of Mrs. Kincaid's house in the process. Later, the structure came to rest behind Glen's Bakery, blocks away in the Ames' building parking lot. Their house was one of the homes that the Ames' family had seen cruising past them.

When the sea finally began to recede, Evans decided it was time to get out before another wave surged in. He carried Maude nearly one hundred feet in water to his chest before finding shallower levels. Seeing the patrolman's flashlight signals, a state highway scoop tractor picked them up blocks later. Mrs. Kincaid and her son were taken to Seaside Hospital and treated for shock and exposure. Patrolman Evans changed his clothes and returned to duty.

MAC MCGUIRE parked his old Ford flatbed truck outside the Long Branch Tavern and walked inside. After watching the initial wave action toss his boat around at the harbor docks, he drove down to buy a pack of cigarettes. As he walked in, Mac observed later: "Gary Clawson was singing and playing his guitar as usual. He was good with that thing. Gary, his mom and dad, another couple (Earl and Nita), his uncle (Bruce Garden), and his girlfriend (Joanie) were having a great time, and they still were celebrating his father's birthday. There was no damage inside, and everyone believed that the worst was over."

Across the street, the lights of the Frontier Chuckwagon were uncustomarily turned off for a Friday night and the structure was dark. After Coast Guard personnel had warned the people at the Frontier, they drove past the Long Branch, but Clawson's group had not yet arrived and no one was there. After conferring with the owners, the Frontier's bartender, Jim Custer, closed down the place and walked over to the Long Branch. By that time, the festive group was celebrating in the bar. Although Custer was invited to have a drink with them instead, he politely declined and left to put on his deputy sheriff's uniform and start patrolling the area. Working two jobs, now Deputy Custer left the Long Branch just minutes before McGuire arrived.

Mac bantered with the Edwards, bought his cigarettes, and waited patiently for his change. As Gary had cleaned out the cash register, Nita needed to dig around in her purse for the exact change. After receiving his money, Mac thought about leaving to check on his boat moored at the docks. Since it would be more fun being with his friends, Mac decided to stay.

The skidding sounds of a car coming to a fast stop outside drew everyone's attention. The people crowded over to stare at the red and blue lights flashing on the California Highway Patrol car. Someone opened the front door. The uniformed officer rolled down his window and yelled, "Get out, now! Another wave's coming!" The window rolled back up. Wheels spinning, the patrol car sped away and disappeared down the road.

As the group continued looking out the front window and door, they watched in amazement as rivulets of water passed by, running southbound over Highway 101. The bright moon lit up strange shadows on top of the watercourse, as the running ocean built up in height and speed. Mac watched disbelievingly as the seawater picked up his truck and pushed it backwards. The vehicle banged with a loud, metallic sound into two nearby cars. Mac wasn't concerned then about the collision, thinking stoically that the truck wasn't worth that much anyway.

At the same time, Gary bolted out the front door in time to see the back of his large, white Pontiac Grand Prix rear up, then slam down on the top of his father's Dodge Dart. Both cars were brand new. The whiteness of Gary's bigger car slowly carried over the smaller, darker one and completely covered it. Hearing a hissing with crashing away in the distance, which then became louder and louder, the once-festive group stared intently outside.

They watched as a churning black mass of ocean rose to rush at them from the darkness. Waves soon seemed to be dancing on top of waves. In fact, more waves traveled behind the main advance, although seemingly on top of the first one. The sea hissed closer.

The moonlight illuminated the larger black waves as they powered over the highway with whitecaps, moving toward them with a speed as fast as cars on a city street. Someone screamed. People ran towards the back. At the same time, the sea lapped into the tavern from the back door, the tidal wave having surged up Elk Creek behind the Tavern. These waters poured toward its backside, then spilled into the structure.

The main tidal wave suddenly burst through the open front door with a roar, and green, brackish water poured into the Long Branch. Everyone jumped up on whatever was nearby. Mac, Nita, and Earl scrambled on top of the shuffleboard table, while Bruce Garden and Gary jumped on top of the bar. Joanie and the older Clawsons ran to the higher, stepped-up lounge.

The lights were still on, highlighting the maelstrom of turbulent sea and crashing barstools and splintering booths that surrounded everyone. The building shuddered from a heavy thud as the bore hit against the west wall facing the ocean. The trapped people watched with a mixture of fear and incomprehension. The brackish waters outside rose above the bay windows, then crashed through with a raucous shattering, flooding the insides with still more saltwater. The ocean thundered in, whirling together large logs and driftwood with the tables and stools.

Nita, Earl, and Mac stayed on top of the shuffleboard table as it floated against the bar. As the sea carried Joanie, Bill, and Gay around, Gary leapt into the water to help his parents and girlfriend get onto the bar. As the currents swept in, the water soon engulfed everyone to their midsections.

It looked to Mac as if he was in a flooded submarine now sinking to the bottom of the sea. The whole west wall of the Long Branch caved in with a splintering crash from the ocean's pressure, and the floor thrust up around the posts. Gary watched the ceiling buckle "like a crumpled beer can." The only support holding the place together was the wood floor. A sole overhead light now reflected off the swirling waters, as the sea worked its way towards the ceiling.

When the surge blew out the wall, the north side of the roof caved in over the bar. There was scant headspace for anyone to breathe. The ocean swiftly rose past their midsections to their chests, then their necks. People grabbed for the roof rafters to breathe and keep their balance.

The last light shorted out, plunging everything inside into total darkness. The Long Branch suddenly ripped from its foundation, and the structure began to move inland with the surging sea. Power lines crackled outside with blue flashes, as the surge snapped poles and then rose to trap the broken lines. Immersed in cold saltwater with debris swirling about, people watched in horror as larger objects passed. Mobile homes from across the street floated slowly past, bobbing along with huge logs, crazy-quilted driftwood, and shattered furniture. Because "it was bright as hell," everyone clearly saw what was happening.

Gary's mother started screaming with piercing shrieks, as she had a deathly, phobic fear of any water. "I can't swim," she cried and cried. A heavy-set woman, Gay Clawson's fears were that she would sink like a stone if she fell off into the sea. Of the eight people, only Mac and Gary could swim. Minutes before, they were raising drinks in toasts and swapping jokes. Who could or couldn't swim was then the last thing on anyone's mind.

From time to time, Joanie and others would yell for help. For the most part, people soon became too stunned to say anything, as the unthinkable had happened: people who couldn't swim were now engulfed in stinging saltwater and trapped in a tidal wave now sweeping inland. Fear seeped inside, and dead silence prevailed.

The sea was very cold, damnably cold. It was the end of March, late at night, and the ocean had swept in with the colder bay waters. As logs big as boxcars and vehicles of all sizes slammed into buildings, no matter how far away, the loud banging sounds echoed to those floating away with the remains of the Long Branch. The flashes from electrical wires shorting out and leaping fires created at a distance offset the dark shadows. Power transformers exploded when seawater drenched them, showering sparks up into the sky.

The building moved swiftly back toward the mountains and Elk Creek, as the main energy from the tidal bore pressed on from the sea. People held onto one another and the rafters for their very lives. Tree branches, lumber, tables, and other hard objects swirled in, bumped against rigid bodies, then eddied back out to disappear into the shadows.

The building had moved nearly one hundred yards when it came to an unexpected stop, undulating in the calmer water's movements. The tidal wave had reached one of its equilibriums. As the structure and its prisoners bobbed up and down, the floor of the Long Branch caught on submerged trees or scrub brush. More of its underpinnings then ground away.

The group could no longer stay inside what was left of the Long Branch. It wouldn't be long before the supports would totally give way, and the roof would collapse to trap everyone underwater. The longer they stayed in the water, the greater the danger of hypothermia setting in. Gary told everyone they would have to get on top of the roof. No one argued.

Mac half-swam, half-floated his way into position at an opening in the roof. Bruce followed Mac. Floating in the ocean up to their necks while holding onto the roof rafters, people carefully made their way toward, then over the bar. Gary led the Edwards, Joanie, and his parents through the water toward the open sky. One by one, he helped them work around the splintered wall, reach up for the roofline, and then float up to the roof. Mac or Bruce then pulled them upward to scramble on top. Gary led his wide-eyed and speechless mother to safety with no resistance. Having succumbed to her fears, Gay's body was nearly limp. Everyone made it to the top of the roof structure. Gary even saved the ledger book and metal cash box, bringing them also with him to the roof.

"This was so overwhelming, people just didn't know what to think. They were stunned by it all," said McGuire later about that time. However, he worried more whether his eighteen-year-old son, Jerry, had avoided their predicament. Mac knew that Jerry had been planning to go down to the wharf earlier that evening. Gary's worst nightmare had already become his reality, as his parents, girlfriend, and other friends were all there.

At the same time, their surroundings were surrealistic. Mac recalled, "It really was a beautiful moonlit night out. You could see everything clearly, from the stars to the nearby hills." Cars, heavy redwood logs, houses, the outlines of animals, and objects of every possible description floated around them on top of more than fifteen feet of water, as the building slowly danced up and down. As fish swirled inside, the salty smell of the sea became nearly overpowering. Nearby fires and the moonlight combined to accent the grotesque shapes of objects and shattered structures.

The question on Gary's and Mac's minds was what to do next. They didn't have to wait long for an answer. The ocean began churning and moved again. The roof with its trailing walls and people took off once more toward Elk Creek, passing several of the cars, house trailers, and tanks that had first moved past them. After a few minutes, the water again became calm and smooth. The roof slid to a quiet stop against a grove of saplings that once marked the banks of Elk Creek. This protective "glove" would keep future ocean movements from carrying them any further. It also ensured that they were trapped on this sea lake.

The nearby fires began to occupy their thoughts. A few blocks from where the Long Branch had once been, Nichol's Pontiac was in flames. Its main transformer had blown up when the ocean cascaded into it. This fire quickly spread to the adjacent Union 76 gasoline bulk station, causing one of the three-story-high gasoline tanks to burst into a towering, flaming inferno that lit up the night. Debris ruptured two of the pumps at the Texaco station, ripping them open to spill gasoline over the ocean. These Molotov cocktails soon exploded in front of their eyes in another firestorm, a scant two hundred feet away.

As the fires burned out of control, the marooned people heard the strong hissing of the propane tanks at the Shell service station, seemingly right next to them. They feared that if these tanks caught fire, the explosion and concussion would surely kill everyone. It was ironic to come this far, yet to still be in such danger. Seemingly calm and benign, the ocean didn't seem to be as much of a threat. The true danger now was from the fires raging out of control near the leaking propane tanks.

Despite this, Mac and Gary didn't want to leave their safe haven. Shivering in the night air, Gary mulled over their predicament. None of the choices, however, seemed to have an appeal. Staying close to the fires and explosive propane tanks appeared suicidal. Trying to swim for it with people who couldn't was equally dangerous. Mac also wasn't very interested in any swimming-out alternative. Trying to pull one non-swimmer out at a time was simply not an option, as it would be hard enough for either to swim out alone. As they talked this over, the fires flared up higher and burning gasoline spread out farther over the sea.

9

Inland over 101 Southbound

Businesses and homes in the Highway 101 South area were the hardest hit, as the surges from Elk Creek joined here with the direct ocean thrusts to form the deepest inundation. The ocean powered over six blocks of sand and sagebrush in some places before reaching buildings, but without structures blocking it as in the downtown, the tidal waves delivered the full force of its blows. The Texaco bulk plant, Nichol's Pontiac, and other structures went up in flames, and the tsunami demolished many of the buildings that didn't catch fire—whether they were trailer courts, motels, or gas stations.

Mrs. Dorothy Dorsch owned the twenty-unit Log Cabin motel, next to a car repair shop. The surges ripped all of the units from their foundations, pummeling some blocks away while dumping others in mounds over Highway 101. The Breaker's Motel lost units when houses carried by the waves slammed into it. The surges completely inundated the Surfside Hotel, battered the Gypsy Trailer Court across from the Long Branch Tavern, and destroyed all of the units at Van's Motel south of the Long Branch. These structures and their remains surged inland, circling with the flow of the currents.

Joseph McKay had lost his job as a cook at Elaine's Restaurant in Los Angeles. The restaurant had gone out of business when the owner died. Joe decided to return to Crescent City with his wife, Eleanor, and find another job. The McKays arrived at 9 P.M., that

Friday, March 27. They asked themselves afterwards why they hadn't stopped at a motel in San Francisco.

They had driven straight through from Los Angeles, a fifteen-hour drive, at best. They were quite tired when they checked into Cabin No. 5 at the Surfside Motel on Highway 101 South. After a quick dinner, they went straight to bed and slept soundly, not hearing a thing—that is, until they heard the ocean crashing against the window, which quickly broke apart from the pressure. The surge ripped their cottage from its foundation and carried the unit towards Highway 101 and the mountains. The bungalow smashed over their car and turned it over on its side. McKay crawled out of the window facing land when the sea began pouring in through the back window.

Its roof fell down on top of the cars originally parked on a concrete apron by the motel buildings. He was standing on this debris, when it surged up and broke apart, seemingly coming apart around his legs "like putty." Joe was badly bruised and cut by the broken jags of debris that pounded up. Grabbing hold of the windowsill, he pulled himself back into the flooded room.

When the seawater sucked back out later to the ocean, Joe and Eleanor were able to crawl out the window and reach the motel office. Their unit was now located in the back of the motel, rather than the front where it had first been. Someone quickly drove McKay to the emergency room of Seaside Hospital for treatment of the serious cuts and bruises he had sustained.

Living at the time behind the Del Norte Ice Company on U.S. Highway 101 South, Joyce London late that night had made a pot of coffee. She and her husband, Paul, were each sipping a cup when their cottage front door suddenly burst open. Her best friend, thirty-six-year-old Lavella (Belle) Hillsbery, and Belle's boyfriend were standing in the doorway.

Belle had come to warn her friend about the tsunami. Since Joyce was having trouble with her television reception, she and Paul had no idea about the tidal wave until Belle then loudly exclaimed, "There's a tidal wave comin'! We gotta get outta here!" Placing a calming arm around her, Belle's boyfriend looked at the coffeepot, then said evenly, "Let's first have a cup of coffee."

Just after 1:00 A.M., Joyce, Belle, and the two men sat down to have that cup of coffee together. The first two small surges had raced over land by now, and presumably the Londons had seen those flows rushing in, but then decided that the second smaller one had ended the ocean's activity for that night. It is also possible that they had left their home before the first "wettings", driven away to eat, then returned to find wet sand and debris, concluding that was the end of the matter. But the worst was still to come.

A few minutes later, they heard the roar of the tidal wave approaching again and rushed outdoors, seeing the mass looming up at them in the moonlight. This wave was the larger third one, but not the last "big one." The two couples raced for Belle's car, jumping in as the first rush of ocean approached. Belle's boyfriend started the car and hit the gas pedal, just as the sea slammed into the vehicle, engulfing the engine and killing the motor. The foursome worked their way from the car in the now high, roiling currents, as it bobbed on top of the swiftly moving sea.

The first powerful waves, unfortunately, pummeled and separated each one from the others, as they tried to swim or float towards higher ground. The tidal bore swept the people inland, somersaulting each over and over underneath the turbulent seas. Huge logs and debris indiscriminately battered at them. A large log smashed Joyce London in the face and nose, while another savagely struck her on the forehead and knocked her out, the others disappearing from one another into the darkness.

PEGGY SULLIVAN had moved to Crescent City from Perris in Riverside County that previous September. She was thirty-one years old, expecting her third child, and in the sixth month of that pregnancy. Her two other children, Gary (age nine) and Yevonne (age two), lived with her. She had been watching television in her unit at Van's Motel on Highway 101 South that night. Her neighbors, Donald and Nancy Colcleaser, were visiting with her when they heard the reports of the possible tidal wave. The Colcleasers soon left for their unit. Although her friends reassured her that all would be fine, Peggy didn't undress to sleep and instead stretched out fully dressed on her bed.

The ocean at the time seemed to sound to her much louder than usual. She had dozed off at about one o'clock when she heard a roar. Looking out the cottage's window, she watched disbelievingly as the black mass of ocean poured towards her. Peggy said, "I grabbed the baby and wrapped a blanket around her. I got my son and by the time we opened the door, the water was two feet deep inside." Turning in the direction of the ocean, she saw the wall of water now crashing toward them, picking up houses and units as if they were miniature toys and pushing them ahead. She stared at the back motel units that spun around and then crashed into one another.

"The water was so swift that I couldn't hold on to my son and he was swept away," she said. "I fell with the baby in my arms, and we were swept under the ocean twice." The sea tumbled her son in one direction, while Peggy and the baby were pummeled in another, ripping away Peggy's shoes and the baby's blanket. She and the baby were swept down the driveway. "A car was parked in front of a market, and we were washed up to slam against the car. I reached up, grabbed the door handle, and held on. Logs pinned us to the car, and I was screaming for help. I just knew that my son was gone."

The cold ocean deposited Peggy against a sports car, one block away from the Wayside Market. Her feet were jammed underneath the car, and driftwood and logs piled up against her back. One hand still held the baby bottle, the other clutched to Yevonne. As the brackish water started to recede, she screamed loudly for help and threw the bottle on the top of the car while trying to free herself.

Electric lines were snapping and crackling in the sea, as they fell when power poles snapped or lines sagged into the roiling ocean. She didn't know that her landlady, Ruth Meindorf, had also been swept away, until she heard Ruth cry out from behind her, "Oh my God, Peg, it's you." As Ruth pulled at the wood pinning her against the car, Peggy cried over the fate of her son.

She then heard her son's small voice murmur from behind her, "Mommy." Turning quickly, she saw a neighbor holding her son. The ocean had savagely swept Gary into the back of a garage next to the office, and the man had rescued him from there. Although severely injured, Peggy didn't feel her wounds.

At the same time that Peggy Sullivan had stepped outdoors, Ruth Meindorf was at the Colcleasers' front door, screaming at them that the tidal wave was coming. As Donald Colcleaser jumped from his bed, the onrushing waves swept away the landlady, Peggy, and her two children. The lights in the units blacked out, and the flashes from the electric line sparks "caused an eerie glow." The floor of the Colcleasers' unit buckled, and the sounds of the shattering, moaning, and groaning wood structures were distinct, even over the rushing water. The ocean ripped their unit away from its foundation, and it lodged against another building.

Donald tried desperately to get the jammed front door to open, but when he did, he said, "It was frightening to find myself looking headlong into another unit's wall, with about twenty inches separating us. As the building was driven further into the ground, water pouring in and walls buckling, I saw hanging electrical wires in the path of our only escape route." Fearing another tidal wave, he jumped anyway into the waist-deep water, as another man held a flashlight to guide him. His wife, Nancy, handed their two small children, Everett and Tina, to him.

Nancy carried their son while Donald held their daughter. The water at times was over their waist, and Nancy became hysterical when she fell into a hole. However, "the man with the flashlight took Everett until she got out, and he then gave our son back to us when we reached high ground." They didn't know or find out who the man was that had helped them that night. Donald Colcleaser wrote later, "There was many a hero born on that terrifying night." Later research showed that Mr. Francis Cussen was the man with the flashlight and their hero.

Some accounts differ over whether there were three or four waves and which one caused what damage. Most experts believe that there were four tidal-wave surges within an overall abnormality of eight land-encroaching movements. Although different areas experienced varying heights and differing "fingers" or severity, the third wave was the one that swept several of these people away—and led to their survival. Had the next wall of water been the near twenty-five-footer that roared in at 1:45 A.M. and unleashed the greatest damage, those people wouldn't have had a prayer of surviving. Those who lived in some of the trailers or motel units and survived would have otherwise drowned, since that fourth wave would have pile-driven their structures into splinters. People who survived would have been listed instead as dead or missing.

Approximately three miles south from the harbor area, the city engineer marked the fourth wave's height at 23.7 feet at the Pozzi Ranch on Highway 101 South. A picture at this remote beach spot shows a stop sign that had been wrenched from its initial position at third and J Streets and carried those three miles south. Any car and passengers that had happened to be on 101 at this time, or caught between the roadblocks, would have never been seen again. Nothing blocked the way of the tidal waves that crashed over land at this point.

IRENE JUANITA WRIGHT was separated from her thirty-year-old husband, Billy "Irish" Wright, for two reasons. First, they were having marital problems. Second, Billy "Irish" Wright was serving two concurrent six-month jail sentences for disturbing the peace and public intoxication. Billy seemed constantly to find himself in scrapes with society and the law. Gary Clawson's father once decked Billy with a punch at the Long Branch Tavern; he had discovered Billy punching holes in the Tavern's bathroom wall. Deputy sheriffs said that Billy Wright was a "bad apple" who had been in and out of jail a number of times and who just couldn't seem to get the hang of not getting into trouble.

Juanita lived in a little cottage house behind the Frontier Chuckwagon, across the street and on the ocean side from the Long Branch Tavern. She was raising her three children at the time, Debbie Lee (age nine), Bonita Ione (age three), and William Eugene (ten months old). Jim Burris, Gary Clawson's friend, had arrived at Irene's house an hour before, finding her worried about the first surges that had flooded the insides of her house and awakened her children.

Jim and Juanita heard the rushing sounds of the next surge. Looking toward the sea, they stared with fright at the looming ocean racing towards them with waves on top of larger waves. Shooing the two small children from the house, Juanita rushed off the porch, carrying her tiny baby, William. The first currents struck them just feet from the cottage, as Jim Burris was leading them towards Highway 101. Debbie Lee was in front of her mother, as Juanita held her baby in one arm, while clutching the small hand of her child, Bonita, with the other.

The sea smacked the group with savage force, splitting everyone apart. When the large wave hit, like the violent currents of a high rip tide churning onto land, the ocean tore Bonita and William from their mother's hands. Juanita and Debbie Lee tumbled away in the surf, as the two babies disappeared under the frothing mix of debris, ocean, and sand. The pounding surge carried Jim Burris off with the others, shaking him like a rag doll underneath the water, bearing them inland and over Highway 101.

As the sea rushed Burris in an angle over the highway, he spotted a telephone pole looming ahead in the moonlight. He managed to slightly change his path, as the sea and Burris collided directly with it. His hand outstretched at the time, the pole caught Jim in his middle, whereupon he quickly reached around and grabbed it with both hands. He held precariously to the telephone pole, as the ocean continued to rage past. With an effort caused by his will to live, to somehow survive, Burris pulled himself higher up the pole as the ocean stormed higher and higher. He held on as best he could.

In the moonlight, he stared as a structure bobbed and raced in the currents, becoming larger as it sailed towards him. As the fractured house spun toward Burris in a black-and-white silhouette, he braced for the collision. He knew he couldn't let go, since he would surely drown in the currents that now engulfed the landscape. The house seemed to move slightly away, as it towered over him, then crashed into the pole. Lumber smacked into Burris's body and one hand, but at first he didn't feel any pain.

Looking up, he saw the roofline above and its tentacles of wood surrounding him. The creaking structure eddied around with the current, then drifted away in the moonlight to disappear into the surrounding shadows. Jim began to feel pain, but kept his body tightly wrapped to the pole. He knew he would have to hold on for a long time if he wanted to stay alive.

AS BILL WHIPPO and LaVelle Torgenson watched television, an announcer broke into the program and tersely said that the tsunami had hit some areas with only a slight rise of water. He announced that information just received from Newport, Oregon, reported that campers on the beach apparently had been swept out to sea. (This was the McKenzie family.)

Hearing sounds coming from the sea that quickly escalated to a "loud roaring from the back of the trailer court," Whippo rushed out the trailer door. He stepped into water that was to his waist. Seeing his pickup truck being carried away, he waded inland through the surging sea to try and get it. Quickly realizing that the current was moving his vehicle away too fast, Bill turned back toward the trailer and saw LaVelle's silhouette for a moment in the doorway.

At the moment he looked back, Whippo saw a monstrous wave thundering over the back of the trailer court with logs, driftwood, and trash dancing on its top. He only had enough time to yell at LaVelle, "For God's sake, get on top of the trailer, if you can." The crush of ocean with driftwood cascaded over him, and as the currents slammed him under, Bill was worrying that LaVelle couldn't swim. From the situation now confronting him, the fact that he could swim didn't seem to make that much of a difference. He knew that this was going to be "some battle."

The huge wave pummeled Whippo underwater, and as the waters tossed him around, he scraped first over the sandy, scrub-brushed bottom, then felt driftwood pound against him. When he finally surfaced, coughing and trying to gulp air, he was swimming free and heading out across Highway 101 on top of the wave. The lights were still on at the service station, and Bill Whippo watched its plate-glass window shatter, leaving jagged pieces of glass around the frame. Looming closer towards him, he surged in the wave's grasp towards the shredded structure of the gas station.

Just when it seemed he would crash through the window and be sliced by the jutting glass and metal shards, a Plymouth seemingly drifted out from nowhere and shot in front of him. The car struck the station and hung up long enough against the building that the boiling water backed up. The currents whipped back into him, as Bill spun around the crashed Plymouth and service station.

As Whippo passed the vehicle in seemingly slow motion, he stared at a person inside, looking back at him similarly with wide eyes. Whippo never would forget the fear on that man's face, then the driver and his car disappeared behind him. Bill shot past the structure as if he was speeding down a steep waterslide at an amusement center. Spotting a large propane tank about one hundred feet to his right and moving with him at the same speed, Bill swam over to the tank to hitch a ride. Although the butane smell "was nearly too much," he grabbed onto the large, seething container and held tight.

Whippo next heard a loud explosion towards his left, as the raging seas drove him and the propane tank inland toward Elk Creek. One of the fifty-thousand-gallon tanks at the bulk tank farm had become a barrel of shooting flames and thick smoke. Thinking that another large tank might also blow up, taking the rest along and spreading burning fuel over the sea, Whippo let go of the propane tank and swam toward Elk Valley Road, away from the flaming fuel.

By the bright moonlight and sharp light of the burning gasoline, Whippo could see tiny shapes by him in the ocean. He wasn't sure what they were, but knew that they weren't dogs or cats. This surprised him, because the trailer court was always full of those animals. He soon discovered that he was swimming through the tops of willowy trees, none of which were large enough to do him any good. Whippo swam right into what seemed like "part of a building." Try as he might, he couldn't pull himself up on it. Since he didn't have the strength to do more, Bill Whippo just held on. "Boy, but was I cold," he said later. "I can't ever remember being so cold and so tired. I didn't realize that the current was so strong, and I could hardly hold on."

Whippo held on for what seemed like ten minutes or more. Then, he felt a strong surge in the water. The building moved at the same time, rolling over and snagging his clothes, pulling him down and under the ocean as it moved forward. Before he could kick free, he ran out of air. Whippo started involuntarily gulping seawater instead of breathing air. He finally broke free and shot to the surface just in time to hook his arm over a large tree limb. Bill couldn't pull himself up into the tree far enough to get his whole body out of the water, but he did manage to bring up both arms, shoulders, and his chest high enough to keep from falling out of the tree if he passed out. Then, he began throwing up the saltwater that he had first swallowed, losing his dentures in the process.

Still gagging, Bill turned to his next problem: He was covered with rats. The small animals swimming in the water were rats that had been making their way through the ocean for safety on his larger body. One by one, he slapped at them and finally knocked the last one away. "It seemed like hours that I hung there," he said. "My lower body swung from side to side in the strong currents like a windsock at an airport."

He clung to a large tree, deeply rooted into the raised bank of Elk Creek. "This tree no doubt saved my life," he said later. At the time he found it, Whippo didn't have the strength to take another stroke. He was frozen but alive, but still in a very dangerous situation. "If I had missed that tree, I would have sailed right out into oblivion and no one would have ever heard of me again," Bill recalled.

Other than the car driver he had passed, it seemed odd to Whippo that he hadn't seen one other person since last seeing LaVelle in the trailer doorway. Where were all the people? It seemed to Bill that people should have been "swarming all over the place," but here he was alone with nothing else around except rats. The answer to his question soon came, as he heard shouts for help coming from his left in the ocean lake holding him captive. Bill answered, "Who are you and what's your condition?"

"I'm LaVelle Torgenson," he heard the reply. "And I'm on the top of my trailer and it's stuck out here. I'm trying to get it to move closer to shore."

Bill at first didn't know whether to laugh or cry. He yelled back, "Thank God, we've made it." Whippo told her to sit down on the trailer roof before she fell off and drowned in the sea. As soon as he had said those words, he felt like a fool in telling her how to behave on top of a trailer.

Although happy that each was alive, their condition was precarious at best.

TWO BLOCKS from Bill Whippo and LaVelle Torgenson, where another grove of trees had captured what was left of the Long Branch with its marooned people, Mac and Gary discussed quietly what next to do. Mac mentioned he owned another small boat, located on land about a mile from where they were. The two decided to swim out and get it. They would use the boat to bring everyone to safety and avoid the fires. Gary told Bruce and Bill to watch out for the others during this time.

Gary and Mac slipped into the numbing cold water and swam away, realizing the water's depth was over twice their height and that they might not make it. They had no idea what the ocean would do next. Each swam through shadowy debris until coming to one that could hold his weight. They would grab momentarily onto it, then find the silhouette of another and swim towards that one. They would grab on the door handle of a trailer, hold onto a car antenna, or tread water while clutching the branch of a large log. Swimming similarly from object to object, Gary and Mac finally made their way back to Highway 101. This had been over a quarter-mile journey.

They found the road flooded but walkable. The ocean had receded somewhat, and Highway 101 had been built in most places higher than the surrounding land. Due to its construction, the thoroughfare now marked the division between the deeper ocean lake they had come from and the sea itself. Depending on the bank contours and road dips, they waded through seawater that varied from their neck to knees. The two men headed away from the city and the old Long Branch location toward Elk Valley Road, being careful to avoid downed electric lines, lumber, and an occasional abandoned trailer that bobbed in their way.

After wading for five minutes, they discovered that the water wasn't as deep as before. The level soon decreased to voluminous wet spots, then to where the highway looked like it had only been rained upon. Traveling half a mile down 101, the men reached the Elk Valley Road intersection. They turned up this road toward the mountains and angled around the large tidal lake that spread for miles around.

Another half mile up, they came to the old weathered house where McGuire operated his "Seaorama" company, selling lacquered sea-life specimens such as starfish and sea horses. The grounds around the house were soaked, but the waters had receded, and Mac's boat was still on the trailer where he had left it. The skiff was small, built comfortably for three to four people, and fourteen feet long. It was made of aluminum with a wide back ending in a sharp prow.

As the ocean already had claimed Mac's flatbed truck, they needed to find a way to get the boat back on water—and fast. They had no idea what the tidal waves were going to do next. The two men walked to an adjacent house and discovered a light shining from a back kitchen. Hailing the neighbor, Mac soon convinced him to haul the skiff in his pickup back to the sea lake.

Highway 101 was still wet but passable in the beginning, and the pickup dodged around the large logs and debris in its path. The water level, however, soon deepened to where the road became impossible to drive further over. The neighbor stopped his vehicle, and they quickly unloaded the skiff from its back. The driver then quickly turned around and sped away into the darkness.

Worried about the safety of his parents and girlfriend, Gary manned the skiff and took the first run. McGuire stayed behind on the highway to open up one more space for someone else to use. They planned to alternate making the two runs they estimated necessary to get everyone back. As Clawson rowed away, the men did not know that neither would see the other again that night.

As Gary rowed towards the captured Long Branch, he heard people crying out for help. Following the sounds of the pleading voices in the dark, he first came across an older man who struggled to stay afloat by tall trees. The man was coughing up saltwater, then began sinking underneath the black sea. Gary quickly reached down into the cold water, grabbed the man, and yanked him closer to the skiff.

At first, he couldn't get the drowning man onto the skiff. With a mighty pull that nearly overturned the boat, Gary finally managed to pull him in part way. The shivering man was so cold and suffering from exposure that the man couldn't move or help himself. While leaning back and tugging the same way, Gary finally manhandled him into the skiff.

Clawson then rowed "thirty or forty more feet" to the second terrified voice. Gary discovered what first looked in the shadows to be a "young guy about twenty" who was stranded on a mobile home in deep water. In fact, it was a woman.

The ocean was up to her chest, and she was standing on top of a submerged trailer. When the woman reached for the boat, Gary grabbed her arm and tugged the woman up. As she kicked upwards at the time, she slipped with less effort into the skiff. Gary told her to start massaging the older man, as he was "near blue" with hypothermia.

Gary had to let these people off somewhere. He needed to get on with rescuing the others. Although nearly everything that could be identified was now underwater, with the help of the moonlight, Gary picked out the outline of a mound. Remembering that a high berm encircled a log pond, he rowed quickly to the embankment. Docking momentarily to the bank, Gary let the two people off. He told them to walk down the berm towards Highway 101. They eventually would find a large sawmill where the berm and Elk Valley Road intersected.

"Go south," Gary advised, "You'll be safe at the mill." He never saw the woman again. However, when the old man met Gary a few days later, he cried when seeing his rescuer approach. It was then that Gary Clawson learned the identity of the people that he had rescued. The older man was Bill Whippo and the woman, his girlfriend LaVelle Torgenson.

After getting the couple to safety, Clawson looked around and knew that he was down from the fires and partially submerged trees. With the licking flames as his guide, he rowed in a northwesterly direction as fast he could toward the inferno and, he hoped, the still-marooned people. Dodging drowned cars and even dead cattle, Gary didn't feel pain or tired, even though he had been at this for some time. Constant shots of adrenaline does that.

Shortly, he made out the outlines of the treetops, the roof structure, and small sticklike people huddled together. Gary pulled harder to close the distance. As he glided up to the rafters, Gary saw his father holding his mother, the Edwards also close together for warmth, and Bruce by Joanie. The dazzling fires in the background created a near-Halloween look to the surrounding tree limbs, roofline angling into the sea, and submerged trees.

People shivered or were numb from the cold air, hypothermia, and uncertainty, and no one spoke as Gary first approached with the boat. His mother, Gay, and Earl Edwards hyperventilated with sharp, whistling breaths. It would be impossible to select who would stay behind for a second run. As people inched wordlessly closer to the boat, there was no question that everyone wanted to get onboard. This would be a tight fit, but making two runs over the burning sea lake didn't make any sense.

Gary said evenly, "Get in the boat." No one at first moved. Then everyone began stirring at once to get into position. From the roofline, Bruce Garden helped the others into the back of the skiff, as Gary assisted them from there. Joanie worked her way to the front, followed by Bill Clawson. Earl and Nita sat in back of Bill. Gay was helped in last at the back. Bruce bent down on his knees to paddle on the right side, while Gary sat on the cash box and ledger book to paddle on the other. With people crowded against one another, the boat sat low in the water.

It was a scene from Dante's Inferno when they pushed away from the tree limbs. The shadowy black-and-white contrasts from the moonlight, the high stretching gasoline and oil fires, the sounds of sirens wailing from land, and the overpowering smell of saltwater and rotten seaweed prevailed. The skiff was overloaded but they could survive. They had no other choice.

The weighted-down boat moved low in the choppy water, and Gary and Bruce had to be careful not to slam into anything that would puncture its hull. They paddled as best they could, Gary navigating the craft toward the business district. With the fear of further explosions happening so close to them, they had to avoid the Texaco gas station tanks and bulk station, which were both burning savagely out of control. Flames leapt higher as continuing explosions shook the air. It looked to Gary like a July Fourth fireworks display gone terribly awry.

They couldn't go back the way Gary had taken, as debris had sailed into the way and now blocked the once-clear path. Too many propane tanks, parts of cars, and redwood logs bobbed in places like mines, and the low-riding skiff didn't have the maneuverability that it once had. The skiff was now three-quarters of a mile inland, and the burning Texaco bulk station was to its left or ocean side. Gary said later: "As I found the way I had come out was blocked with debris, I spotted a smooth place about seventy-five feet wide right up to Front Street. We took off that way with everything smooth and quiet. The waters were smooth as a glass tabletop."

To avoid the Texaco fires and angle toward Front Street, the skiff had to cross over Elk Creek, now totally inundated by the washes of the last great wave. Elk Creek angled toward downtown from behind the old site of the Long Branch. It bound the burning buildings on 101 in a parallel course, curving to the west to intersect Highway 101 at the Elk Creek Bridge and running eventually into the sea. Highway 101 at M Street forked sharply to the right where Elk Creek crossed underneath the bridge.

A direct course to avoid Elk Creek would move them uncomfortably close to the fiery holocausts. Turning around in the opposite direction would take them straight out to sea; going east moved them away from the populated areas. There were no good options, except to row in the original direction that the Long Branch had been thrust, angling towards the left and downtown but across Elk Creek and away from the fires.

This was an instinctive decision, and no one thought or said anything about where Elk Creek was. The laden-down skiff proceeded in that direction with its huddled, shivering occupants. Gary had been too busy to worry, although at times the thought flashed through him whether he would ever make it out of this alive. He maneuvered the skiff around the flames, heading it towards the reflected landmass that was ahead.

Spirits seemed to lift as the boat narrowed the distance. People thought they were going to survive, despite the horrors that they had already endured. Joanie turned her head away from the flames toward Gary and for the first time since the disaster gave a hopeful smile. He even kidded his father about their lost bar, joking to his father, "How does it feel to be in the grocery business? You're now a half-owner of Gary's Grocery." Staring intently ahead, Bill didn't answer.

10

Raging Infernos

Dangerous fires ignited throughout the city, especially to the south. As one observer recalled, "Electrical wires popped and crackled all around, and there was the danger of the ocean spreading the flaming oil and gasoline throughout the city." People estimated that at least fifteen and up to twenty different fires occurred during the night. Luckily, most were finally extinguished, either by nearby firemen and residents, or even by the tidal waves. However, the biggest contagion was reserved for Highway 101 South and these could not be put out.

The large Texaco gasoline bulk-tank station was below the downtown section, one-half mile down on the inland side of Highway 101 South. On the city side of the bulk station was Nichol's Pontiac dealership, on the other a Union Oil service station. Heading due south from the Union station was a Texaco service station, a repair and paint shop, a Shell station, and then the Long Branch Tavern. The Del Norte Ice plant was on the ocean side of 101, with tourist shops, a trailer court, and motels heading south on both sides from there to the highway's intersection with Elk Valley Road.

The ocean's third wave crashed over a transformer at the Nichol's Pontiac dealership, electricity surging directly into the building's main electrical box. This junction box shorted and caught fire, causing the Nichol's building also to start burning. The flames eventually consumed the structure. The churning, high seas at first kept the fire under control, but it then burned without restraint when the ocean receded and the flaming gasoline spread.

At the same time cars and logs pounded against the three-story, huge bulk tanks at the Hussey-Texaco bulk station that was directly adjacent to Nichol's Pontiac. There were five such tanks, each ten feet in diameter and containing 50,000 gallons of fuel. One six-foot-wide massive log in particular swept in and smashed one of those bulk tanks, causing it to rupture and spill gasoline over the sea. Other debris ruptured one of the feeding pipelines with more fuel spilling on top of the roiling waters.

Sizzling electrical wires and the burning dealership ignited the fuel that eddied over the ocean and now spilled out of the ruptured pipes and tanks. Whether on an ocean trawler, at Seaside Hospital, in downtown Crescent City, or far up in the mountains, anyone could see in the night's sky the series of fiery explosions that lit up the air, now visible from tens of miles away.

Two of the bulk tanks exploded in showers of flames, the firemen helpless to battle the blaze. Over time, all of the bulk tanks exploded. Gasoline floating on top of the waters burst into more brilliant flames, creating the danger of further fires and explosions throughout the area, especially as the tides swept from one place to another. The flaming seawater and collapsing, burning bulk tanks were a constant danger in spreading the contagion. One resident said that this scene looked like a "naval engagement at night with ships burning with towering flames as the sea spread the flaming oil around."

Next, the ocean powered a colossal, eight-foot-diameter redwood log through the back gate of the Union Oil station. This huge log smashed through everything in its path, finally slamming into a large gasoline truck parked at the station. The projectile hit with such force that it knocked the truck fifty feet back, the vehicle coming to an abrupt halt against debris by one of the bulk tanks. It wasn't known whether this gasoline truck exploded by flaming gasoline or if one of the bulk tanks accomplished the task. Regardless of how the vehicle burst into flames, the heat from the flaming bulk tanks and truck literally melted it down.

The question was just when the nearby Union Oil station would catch fire. It soon did. The holocaust of burning bulk tanks set the station's fuel tanks ablaze. These tanks burned for several hours, until the tidal waves subsided enough for the fire department to put those fires out, just before they burned completely through the tanks. The underground fuel tanks and pumps of the Texaco station also caught fire, and nearly every structure except for, surprisingly, the main Texaco building was in flames.

The tidal wave swept trailers, logs, and even people into the Shell service station. Cars and debris plunged into the station, shattering its front bay windows. A large trailer sledgehammered two gasoline pumps from their cement foundations, spilling more gasoline over the sea. Spinning cars and lodged wreckage knocked other gasoline pumps off at weird angles. The Shell station's smaller storage tanks sustained heavy smoke damage, but they miraculously didn't ignite. Butane tanks spun around in the high seas in front of the station, including several that hissed leaking flammable gases into the air.

Fortunately, the Shell service station didn't catch fire, due to the different ways the ocean currents moved in this area. The currents first surged in from the sea, around the station, and flowed towards the flaming bulk tanks in one sweeping motion. When the ocean pulled back, the flaming seas receded in a different route away from the bulk-tank farm over areas with not as many structures as before—the tsunami having already swept away most of the buildings and homes that were combustible fuel.

Fire authorities allowed the monstrous bulk fuel tanks to burn out of control for four days, eventually consuming all of the stored fuel. When the fires eventually extinguished themselves, the flames had consumed the city's entire supply of gas, diesel fuel, and stove oil. Nichol's Pontiac burned to the ground, the Union Oil and Texaco stations sustained heavy damage, and even a nearby Union Oil bulk plant sustained extensive fire damage.

The scorched tanks resembled what remained after a wartime bombing attack on an oil-supply depot. The pictures of the crumpled, burned-out shells of the tanks—several twisted on the ground or leaning at crazy angles with one still filling the air with acrid smoke—is one of the hallmark pictures of this disaster. For days afterwards, the city's residents endured the pungent smell and pall in the air from the dense, black oily smoke.

ALTHOUGH THE TEXACO service station was located close to the Nichol's Pontiac dealership, bulk oil tanks, and Union Oil station, it was situated further back toward the mountains than the others and on somewhat higher ground. Al Stockman that night was the Texaco attendant. He was filling a gas tank when a resident drove in and told him that a tidal wave was projected to hit the city at midnight. Al told the customer that they had experienced false alarms before. The man said he wanted to see the tidal wave from high ground, so he could get a good look at it. Stockman directed him to Pebble Beach, which he thought would have a good view. He laughed when other customers asked him if he intended to close the station down right then and run for safety.

Around midnight, Stockman peered down the street toward Elk Creek and watched the sea splash down Highway 101. He said, "It started as a little stream of water, then suddenly water was all over the place, with logs slamming into cars and people shouting. When the water came right to the edge of the drive, I began to worry, but this soon subsided."

He called the owner, Sonny Hussey, who also owned the Texaco bulk-tank farm. Sonny said he wasn't too concerned, because the ocean hadn't flowed up the driveway and into the station. He said he would come down to check the lids over the underground gasoline tanks to ensure that they were still watertight. Stockman then checked them just before Sonny and his wife arrived and the underground tanks were fine.

The Husseys arrived before another wave started down the street, shortly after 1:00 A.M. In a quick decision, Sonny told Al to run their car up on the last grease rack, just in case the water surged higher. Stockman already had one car on the rack, about to start repairing it for its nearby, impatient owner.

This wave flooded Highway 101 and flowed up the driveway to

a depth of one-half foot inside the station. They worried for the first time about the danger of fire and electric shocks, but these fears lessened as the ocean again began to recede. Thinking ahead, Stockman drove his car to higher ground, as Hussey moved a gasoline truck away from the driveway. Al then called another employee to come down and drive the truck away to safety.

While they were waiting for their employee, a large wave surged in. Sonny and his wife jumped inside their car on the service bay, as Stockman raised the rack all the way to its top. He started raising the customer's car on the second rack, as the ocean surged into the garage. When cold seawater raced over his knees, Stockman climbed on the higher tire-changing rack. The water kept rising, so he jumped off that and climbed onto a service rack, pulling the customer up with him. They grabbed the overhead tire rack on the ceiling and held on.

The lights were still on outside the service station, so everyone stared at the huge logs, cars, debris, and even trailers floating down the street. The thirteen-ton gasoline truck just parked in front surfed away like a boat. The water level rose to over eight feet inside the garage, as water inundated Stockman to his chest while on his high perch, and the car with Sonny and his wife rocked back and forth from the currents.

The lights suddenly flashed off, throwing everything into darkness. As his eyes tried to adjust in the moonlight, all Stockman could feel was the surrounding cold water. The fears of an electrical fire bubbled up inside him and the others, but that thankfully hadn't happened yet. The people watched a fire flicker outside through a side window, then increase in intensity. They stared at the outside flashes of shorting electrical lines in the darkness. After what seemed to be a long time, the ocean finally began to recede.

The people climbed down from their roosts and waded through three feet of water. None of their equipment was operable, as all of the electrical power had cut off. They waded through the ocean towards the fire, past the Union service station and bulk-tank farm.

They then realized that the flames were coming from the Nichol's Pontiac dealership and stared in the moonlight at the dealership's garage door; the ocean had rammed a gasoline truck straight through the now shattered doors. According to Stockman, "A junction box inside the door had broken loose and caught fire." Watching the flames spread toward the truck, Stockman spotted a fire extinguisher on the vehicle. The broken electrical wires hanging overhead and strong smell of gasoline, however, quickly eliminated any further thoughts of trying to put out that fire. They quickly retreated.

After wading back to their station, the men discovered that logs and out-of-control cars had completely knocked over two of the Texaco gas pumps. They momentarily stared at the gasoline leaking into the sea and its oily film spreading over the water. "That was it," thought Stockman. He quickly retrieved his car, and everyone jumped inside. Tires spinning and not catching on land, he drove through the seawater still covering Highway 101 to the downtown area, dodging floating debris on the way.

As he drove into downtown Crescent City, the group heard thundering explosions behind them and turned to look outside the car. Flames were shooting high into the black sky. Not only had one of the bulk tanks started to flare up in fiery light, but the gasoline storage and gas tanks under their Texaco gas pumps had also burst into flames. They had left not a minute too soon. The Union Oil station then erupted in its inferno. Later that morning when conditions were safer, Stockman and Hussey checked out the devastation at their Texaco station. Stockman wrote later, "We found everything but the station itself in flames, and our fuel tank burned for three or four days. It was a kind of torch to show people the way back to Crescent City, 'Comeback Town, U.S.A.'"

Able to see the flames in the night sky and having heard the explosions, firemen didn't need to receive fire alarms. Before alarms were received, fire crews were already on the way, guided by the infernos that lit up the sky. Although the city had marshaled as best it could all of its available men and equipment for this fight, the obstacles in its way were considerable.

The ocean, especially the large, fourth wave that rolled over Highway 101 between the fire station and the fires, had already left a minefield of debris on the southbound route. Cutting off the normal routes to fight those fires, this blockage greatly delayed the response time of the men and their equipment. Firemen had to drive their fire engines over time-consuming alternate routes, constantly dodging off one road, and then turning onto another to avoid the large logs and debris in the way. The strewn wreckage stymied several attempts in getting close to fight the worst fires, and the firemen worked to find some route that would get them there.

One fire crew responded to the first fire at the Nichol's Pontiac dealership before the last major surge. They had started hosing water down on the flames, when one of the men shouted a warning. Looking over their shoulders towards the ocean, they watched the black mass of the fourth wave barreling towards them. The firemen had to drop their hoses abruptly and race back at speeds of more than forty miles per hour towards safety, the wave in close pursuit. They were able to reach higher ground only seconds in front of the grinding tidal wave—still climbing up after them.

When fire crews finally reached the Texaco bulk farm after it first exploded, flaming electrical wires had by then ignited the gasoline spilled over the waters. The flaming gasoline flowed around the fire engines and spread, quickly trapping the firefighters. It became too dangerous for the men, who had to turn quickly around and leave for their own safety. Even when back on the scene, the firemen needed to be ever mindful of more tidal waves returning. In fact, after fighting the fires at this area for three hours, all of the units raced back to higher ground when a report came in that another tidal wave was on its way. This proved to be a costly false alarm.

The city's Fire Chief was Bill Marshall, Jr.; the First Assistant was Wally Griffin, who owned the *Crescent City American*; and Bob Ames, Jr., was the Second Assistant. Neither assistant was available. Wally voluntarily helped out the fire department, but this time he had to work through the night so an extra edition of his newspaper could be brought out that following day. The tidal wave already had caught Bob Ames and his family, causing them to fight for their lives, both inside their building and out.

Among the first fire alarms received that night by the fire department, one involved a home at Front and J Streets; another electrical short had started those flames. At the beginning of the conflagrations, Marshall and his firemen raced to the house and began to hose down the burning residence. The ocean suddenly rose quickly up again. Without a moment's hesitation, Marshall ordered his men to put down their hoses. "Put this thing in low gear and let's get the hell out of here," he ordered. "Don't stop for anything."

As the last big surge steamed over land, the fire engine and its crew raced up K Street with the tidal wave in hot pursuit. This surge actually overtook the fire engine, washing over the running board of Engine No. 5 at one point. However, the fire truck was able to keep moving and won the race.

Fire Chief Marshall's main concern was to save the fire truck in case the fire spread through the city. He made the right decision: this was the same fire engine used later to fight the Texaco bulk-tank fire until high waters again forced those firemen to retreat. Unfortunately, the Front Street residence burned to the ground, as fears of more waves returning and the devastation kept fire-fighting efforts at bay.

The infernos on Highway 101 South remain strong in residents' memories. The towering flames were easily seen and highly visible in the sky. Nearly everyone who was in Crescent City at the time recollects the power and impact of those explosions and fires at night—they brought home the fact to everyone that their city was under terrible siege. Understandably, people went out of their way to avoid being too close to the flames, including the boat from the Long Branch that detoured away to miss the towering blazes.

THE LOADED DOWN skiff continued on its laborious passage. Fairly quickly, Gary Clawson and the others saw land dead ahead. The sights were clear to everyone. Houses bobbed by others, lumber floated everywhere, but the distinctive shape of the Ames building and other structures took form. They were close to safety, and Gary and Bruce paddled harder. It would only take another minute or two, and their spirits quickly lifted.

Suddenly, the seawater surged back towards the ocean with that abnormal, deep "sucking" sound that happens after the thunderous advance of a tidal wave. Gary said, "We were about two boat lengths, just twenty feet or so, from the bank and safety when the ocean started to recede. In that instant, I realized that we were in the worst possible place we could possibly be: right on Elk Creek. And directly above the culvert through which the river passed under the highway."

The skiff was angling over the creek when the sudden backwash of waters hit, surging from right to left, and caught the skiff broadside. "We didn't have any time to turn the boat, and we were pulled down sideways towards the bridge at the mouth of Elk Creek. It was only a hundred feet to the culvert when the waters caught us."

The ocean's retreat became a frothy, raging torrent heading back to sea. The boat had nudged to the point to where all would be safe. But at that very moment the tidal surge tore away at speeds escalating to forty miles per hour. The skiff hurtled towards the low-lying bridge, underlying culvert, and ocean. Everyone knew about the steel grate on the ocean side of the bridge, waiting to stop anyone or anything that made it underneath. Anticipation and anxiety bubbled into horrifying terror.

It would be all too easy to row over what used to be a river and not know it. No matter where you were, the water level would be the same. The unspoken tenet would be to get onto land, to survive, to live. Once the receding waters ripped the boat from its course with savage speed, there was no chance to leave the swirling waters that followed Elk Creek's outline. Tidal waves gravitate up and down tributaries, attracted by the pull of their underground contours, and this one was striking its way back the same way it came. Millions of gallons of seawater pulled back to pour off the land, a mass over two miles inland and twelve miles in length.

The bridge cleared the river by fifteen feet during normal times. The sea currents now pounded through the culvert just underneath it, surging over, around, and to the sides of the man-made obstacle. The ocean swirled over Highway 101 farther up and down from the bridge, its levels reaching toward the very height of the bridge's belly. The sea became a flash flood in its retreat.

The mouth of the bridge with its metal guardrail soon loomed high in the moonlight. Silhouetted over the skiff, the concrete abutment raced towards them, then smashed the boat with a loud "smack" from the impact. The water level was so high that the skiff slammed astride the culvert's narrow opening at its very top.

Bruce Garden happened to be on the side that hit. Seeing the bridge speed toward him, he instinctively stood up just before the collision and lunged forward, at the moment the boat sailed into the bridge. Taller than most, he grabbed at the structure and guardrail, while the boat slammed into the opening. The force of the impact was so strong that this collision broke two of his ribs. Garden frantically pulled himself onto the bridge, the skiff wedging momentarily between the ends at the culvert's opening.

The ocean waters thundered against the boat and swiftly lifted it high up. The skiff hung momentarily in the air, then the ocean spun it over. Everyone in the boat spilled head over heels into the cold churning sea. As Gary tipped over, the metal cash box opened up, showering cash and checks around. The box hit him squarely in his face. His mother, father, Nita, Earl, and Joanie joined him in being instantly sucked by the currents underneath the boat, then ripped down into the underground stream that surged through the culvert.

The chilling water churned the hapless people around like a washing machine, the currents tearing one after another down toward the bottom, then forcibly propelling them back up as if they were ragdolls on a hellish roller-coaster ride. The undulating ocean slammed the six around, then up and down. For an instant, the surging waters threw everyone into a small air chamber under the bridge and a "good way" inside the culvert. Faces stared in horror or with incomprehension for a second or two at one another, before each was pulled back down into the sea. The waters were "frothing white and violent," as Gary described.

He numbly watched his mother, father, and Joanie struggling frantically about thirty feet in front of him, as the tidal wave raged through the culvert with powerful eddies and swirling underwater currents. From that time on, however, Gary didn't see Nita or Earl again. The currents pummeled the six people underwater for the length of the bridge and its underground channel—a full two hundred feet—as two streets joined above ground at that point to form Highway 101. The metal grate at the other end awaited each person's arrival.

The city constructed the grate in a straight line that veered slightly at an angle from the bridge, starting six feet away on the ocean side. The contractor built it well. Steel posts were pounded 1½ feet apart into the creek bottom and set solidly in concrete. A strong I-beam was welded on top, binding the line of posts for seventy-five feet, from one bank to the other.

The authorities designed the grate to keep debris from being pushed up the river by tidal surges. The irony now was that it trapped anything or anyone pulled down from the other side toward the ocean. The grate already had entrapped huge logs, lumber, merchandise, refrigerators, and other debris being pulled back by the tsunami. Outside the grate, the waters steamed down Elk Creek as it curved in a reverse "S" for four hundred yards down to the beach.

Incredulous at what was happening, Gary Clawson was conscious the entire time. The white water hitting the wreckage lit the area up like a neon light. Time seemed to stand still. "The phosphorus in the saltwater sprayed against the debris and moonlight into a brilliant, blue-green light at the end of the tunnel," he said, reflecting on the explosion of sights and sounds he experienced. As each person churned toward the debris piled against the steel grating, dancing lights, thundering sounds, and drowning water engulfed each.

It was seconds after hitting the air pocket that people sailed into the grate and its trapped prizes. Before smashing into the logs and debris, Gary heard Joanie's voice agonizingly scream his name for one last time. The force of these currents is nearly incomprehensible, similar only to smashing into underground rocks if someone fell into a swollen flood's worst rapids. Then add that the person is inside a culvert filled with the raging ocean.

Like the others, Gary hit the grate and objects with tremendous force. The impact knocked the wind out of him, but what kept him from more serious injuries was that he instinctively threw up his hands to protect himself, just before slamming into the wreckage. The ocean's currents momentarily flattened him against the debris pile, then dragged him underwater. The churning water trapped him under the logs where he swallowed "seawater in gulps."

The ocean smashed against the trapped wreckage in huge torrential sprays, then surged underneath it with full force to pound through the steel posts or gouge openings through the sand beneath the pinning concrete. Anyone slamming headfirst against the pile would be knocked unconscious and quickly drown. Or worse, they still would be conscious with the air in their lungs knocked out. The buffeting action of the raging waters would force in gulps of suffocating saltwater. The terrible sensation of drowning would take over, as each fought savagely, fearfully, to survive. Gary Clawson was no different. He said in a measured voice later:

> I couldn't get through the logs to get back to the surface. The currents pinned me against the debris, all underwater. I could look up around the logs and still see the white light at the top. I was under some eight feet of water at this time, trapped under all of the rubbish. I sucked in more saltwater, gagging without air, and I thought to myself, "Son of a bitch, I'm drowning." When you take in water, it may only be a matter of a few seconds, but to you it's an eternity. I felt a shot of terror.
>
> I don't know why, but I pushed down for some reason. If I couldn't go up, then I must have been unconsciously thinking, "Let's go down." But that didn't work. So I reached up against something above me and pushed down a second time, this time as hard as I could and toward the bottom. Fear gives you a lot of strength, and the second push did it.
>
> The current sucked me feet first, upside down, with tremendous force. I felt I scraped the bottom of the grate, then I was swept through a hole between the posts. I felt myself whirling about, then up. I fought my way toward what seemed to be the surface and poked through. I looked around, as I coughed and coughed up seawater. I was on the opposite side of the grate. I was alive, although I wasn't so sure at the time.
>
> I looked around. It sounds unlikely, but I could see everything then as clear as a bell. I could see straight out to Seaside Hospital, as plain as if it was day, and the hospital was located one-half mile away. Although the time wasn't close for the sun to rise, it seemed to be light out, lots of light out. And everything was in an orchid color . . . a light purple, orchid color. Everything around me was bathed in that beautiful color.

11

Of Fishermen and Docks

THE FIRST WAVE washed over the inner jetty and sand barrier, flooding Citizen's Dock under one foot of water but causing no serious damage. It dragged boats from their moorings and smacked them against others. The first wave action, however, apparently didn't mount the outer breakwater on the lighthouse and Seaside Hospital side of the harbor. Although littering the docks and beach with debris and some boats, the second didn't contribute to the disaster either, being smaller than the first.

The Coast Guard cutter *Cape Carter*, a lumber tug, and a few fishing boats managed to escape the harbor and ride out the next waves in the open sea. The tsunami caught all of the other vessels. Although the Coast Guard did the best job it could, the limited amount of warning, and the reluctance of people to act countered their efforts. Chief Matthews of the *Cape Carter* stayed behind when his cutter cruised out to sea. He cleared the dock area, warning people of the impending tsunami and its dangers. When fishermen tried to reach their boats as the waves came in, Matthews and his volunteers turned many of them back. However, they weren't able to stop everyone.

The third wave started the serious destruction of the harbor. In fact, when the third wave emptied out, the ocean's movement sucked the entire bay dry and left many boats lying on their sides in the mud. When the fourth wave surged over every jetty and breakwater—returning lumber, cars, boats, and debris—what was left in the way was then crushed. The constant surging and ebbing of the seas compounded the devastation, and this destructive cycle occurred at least six times.

Whether they worked on the ocean or not, Crescent City residents weren't "city folks" and were used to the outdoors. Although most weren't college-educated, they were hardy people with practical instincts. When it came to survival, they didn't have to think about what to do. Those who were fishermen were used to riding out rough water or being dumped in it, and they didn't give in to panic as a rule. This is why these people survived through their incredible experiences.

One fisherman, Larry DeWolf, tried to motor his boat out to sea as the currents surged in, but lumber spilled onto the water from the huge barge and inland mills blocked his way. He threw out his sea anchor, but the swift currents kept it from catching bottom. Knowing that his larger forty-foot boat was now a liability, the man jumped into his skiff and abandoned the bigger one. However, the fourth wave and large debris smashed into the skiff, sinking it and tossing him with his heavy boots still on into the raging waters. De Wolf bodysurfed over lumber and debris while the tidal wave roared over the beach and land. The tsunami swept him several blocks over Highway 101 South, where he managed to catch onto a tall tree. The man stayed there until he could make his way to safer ground. DeWolf said later, "Don't believe you can't swim with your boots on!"

Marty Holenbeck tried to row another small skiff from the boat basin out to his commercial fishing boat. Barreling in the other direction, the tsunami swept it up from there to Elk Creek. It pushed him towards the grate at the Highway 101 intersection with the Elk Creek Bridge, but the surge then stopped and eddied around. He stayed in the boat. When the ocean receded, it sucked the skiff and Marty out to sea and Muscle Rock—three-fourths of a mile from shore.

Jack McKellar was watching the Friday night fights on television. When Jack learned about the threat, he phoned Ray Thompson who owned the sailing sloop the *Ea*. Ray, Jack, and Ray's fourteen-year-old son, John, drove down to the harbor in Ray's jeep. They parked the jeep by the south jetty, and Ray and Jack rowed out to the boat to take it to deeper waters. Ray told his son that if any waves came, he was not to try and outrun them, but to jump on top of the jeep.

As the two men loosened one mooring from the *Ea*, a second one snapped from a violent tidal surge. Another surge spun the boat around like a top, and as the ocean receded to prepare for the big fourth wave, the strong currents shot the boat from the harbor toward deeper ocean.

John during this time waited on shore for his father, who was now out to sea in the currents. As the ocean roared over the jetty, John climbed to the top of the jeep. Two other fishermen, Pat Grogan and Calvin Bradshaw, came down to the jetty to check on their boats. They discovered that the third wave had sucked their boats out to sea. As they drove away, they came across John who was sitting on top of the jeep.

John jumped from his perch and ran over to the other vehicle. As the threesome sped away, the fourth tidal wave surged after them and raced up to their car's muffler. Although the ocean pushed against their bumper and over the muffler, they made it to higher ground. Speeding at upwards of fifty miles per hour, they outraced the tsunami.

Meanwhile, Jack and Ray spent the night on the *Ea*, mutually reassuring each other that John was smart enough to have followed his father's advice. They decided to stay in safe waters, knowing it would have been foolhardy to sail back into the harbor under these conditions, especially with the explosions and fires on land that they were seeing.

John finally found a working phone and telephoned his mother at 4:30 A.M. to tell her that he was safe. With the help of the Sheriff's Department and radio station KPLY, this news was broadcast over the radio. A fisherman sailing by heard the news and sailed over to the *Ea* to tell Jack and Ray. They were overjoyed, of course, at hearing about John's safety. However, it took two days before the boat could wind its way around the floating obstacles and back into the harbor.

MICK MILLER had borrowed his dad's Lincoln Continental that evening to take his girlfriend to the drive-in, the same one that Guy Ames and his buddies were at. Afterwards, he drove to the beachfront and parked. The beach area at the time was completely undeveloped with two dirt roads that snaked though scrub brush, beaten driftwood, sand, and silt.

They were engaged at the time in some "post drive-in activities," when he heard "tapping sounds" at the side of the car. As it grew louder, Mick opened the car door to look around—and water gushed in. He started the ignition and luckily the car started up. He turned the Lincoln around, but his brakes were too wet to work.

As he drove back toward Front Street, the water was three feet high behind him. Mick was lucky in that this was the first and smallest wave that had caught him at the beach. The last one would have been over twenty feet high. However, he was speeding over a one-way, narrow dirt road, and a police car with its red lights flashing and headlights bouncing was accelerating toward him. There was no room for either car to pass one another, and Mick's brakes were gone.

The young man flashed his headlights and honked his horn to alert the policeman. However, this didn't seem to make any difference, as the patrol car sped toward him, its headlights becoming larger in the night. At the last moment, Mick spun his car to the right and swerved onto the sandy embankment, as the police car flashed past. Unfortunately, his dad's Lincoln Continental was now stuck in the sand.

The policeman backed up his car and yelled out the window, "Run for your life, there's a tidal wave." Fortunately for him, the area where he was stuck—in front of the Surf Hotel, some one hundred feet from Front Street—was on slightly higher ground and they were still dry. Mick and his girlfriend abandoned his father's "limo" and ran the rest of the way to Front Street. By this time, people had poured out of the restaurants and bars to check out the ocean's actions, including Gary Clawson and his party, and the ocean was lapping already up to Second Street. "After all these years, scares, warnings, and false alarms, it was actually happening," Mick said later.

A friend picked up the two, took his girlfriend home, and then drove Mick home. Mick decided to get his father's Lincoln Continental out of there, feeling that, "A tidal wave was small potatoes compared to the wrath of my old man." His father was sound asleep. "Usually, waking a sleeping gorilla is not a sound idea under any conditions," he later wrote. "These were, however, very unusual circumstances."

Once awake, his father became more upset over the policeman's reckless driving than about his son's reason for being there in the first place. With Mick and his friend in tow, his father drove their four-wheel Land Rover into town. The second and third waves had hit the town by this time. Mick said, "Elk Creek had backed up, creating a whirling undertow that was destroying the foundations of the old buildings. Stores had six feet of water inside, merchandise was floating outside, and skiffs and small commercial boats from the harbor were rushing up L Street toward Third." As the party stared at collapsed structures, his father tried to avoid the police barriers erected blocks up, as the officers tried to bring "order out of chaos."

However, his father was now more interested in finding the cop who had forced his car off the road, than trying to rescue the Lincoln Continental. He would slow down at a roadblock, splashing saltwater over "angry flashlight-waving lawmen." He ordered Mick to identify the guilty party. Mick's friend, Steve, and Mick himself pleaded with his father to forget it—but he wouldn't. "To try and put my father's behavior into some perspective," wrote Mick, "you should know he was the only man I ever knew that physically forced a policeman off the road and placed him under citizens' arrest for speeding."

Finally, they found the unfortunate young policeman. "After standing in running saltwater halfway to his knees, nearly getting arrested by one cop and shot by another, my father finally moved on," Mick stated. They drove down J Street to the Surf Hotel, then onto the dirt road and finally located the stuck car. Although it was still intact, they couldn't pull it from the sand dune. His father threw up his hands and said, "The hell with it. Roll up the windows and lock the doors, we'll get it in the morning. I'm going back to bed." With that, he had Mick drive him home.

However, Mick wasn't finished. Steve and Mick found another friend, Steve Burtschell, who drove a jeep with a V-8. They again went after the now-famous Continental. This time, the threesome was able to free the car. However, Steve Burtschell saw something in the darkness, and yelled out, "Let's get out of here, I think it's coming back in again." Tires spinning in the wet sand, the two cars sped up the unobstructed road, as the last wave had sucked everything back into the bay. At that time, the ocean was continuing to surge out through the funnel created by the inner and outer breakwaters.

The two teenagers drove rapidly away and made it to the high ground over the town. Mick and Steve Burtschell watched quietly from there, as the big one surged in. The area they had just left was now completely inundated by a raging torrent of boats, logs, cars, parts of stores, and boiling water. It was only then that Mick realized how close he had come to real danger. Stunned, he watched the swirling sea rise to seventeen feet against the Surf Hotel, right where he had been before. There was now an overwhelming "briny smell" of saltwater and seaweed, that then changed to the stench of gas. As the ocean snapped electrical lines into the sea, jolts of exploding lightning streaked from pole to pole over the power lines along Front Street. Other explosions occurred and the "whole end of town seemed engulfed in flames, casting an eerie, evil glow over the water." After the water receded, Mick drove his dad's car safely home and he and Burtschell went back down to help in the clean up.

Joe Pitt and "Bricky" Proctor lived directly above the Klamath River. Hearing the sharp crash of ocean raging up the river, Joe woke his neighbor, Bricky, and the two men ran to Joe's pickup truck. His rowboat was tethered on a trailer behind the vehicle. Navigating gingerly over a dirt road that led down to the river, Joe stared intently ahead as Bricky leaned out his window, straining to hear or see what was causing the commotion. The moonlight painted the surrounding landscape with black and white streaks, outlining the distinct shapes of the tall evergreens, along with the surrounding chaparral.

Joe stopped the pickup at a ridge close to the river. The engine idled as the lights cut through the late night. Looking down and silhouetted by the moonlight, both men "saw what appeared to be a large log with two people on it, on the south side of the river."

Pitt quickly drove to the river's edge, his car lights sweeping over the raging currents, but the log and its occupants had disappeared from view. The men smelled the salty air and saw the ocean boiling up and over the banks of the river that normally was gentle. The choppy water was full of huge logs, debris, and foam, as the currents moved up in the wrong direction.

Without hesitating, both men set the rowboat into the water, jumped in, and immediately were swept up by the flowing sea. It was as if a flood had leapt the banks by over ten feet, swirling with deep encroachments into what once had been protected land.

"Can you hear me?" yelled Proctor, trying to project his voice over the noise. He heard no answer. Both men continued yelling, as they dodged debris and worked their way, stopping to hear only the thump of floating objects bumping into one another. Then, the river stopped moving and became quiet.

They heard a "voice answering their cries, but now on the north side of the river," or opposite from where they were—on the Crescent City side of the Klamath. Proctor yelled as loud as could, "Hang on, we're coming," and Joe Pitt rowed in the direction of what seemed to be two voices. Before he could go any distance, the currents began frothing again. With a rush, the sea heaved back towards the ocean, picking up the boat and its shocked occupants with a lurch. Joe put his muscle into trying to keep the rowboat on course, but his efforts weren't successful as the current had turned into rapids. The diagonal route of the boat, however, took them eventually to the opposite side of the river.

They heard a plaintive cry for help—barely audible over the

rushing of the currents—to the land side of the boat. Working against the current with the oars, Joe tried to maneuver the boat towards land, as the moonlight partially illuminated a large rock with what appeared to be a man clinging to one side. The rock was some six feet from the receding currents in eddying water.

The boat clunked into several rocks to one side. Scampering into the cold ocean, Proctor waded to the rock. The man gasped for air and "was in a state of shock," as Joe and Bricky said later. He trembled as they picked him up, unable to answer their inquiries as to what had happened. Finally, the limp man said with considerable effort, "My buddy is still out there," and pointed back towards the black morass. After he was wrapped in a blanket, the man told them his name: Stuart Harrington.

Despite being tired from their previous efforts, Joe and Bricky pushed the rowboat back into the currents with Stuart to search for Harrington's lost companion. Bricky rowed out into the currents, venturing even farther toward the river's mouth. Despite the risk of being swept out to the sea, they continued their search.

Shortly, they realized that they couldn't navigate in the choppy waters, so Pitt and Proctor took turns rowing back to a boat landing that was close and approachable. Once there, they bundled Sgt. Harrington into a waiting car that raced him to an area hospital.

They started out a second time into the froth of saltwater to continue searching. Strange objects bobbed around in illogical directions due to the eddying currents. Being locals, they knew full well the treachery of the river's mouth and the dangers of venturing out into it. Nevertheless, they continued their search on the Klamath River for Sergeant Donald McClure.

After a long struggle against the abnormal pitching and flowing of the Pacific Ocean, Pitt and Proctor finally gave up their efforts at approximately 5 A.M., March 28th, that Saturday morning, still rowing in the dark.

ROY MAGNUSON and his wife, Marilyn, were visiting her parents in Ferndale, south of Crescent City. He had heard on the news that there had been an Alaskan earthquake and a tidal wave. Although

Roy was a local high-school teacher, he also owned a thirty-two-foot commercial fishing boat that he used in summer to catch salmon for extra spending money. It took two hours to drive back to Crescent City. When he approached town, red flares already marked the road and considerable debris was scattered over Highway 101.

"It's too late," he said to his wife. "It's all over. And this one's really different." Most of the tidal wave scares before had not resulted in such major flooding over Highway 101. He drove further down and parked his Volkswagen across the street from the Curly Redwood Motel, close to the Lighthouse Sporting Goods store on Citizen's Dock Road and 101. Sheriff deputies waved him through when he told them they were going to check out their boat.

Roy left Marilyn behind in the car and started walking on Citizen's Dock toward where his boat was moored. He was about two-thirds of the way down, when he heard a noise sounding like huge rapids inside a narrow canyon. A man driving a heister—a small vehicle that can raise its forklift ten feet or more to pick up and move large lumber stacks around—rumbled past him in the other direction. The operator yelled out, "Here comes another wave."

Roy stared at the wave quickly sweeping in, frothing and about two feet high. Behind it, other waves were racing toward him on top of those. As this mass came over the dock, he heard a terrible grating sound and next saw the Dock Cafe restaurant sliding across the wharf. The ocean was right behind it and seemed to be running southeast, nearly reversing its direction from when racing onto land. Roy started running for his life, as the ocean quickly ate up the distance. He jumped into the Volkswagen and started to drive away. "No way," he said, looking at how close the black mass was. Roy and Marilyn hopped out and raced to the adjacent Curly Redwood Motel. They scrambled up its staircase to the second story just in time, as the sea cascaded into their car. It floated away, the water rising toward where they were standing.

A large bundle of lumber, ten feet long and six feet wide, drifted against the floating car. However, this seemed to protect the Volkswagen, by keeping it close to the motel. When the water began to recede, Roy heard and saw the oil tanks and transformers further south of them blow up with skyrocketing fireworks. Amazingly, once the ocean receded this time, he was able to start up his car and drive away. Roy and Marilyn couldn't drive into town, due to the destruction, debris, and possibility of larger waves surging in, so Roy drove around the city on Elk Valley Road back to his house.

AFTER ROY MAGNUSON arrived home, Gary Clawson was now outside the Elk Creek Bridge and swimming with all his might against the currents surging out to sea. Although the ocean was actually returning fast with a strong pullback, it seemed to Gary to be going by slowly. Coughing mightily and in fits, he treaded water while searching for other survivors. Angling his way toward the closest bank, he swam against the current. Gary spotted nearby what looked like the shape of a body, floating down with the currents. He swam to the silhouette. Grabbing and shaking it, he felt no response. As he turned the body around, he saw Earl's face staring back. The waters had pushed both through the gate, one seemingly dead and the other one alive.

Gary swirled around and around, but didn't see anyone else. With Earl in tow, Gary swam to land. He pulled Earl on shore, then felt a growing tiredness and throbbing inside his body. He started coughing and fell to his hands and knees, as if hit by an axe. Aching from the cold, bruised and dazed, Gary kept coughing up brine from his lungs.

As he coughed, he numbly realized he was on land. He had survived, somehow. Trapped underwater, grabbing at unknown objects to push yourself down to the bottom; taking in saltwater the entire time, but keeping your cool so that you can live: this reaches levels of survival rarely seen. Try to imagine the panic from being churned around, smashed into huge objects, driven down and held deep underwater, gulping in drowning seawater, arms and feet flailing, lungs filling with water, roaring sounds, pinned in darkness, flashes of light, and dying. This is a horrible way to die. Yet somehow Gary Clawson survived.

Hearing a noise echoing from the bridge, he pulled himself up slowly and looked toward the sound. Bruce was staring down at him. Gary yelled to his friend to come down and help him. As Bruce scrambled down the embankment, Gary started artificial respiration on Earl, pushing hard and down on the man's upper back. No matter how hard he tried, the man didn't move or react. Froth poured out of Earl's mouth and nose on the wet sand, as Gary continually worked on him. Looking down at Earl, Gary was struck by the fact that the man had no marks on him, except for "one little two-inch cut over his eye."

With no response to his lifesaving attempts, Gary called Bruce over to continue the resuscitation. Clawson then ran up the banks and back to the bridge. He stared into the raging waters inside the grate, outside it, and down to the ocean, but there was only debris piled up. He desperately looked for some sign of the others, but Gary found none. He wished there would be more light. The sun should come up sometime soon, he thought, estimating the time to be somewhere around 4:30 A.M.

Again without concern for his safety, Gary leapt into action. He jumped from the bridge onto the wreckage packed into the grate, then worked his way over to the connecting I-beam. From there, he began frantically digging through the tree limbs, clothing, store merchandise, and other debris in his way. He ended up to his shoulders in the rubbish, as saltwater sprayed and surged around him. However, this time he was on top of the logs. Although he tried everything in his power to find the others, he didn't come across any signs. Tired, spent, with a gnawing feeling inside him, Gary gave up and made his way back to the bridge.

Meanwhile, Bruce's efforts to revive Earl also had not worked. Knowing that there was nothing further he could do, Bruce came back for Gary. After all that they had endured through the night, both men reluctantly concluded that their friend Earl was, in fact, dead. And that everyone else in their group had disappeared.

They walked away from the bridge on Highway 101 toward Front Street. Coming across two deputy sheriffs, they brought them back to the bridge and pointed out where Earl's body lay below. Taking one look at the bruised and bloodied Gary, then at Bruce, the sheriffs tried to convince them to go straight to the nearest hospital. The officers would even drive them there. Both Gary and Bruce declined. The two men stumbled to Bruce's nearby home, changed into dry clothing, and returned immediately to the bridge.

The California Highway Patrol now stood guard over the span. Despite their pleas to be let back in, the authorities refused to allow them to continue their search. Gary became so enraged at this turn of events, the sheriffs had to physically restrain him from wrestling his way back. He couldn't believe that they wouldn't let him find his parents, friends, and lover. In more normal times, he would have been arrested on the spot.

In defense of the authorities, they were quite concerned over the abnormally high, in-and-out tidal surges still pounding through the culvert. Worried that another series of fatal waves would rise up, they cordoned off numbers of places around Crescent City, including this bridge. The search and rescue efforts would have to wait until the sun rose.

HIGH UP THE TOWER of the Battery Point Lighthouse, Roxey and Peggy Coon watched with horror as the receding waters sucked out the guts of Crescent City and as explosions and broken electrical wires cast a weird Fourth of July display. The lighthouse was not damaged, because the tidal waves stretched around the high island, flooding lower parts of the island but not touching the much-higher lighthouse structure.

The lighthouse had been in continuous operation since 1856, and the Coons were the lighthouse caretakers working for the Del Norte Historical Museum that maintained the facilities. Peggy had awakened just before midnight and stood at the window of her bathroom. A full moon shone on the bay and the shimmering waters below. When she saw the ocean, Peggy immediately knew that something was wrong. The rocks around the island had disappeared under the sea. She knew that it was time for high tide, but the rocks had always been visible, even in the severest of winter storms.

She awoke her husband, they dressed quickly, and both quickly ran outside. They watched in awe as the first "huge wave" crested over the breakwater with its debris and churned toward the town. Within minutes the wave came back, as fast as it had first headed in.

Peggy wasn't sure how long it was before the next wave rolled past, but it surged by the lighthouse with more logs, driftwood, and debris than before. Lights flickered out on shore, as this one streaked further inland. When the back flow of the ocean started for the second time, they stared as the water drained from the bay. This time, the water receded even further.

The third wave was larger. The flashes and sparking of downed power lines at the south end of town sparkled in the night. A fire started, lighting up the sky, and more lights blacked out through the town.

Peggy Coons wrote:

> The water withdrew as if someone had pulled the plug. It receded a distance of three-quarters of a mile from the shore. We were looking down, as though from a high mountain, into a black abyss. It was a mystic labyrinth of caves, canyons, basins, and pits, undreamed of in the wildest of fantasies.
>
> The basin was sucked dry. At Citizen's Dock, the large lumber barge was sucked down to the ocean bottom. . . . In the distance, a black wall of water was rapidly building up, evidenced by a flash of white as the edge of the boiling and seething seawater reflected the moonlight. The Coast Guard cutter and small crafts, before riding the waves a safe two-miles offshore, now seemed to be riding high above the wall of seawater.
>
> Then the mammoth wall of water came barreling towards us. It was a terrifying mass, stretching up from the ocean floor and looking much higher than the island. Roxey shouted, "Let's head for the tower!"—but it was too late. "Look out!" he yelled and we both ducked as the water struck, split and swirled over both sides of the island. It struck with such force and speed that we felt like we were being carried along with the ocean. It took several minutes before we realized that the island hadn't moved.
>
> The wave crashed onto the shore, picking up driftwood logs along the beach and roadway. It looked as though it would push them onto the pavement at the end of A Street. Instead, it

> shoved them around the bank and over the end of the outer breakwater, through Dutton's lumberyard. Big bundles of lumber were tossed around like matchsticks into the air, while others just floated gracefully away.

The ocean covered the outer breakwater as it rolled over Dutton Dock. The surges left the huge lumber barge resting on top of Citizen's Dock. Once attached to a dock, the Citizen's fish storage buildings were now dancing over the ocean. Moored fishing boats bobbed up and down, and one boat tore up Elk Creek as if it was motorized. This was Marty Holenbeck's skiff.

Peggy Coons continued:

> When the tsunami assaulted the shore, it was like a violent explosion. A thunderous roar mingled with all the confusion. Everywhere we looked, buildings, cars, lumber, and boats shifted around like crazy. The whole beachfront moved, changing before our very eyes. By this time, the fire had spread to the Texaco bulk tanks. They started exploding one after another, lighting up the sky. It was spectacular!
>
> The tide turned, sucking everything back with it. Cars and buildings were now moving seaward again. The old covered bridge, from the Sause fish dock, that had floated high on the land, had come back to drop almost in its original place. Beds, furniture, televisions, mattresses, clothing, and other objects were moving by so fast that we could barely tell what they were. The next wave rushed past us into town but appeared to do no damage. The rest of the night, the water and debris kept surging in and out of the harbor.

Until that night, Roxey and Peggy Coon had never seen as many violent and monstrous changes in the tide as had then occurred—and they never would again.

PART IV

Hardship of Renewal

12

When the Sun Rose

The tsunami roared past Crescent City and hustled south during the night. The quaint harbor town of Trinidad is located about an hour's drive south from Crescent City. This town reported an eighteen-foot surge, comprised of a fourteen-foot wave on top of the four-foot high tide. However, the city is situated on the high side of a hill that's well above sea level and didn't incur damage. A two-hour drive to the south, the boat basin at Eureka also reported little damage, although the highest surge was eight feet over the low-lying streets of that town.

Located 125 miles away and halfway between Eureka and San Rafael/San Francisco, Noyo Harbor at Fort Bragg in Mendocino County was especially hard hit. As in Crescent City, it experienced four major waves over a period of nearly two hours. At about 12:30 A.M., or one-half hour after the tsunami rolled into Crescent City, the first wave surged into this harbor and over pilings normally ten feet above high tide. This initial surge sunk six large boats, snapped off pilings supporting the dock and boardwalk, and washed four skiffs out to sea. The second and third bores speeded upriver at thirty-five miles per hour in a series of stepped-up jumps. Overall, the tsunami sunk fifteen boats (half of them commercial fishing boats), damaged another one hundred (from slightly to total), and caused over half a million dollars of damage. The surges spun the forty-two-foot long, drag-fishing boat *Lapaz* around like a top, hurled the vessel one-quarter mile up the Noyo River, and drove it over a smaller boat. Fortunately, no deaths or injuries were reported.

There were four major crests around San Rafael, and the tsunami damaged or sunk over three hundred boats at Loch Lomond on San Pedro Point off San Rafael. The damage was estimated in excess of one million dollars. On both sides of the two-mile-long San Rafael Canal, the surges tore away all of the docks at this huge harbor from their moorings. At about 2:30 A.M., the tidal surf boiled past the breakwater through the wide mouth of the Loch Lomond Basin. It broke the end off a dock with twenty boats still moored to it. This crashed into a neighboring dock, causing that structure to crumple. The ocean movements lifted another dock over a levee with thirty boats attached to it, then drove this mass one-quarter of a mile away. By mid-afternoon the following day, debris littered the area and the ocean was still churning.

No injuries or deaths had been reported up to then in this area. In Bolinas, on the coast north of San Francisco, a man drowned at 3:00 P.M. the following afternoon. Isaac Dirksen lost his footing when a surge caught him during high tide. At the time, he was attempting to wade across a low-water channel. The thirty-four-year-old man was thirty feet from shore and wearing rubber-fishing waders. A three-foot high bore surged in, smashed him down into the ocean, and filled his waders with seawater. Dirksen couldn't get up due to the current's power. He disappeared from view, the ocean currents dragging his body out to deeper water.

When the tidal wave reached San Francisco Bay, it roared through the narrow Golden Gate opening and spread throughout the bay into the smallest inlet. Beneath the Golden Gate Bridge, the water level dropped eight feet in a matter of seconds prior to the coming of a four-foot wave. Newspapers reported that ten thousand people had lined the entire bay at the time to see the tsunami. They were lucky in that the first surge was the highest wave experienced there.

A forty-foot Coast Guard patrol boat was cruising near Belvedere opposite Angel Island, when the captain found his boat standing still, its props churning the mud at the bottom of the bay. The tidal wave had whipped the water out from underneath the vessel, damaging the boat's propellers. A four-foot wave then rolled into Sausalito, causing boats to capsize, docks to rupture, and 100,000 dollars in damages (or over three-quarters of a million dollars in today's money).

Starting at 12:15 A.M., eight-and-a-half-foot-high waves rushed in twenty-minute intervals through Monterey Bay south of San Francisco, but there were no reports of damage or injury as all of the boats were already out to sea. From Half Moon Bay and Santa Cruz to Cayucos and Morro Bay on the California coast, boats were sunk, docks splintered, and fuel docks destroyed. The tide changed ten feet in ten minutes in Morro Bay, causing the harbor's floating yacht club to splinter against its dock and sink a number of smaller boats.

The tsunami pushed further south and sank boats and damaged docks from Santa Barbara to Santa Monica and Marina del Rey. A mighty surge of ocean at Marina del Rey ripped out 450 feet of the dock that was operated by the Union Oil Company and shoved it one-half mile up the channel. At the Terminal Island complex near Los Angeles, surges of five to ten feet pummeled through the narrow Cerritos Channel, ripping away boats, docks, and walkways.

A longshoreman was killed in Los Angeles harbor when a cable snapped while he was loading cargo onto a ship, probably caused by the stresses on the cable from the vessel's violent rocking in the high waves. While being moved by tugs, the huge Union Oil tanker *Santa Maria* ripped out a 175-foot section of the dock when the currents pushed the vessel against it. The backlash from its propellers then sank a nearby eighteen-foot boat. The surges disintegrated an entire dock landing and swept a row of twenty large boats, including one unmanned 110-footer, in a whirlpool out to sea. Abnormal tidal surges in San Diego Bay caused extensive damage to boats and floating concrete piers. A sixty-foot schooner, the *Hispanola*, broke loose and smashed into three pier pilings and an albacore boat.

The waves spun out from the Alaskan earthquake toward Hawaii and Japan in the opposite direction. The Honolulu Observatory (Pacific Tsunami Warning Center) estimated that the waves would hit Hawaii within five and a half hours, or about one hour after they began pounding into Crescent City. After the alert sounded, Governor John Burns, in a special radio broadcast, urged everyone to evacuate; 150,000 Hawaiians raced to higher ground in the middle of the night.

Fortunately and ironically, this tsunami caused no deaths in Hawaii, very few injuries, and only minor damage. Due to the orientation of the generating fault and strike line, the wave heights were smaller and caused little problems. Observers reported a maximum wave height of 12.5 feet (3.75 meters) from six surges starting at 1:00 A.M. in Hilo, Hawaii, with only four Hilo restaurants and a residence being flooded. Maui experienced some flooding, primarily to its immediate waterfront area. At 3:00 A.M., PST, the Honolulu Observatory sent its final bulletin. This was an all-clear message for Hawaii with all other "participants" (or countries) being advised to assume the same all-clear status two hours after their tsunami ETA, or estimated time of arrival, "unless local conditions warranted a continuation of the alert."

Coincidentally, an earthquake reportedly struck portions of southern Louisiana that same day, causing sudden waves six feet high to churn up their rivers and bayous. Some small boats were overturned or smashed, but there were no reports of injuries or major property damage. Similarly, strange tides also hit Texas when six-foot tidal surges followed rough and choppy seas. At Port Arthur, Texas, a watchman reported that the tide dropped six to seven feet that night and a fully loaded grain ship "bobbed up and down like a cork." Crews on oil rigs in the Gulf of Mexico reported five-foot drops in the tide with corresponding rises. These effects were also attributed to the Crescent City tsunami.

After the tsunami coasted into Japan around 3:00 A.M., the tidal surges reportedly did cause damage to pearl and oyster beds. However, Japan reported minimal damage; the sea wave here being no more than ten inches high. An eight-foot wave (2.4 meters) surged later into Ensenada, Mexico, as the tidal wave continued on its journey around the world. Sixteen hours after the earthquake, the tidal wave reached La Punta, Peru. The surges increased slightly in height as the waves raced into South America, and hit a maximum of seven feet (two meters) in Antarctica. The tsunami then coursed around the world again, but with much less force or effect.

All in all, only two people died after the tsunami roared past Crescent City. The tidal waves had slammed into Crescent City with more damage and fatalities than in Japan, Hawaii, and all other countries combined, reversing the experiences of past global tsunamis.

WHILE THE TIDAL WAVE ran south and hit other regions, radio station KPLY in Crescent City received telephone calls both from concerned residents and out-of-state people. When the tsunami severed the cables to wide areas of the city, its telephone lines and communications were also lost, but the station could continue operating since its electrical power was still on. Reverend John McMath, whose house was located across the street from KPLY, still had telephone service, so he volunteered the use of his phone for messages. After the station broadcast the Reverend's telephone number over the air, information and bulletins were phoned in to him, then he ran them over to KPLY. Bill Parker then could pass on his important bulletins to Reverend McMath, who in turn ran them over to Virginia Deaver, and she announced them on the air. A portable two-way radio was put in use later between Reverend McMath and KPLY, speeding up the information transmitted—as well as making it easier on the good Reverend.

People jammed into KPLY's studio trying to find missing loved ones or wanting somehow to assist. After the second wave retreated, the order to call the National Guard into action and all the doctors and nurses to the hospital went out over KPLY. People at the studio ran out to personally contact hospital personnel to ensure that they received the news. Responding to door knocks or telephone calls late at night, those in the outlying areas were shocked when they heard the news about the disaster.

KPLY focused on locating missing persons, then relaying this information to worried spouses and family members. The station was instrumental in helping to track down residents, as well as directing their listeners where to go for food, shelter, and clothing. Later, it broadcast valuable information on the cleanup, sanitation directives, housing, and the location of Red Cross facilities and food centers.

During the night and into the following day, it was unnerving for people who didn't know what was going on to try unsuccessfully to find KPOD—it just wasn't on the radio dial where it should have been. Then, when the listeners turned to station KPLY, they would hear:

> Does anyone know where the two little children of Emma Post are? They were with their mother in the alley behind the Surf Hotel, when they became separated by the second wave. Please call any information in to us, as soon as you can. Also, Frank Tolscomb is trying to find his wife, Roberta. The third wave caught their car when they were driving on Second Street and overturned it.

FURTHER UP the Oregon coast, continuing high waves, surges, and abnormal tides sweeping back and forth during the night discouraged and disrupted efforts to locate the missing McKenzie children. The main search had to wait until daybreak. Rita McKenzie was listed in fair condition at the hospital in Newport, Oregon, having sustained deep cuts and abrasions from the pummeling by logs and rocks, both on land and in the ocean. Doctors treated both adults for shock at the hospital, although Monte McKenzie did not need to remain hospitalized.

The search intensified when the sun finally rose. Hearing about the lost children, people drove to the spot and offered their assistance. Other drivers simply stopped on Highway 101 and watched solemnly the rescue efforts going on below. Later that morning, the police discovered the body of Ricky, age six, buried under debris down the beach.

Newspapers across the country carried the accounts of the search over Easter weekend for the still-missing three children, as Lincoln County sheriff deputies, State Police, and Coast Guard personnel continued the search. The bodies of the three remaining children—Louis, age eight; Bobby, age seven; and Tammie, age three—were never found. Police discovered only remnants of the children's clothing under a pile of driftwood along the beach. The family dog also had disappeared forever into the sea.

In Crescent City, Jim Burris couldn't remember later how long he had held onto that telephone pole, but as the seawater mercifully retreated back, he stared down at his hand. The crush of the house against his life-saving perch had cleanly severed off one thumb.

Rescuers later discovered Juanita Wright in a state of shock, sitting on top of a car and holding onto her oldest child, Debra Lee. She and the child were taken to Seaside Hospital that night and treated for shock and exposure. Sadly but understandably, Juanita ebbed between bouts of hysteria and episodes of frozen shock over what had happened. The following morning, police discovered the drowned bodies of her baby boy, William Eugene, and little girl, Bonita Ione.

A gripping newspaper photo pictured the little baby boy's body, wrapped in a soggy dark blanket, as it lay over the top of a black-and-white police car. A black-jacketed, white-helmeted policeman is staring down at the ground by one tire, gloved hands gripping his pockets tightly. One black boot rests on a large but crushed can. He can't bear to look at the child's body and the sadness of it all.

After being knocked unconscious, Joyce London didn't remember anything until just before the dawn. Finally regaining consciousness, she discovered she was buried under a pile of logs across Highway 101, blocks away from where her home had once been. The ocean had carried her past the Shell Oil Station, close to where the Long Branch Tavern used to be, then swept her into wreckage and finally deposited her on top of it as more currents surged through.

Joyce was in great pain and cried out for help. Lapsing in and out of consciousness, she remembered finally being discovered by "some kid that was playing his guitar in a restaurant the night before. He found me and had to drag me into a cabin."

She suffered a broken hand, two broken legs, seven broken ribs, deep facial bruises, brain damage, and numerous bruises and abrasions. Although the prognosis at first was poor, Joyce London lived, although she didn't make a complete recovery from her injuries. She was hospitalized in Seaside Hospital for weeks, being seen later by Congressman Don Clausen when he visited the severely injured. But Joyce was the lucky one, as the surging shrapnel of debris, huge logs, and structures killed her best friend, Belle Hillsbery. London had no idea what had happened to Belle after the tidal wave separated them, nor did anyone else. The raging ocean also injured her husband, Paul, and Belle's boyfriend, but both later recovered from their injuries.

By now, Peggy Sullivan was also at Seaside Hospital. She had broken her ankle and suffered numerous deep cuts and abrasions from the pummeling by the logs and debris. Her daughter received severe abrasions, as well, but both would eventually recover. Although her son was relatively uninjured, Peggy Sullivan, unfortunately, lost her baby. The unborn baby girl's death was not listed as part of the official death total.

WHEN THE early morning sun rose to cast its warming hues on the city, the sights of the destruction and havoc wrought there seemed unreal and surrealistic. Splintered houses, crushed cars, twisted buildings, and smashed boats lay scattered over land and sea to the distant horizon. The Texaco bulk plant and gas stations still burned furiously with thick clouds of black smoke hanging over the town, the stench of the ocean and rotten fish filling the air. As people desperately searched for missing loved ones, flashing red lights and the Highway Patrol guarded the town. Structures or their remnants were left in crazy-quilt angles by and on streets. The city resembled a World War II disaster zone, and massive redwood logs, trees, and debris made passage by car impossible. That night, Armageddon had visited Crescent City.

Rescue operations commenced throughout the city, including the inland and ocean sides of Elk Creek Bridge. Divers in wetsuits bobbed back and forth in the river like so many seals, trying to locate bodies and confirm missing people. A large scoop or clam shovel clattered noisily into position on the bridge. The equipment soon began sifting through the wreckage packed between the bridge and grate.

The engine grumbled long and loud from the deep digging efforts, as diesel smoke poured out from the exhausts. Debris soon piled up on the bridge. Mac's skiff was the first object to be located.

The surge had pushed the boat through the culvert and under the main pile at the grate. The large shovel picked up the skiff and laid it carefully on the bridge, next to the other finds.

The next discovery was the body of Bill Clawson. The clam shovel unearthed the body of Gary's father from deep inside the debris. He had been trapped like Gary under the same wreckage, but Bill had not been able to work his way out. After the authorities had restrained Gary Clawson a second time from getting into the recovery zone to search for his parents and friends, he and Bruce Garden went back again to Bruce's home.

An hour and a half later, searchers located his mother, Gay. The tidal surges had washed her body back from the grate to the land side of the bridge and on the north bank of Elk Creek. They discovered her body buried under a mound of driftwood.

Nita and Joanie's bodies were next located. Washed underneath or eventually through the grate, Nita's body moved halfway down the river to the ocean, or some two hundred yards from the bridge where it was assumed she had died. The currents washed Joanie Field's body into the harbor, all the way to the rocks of the breakwater. Head injury wounds on her body were massive, and the medical examiner couldn't determine whether she had died from those injuries first or by drowning. The scattering of the bodies underscored the power of the ocean's force that night.

That past night, Mac McGuire had waited for Gary's return with some of the others. He courageously swam back two times trying to find the skiff and his friends, as the waves surged monstrously in and out. Given the currents, uncertainties, obstacles in the way, and efforts required at night, these were not simple feats. When he couldn't find anyone, Mac gave up and went home. Once there, he found out that his son, Jerry, had taken his advice that if the waters ever looked unnatural, it was time to "beat it." Jerry had done this in the nick of time.

Having given up drinking six months before, Mac fought the urge to have a drink "every five minutes for the next twenty-four hours." His determination won and he stayed sober. Mac felt guilty that it was his boat that had overturned. "It was my skiff in that picture up on the bridge over the highway," he said. "That was the one reason I had so damned much trouble later, as I was blaming myself for it." However, Mac had done as much as anyone could ever have expected.

Workers also discovered the remains of the Long Branch Tavern that morning. The remnants were left exactly where Gary and Mac last saw them: in the grove of trees by the edge of Elk Creek. The structure was so mangled, the authorities burned everything on the spot. Gary's green ledger book carried through the grate and washed all the way to the ocean. It sailed in the currents halfway to the jetty before washing up on a beach. In fact, checks made out to the Long Branch Tavern were discovered later, dried out, and handed back to Gary, along with some of the cash found in the rubble by the grate.

Later that day, Gary left Bruce's house and headed to the home of his Uncle Fred, his mother's brother, who lived in town. A doctor gave Gary a sedative shot there to settle him down, and he next drank one-half of a bottle of V.O. Scotch. However, nothing seemed to work. Nothing seemed able to stop the pain that Gary felt over his losses, especially when the reality of it all came crashing down. His sister, Ginny, was recuperating at the time in a Novato, California, hospital. She learned about her mother's death while watching the cleanup efforts on television. The reporters were there when Gay's body was discovered on the banks of Elk Creek and identified, and they quickly announced the news to Ginny's shock.

After the workman discovered the bodies, Gary was walking slowly over the bridge in the afternoon. Logs, soiled merchandise, and driftwood were strewn over the structure, most dropped there by the steam shovel rooting through the rubble, some deposited earlier by the ocean's overflows. He spotted a white object lying upright among the wreckage and between two large logs. It stood scant feet from where his father died.

On closer inspection, Gary discovered this to be a small, twelve-inch high statue of Jesus Christ. He first thought that the tidal waves had washed it from a curio shop. "There it was, standing so tall, amidst the ruins," he said later. "It didn't have a scratch or any discoloration from the ocean. The only thing it was missing was the felt backing, and that was easily replaced." He didn't know that national newspapers across the country had run the story and picture of the "small statue by the skiff on the bridge" until years later.

With funerals to plan and attend, Gary Clawson encountered his friend, Jim Burris. When they went to inspect the telephone pole where Jim had lost his thumb, they discovered that the severed appendage was still attached to the pole by the severing metal. Although they delicately removed the thumb, it could not be surgically reattached.

DAYLIGHT CREPT into the wreckage of Mabel Martin's home. Peering upwards through the debris, she saw that the currents had ripped away an entire corner of her room. Parts of the roof, ceiling, and other debris still covered and pinned the old woman down painfully to her crumpled bed. As the sun rose in intensity with its warming colors, she saw "dirty rocks and gray mud outside." Due to her hypothermia, she didn't feel as cold now as she had during the night. Mabel said later, "I also saw the old electric light plant put up by the Hobbs and Wall Company. Then I realized how far I had gone. In all, my home had traveled over three blocks, and I was now near the Hamilton Brothers Mill."

Her watery journey had come to an end in the middle of the field, west of the McNamara and Peepe Lumber Mill in the graveyard of debris deposited by the sea. Cars, houses, boats, furniture, clothes, and everything imaginable had been dumped here—including dear Mabel Martin with her mattress and the remains of her home. However, she was fortunate in landing where she did and not being dragged back into the sea. This would have happened if the house hadn't caught on land, along with the other bounty held captive, before the sea reversed itself.

She wasn't discovered until mid-morning that following day, over eight hours after the last wave hit. Mabel wrote later: "I was found at 10:30 A.M. the next morning with the nightgown I had on, my blankets, and mattress. I began to call for help, again and again, and finally a woman looking for her cow found me. I don't know who she is, but I would certainly like to, and even feel like kissing her cow. Bless them both."

It is possible that "the woman looking for a cow" had come by and then immediately left Mabel to find help. Ray Schach of Crescent City Lumber, Bernie McClendon, and two others, however, are the ones credited with hearing her cries and coming to her aid. Ray said, "When I heard her sounds, I thought that they had been made by a lamb." It was ironic that Bernie McClendon helped pull the rubble off and free Mabel; not only was he her landlord and head of the local California National Guard, but he was also the last one to see her when he gave her the Easter candy. Rescuers immediately drove her to Seaside Hospital.

Once there, Mabel Martin was "so cold that I thought I would never get warm again." While being treated for exposure, she took a cup of coffee but said, "I couldn't even hold the cup, because I was shaking so badly." Mabel had survived a trip, however, that even a young person would have found arduous, and she spent weeks in the hospital before recovering.

While a doctor stitched up their father at the hospital, Doug and Steve Pyke began drying out money at their grandmother's house. The family had retrieved it later from their building after the tsunami left. It took a day or so for the money to dry out. The Pyke brothers recalled that sand had been piled over the floors, streets, and around the buildings in their area. However, it was the fish that stood out. "They were everywhere," said Doug. "The ocean had left flounder, perch, and all other types around and inside our store—in fact, some were wedged inside the walls. I don't know how they ever got there, given the small size of the cracks."

His Uncle Bud had parked his brand new Jeep Wagoneer by the store, and the tidal wave had taken it away. The family discovered it later at the Safeway parking lot, deposited right side up as if it had just been picked up for a drive. When they first looked for the Jeep at their parking lot, the Pykes noticed that other people's cars were smashed upside down or jammed on top of one another.

As the family stood in waist-deep water, hearing glass break and debris grind against the walls, their Uncle Bud suddenly remembered that a 1,100-dollar check (from selling the family's electric organ the day before) was still in his wallet in a coat pocket. In the panic, Bud had left the coat draped over one of the cash register stations that was now probably swirling in the sea. The next morning, when the family searched through the rubble in their cleanup, they found the coat on the cash register—still dry with the check and wallet inside just where he had left it.

Ernie Pyke went directly home after being stitched up. That morning, the family headed back to clean up their store, startled at the destruction and debris they found. That day they encountered one of the rare problems with looters. The Pykes were taking merchandise out to dry in the parking lot, when "some people from Brookings" came by, grabbed some of their goods, and ran. "We were so tore up then by what had already happened, that all we could do was watch—but I could have shot them," recalled Ernie.

However, Don Mather, Jim Howland, and John Howland guarded the cash in the registers and the safe at the Bay City Market that night, their loaded shotguns trained outside into the darkness. Any would-be looters were lucky to have avoided that place! Although the men represented the "private" army that had emerged to patrol and guard their stores and the town quite effectively that night, formal law and order needed to be reinstated.

Joe and Eleanor McKay lost everything to the ocean: all clothing, wallets and money, car keys, their glasses, and even the tools of his trade (he had brought along his cooking utensils). In fact, their only possessions were what they had on when jumping for their life from the motel unit, Joe wearing only a bathrobe, his wife grabbing a simple coat to wear over her nightgown. After a doctor stitched up Joe, the Reverend John McMath took the couple to the El Patio Motel for the night, and others gave them needed clothing.

The grader dropped Ruth Long off that early morning at the very top of L Street, away from the destruction below. Depending on their needs, evacuees were helped from there into awaiting cars for transport to the hospital or to the county fairgrounds where cots and tents were being set up, per Bill Parker's emergency plan operation. She then recognized her dentist as one of the volunteer drivers, all being part of the plan. He drove Ruth, her baby, and their dog in his jeep to her aunt and uncle's house located on higher ground. By then, Dale had located his mother, and they rejoined his family there, staying the night.

Diane Anderson had watched the tsunami from the upstairs window of her parent's house, next to Seaside Hospital. Since she had worked at the hospital in admissions for several months before finding another job, she went to the hospital to help out. Injured people were coming in so quickly that Diane could only tape their names on their wrists and put them to bed or in a waiting area for further treatment. She vividly remembered Mrs. William Wright in the emergency room, "hysterical" over losing her two young kids and being treated then for shock.

Later that night, Roy Magnuson happily discovered that his house had not been damaged. After picking up a friend, they returned to help in the search and rescue efforts. At a beach motel, Roy searched through the ruins. "It was pitch black, as I remember it, and a very strange scene," he said. They walked through dark rooms, water damage and destruction surrounding them, with no lights to guide them except for their flashlights. They saw "lots of things scattered about, like alarm clocks, luggage, clothing, and suitcases—but there were no people. No one was there."

Near daybreak, Roy and his friend left for home, hoping that most everybody had been able to get out safely. Roy discovered that morning that the tidal waves had sunk his thirty-two-foot salmon boat. Tied to concrete mooring pads, the high surges ripped it apart when the boat couldn't rise past its moorings. Some fishermen were able to refloat their boats by pulling them toward land during high tide, then repairing them when the tide was low, and refloating the vessels during the next high tides. Unfortunately, his was not one of them.

Richard Wier was ten years old at the time; his parents' house was located outside the inundation area, so his family was one of the luckier ones. He remembers when the police awakened his father that night to help with the dead and injured. His father not only owned Wier's Mortuary, but the local ambulance service as well. As the city's sole ambulance had just broken down, this meant that his father also owned the only other ambulance in town. It was in use the entire night and for several days afterwards.

The day after the sea wave hit, Richard and his friends played in the slough by his dad's mortuary, located at Fourth and G Streets. An open swale or "indented" swamp area of two square blocks was across the street from his dad's building. Tons of merchandise, including the canned goods and products from the Bay City Market, swirled around and had been deposited there. As kids, they had fun exploring what had been left there, from picking over the merchandise to finding one Confederate dollar. As Richard said, "It was like a 'gold mine' of things for kids to explore and find."

Upon returning to his store in the morning, Glenn Smedley of G&G Liquors found only heaps of broken glass inside. The liquor left on a top shelf had the labels washed off. Health officials then condemned all the food and bottles that were even left in the downtown stores that night. "They dredged out a spot at the landfill," he said. "The trucks dumped their loads of bottles and debris into it, and then a Caterpillar tractor ran over each load. Whatever was flammable was burned." Glenn remembered the cleanup as a time when the whole community worked together. "There were so many people affected by it," he said, "that it brought the county together."

WITH INFORMATION now speeding in, the full extent of the deaths, injuries, and destruction was staggering. Eleven people had died, scores were missing, and over sixty people were injured. "Frenchy" Arrigoni and James Parks died in the same area near Seaside Hospital, the site of savage currents that reached the steps of that building. Bill and Gay Clawson, Nita and Earl Edwards, and Joanie Fields drowned on the western side of town under the Elk Creek Bridge. Lavella (Belle) Hillsbery and Juanita Wright's two children died in the Highway 101 South area. Given the unsuccessful results of the searches, the authorities presumed that Sergeant Donald McClure had drowned in the Klamath River, fifteen miles away.

Not counted in the official Crescent City account is the loss by Peggy Sullivan of her unborn child. Orin Magruder, 73, died at home of a heart attack and is sometimes mentioned as a casualty, although a few accounts report that he died quietly in his sleep. The four McKenzie children drowned further north in Oregon.

People who chose to stay inside and ride the waves out had

fewer injuries, although this depended entirely on where their home was located and whether it was in the direct path of the ocean. Most fatalities occurred when people fled outside with nowhere else to go. Some rode the waves on extraordinary journeys, living to tell about it. Those who died carried their stories with them forever.

The tidal surges didn't stop, even after the last big wave receded. During that early morning and into the following day, the bay and Elk Creek experienced extraordinary surges as the ocean tried to regain its equilibrium. Searchers and shocked residents alike kept a wary eye towards the abnormal seiching and rapid in-and-out tide movements. In fact, several rescue and cleanup operations shut down entirely when the nearby boiling surf became too unnerving.

Family members poured into the Sheriff's Office or tried to talk their way into the downtown areas, searching for missing loved ones. The official list of the missing at first was set at fifty and even higher by some newspaper accounts. The numbers of transients and tourists passing through or in the bars and motels hit by the waves made it difficult to establish a clear casualty list.

The man who Guy Ames and his friends watched disappear was never seen again. When the teenagers later matched descriptions of that individual with the official missing list, there was no record of him. Not being listed as officially dead or missing is misleading. In order to make the count of who was "officially" missing, the authorities needed to know that a specific person was in town that night, he or she wasn't around afterwards, and their whereabouts could not be ascertained later.

Bill Whippo and Deputy Sheriff Jim Custer later tried to locate the driver and the Plymouth that the tsunami sped Whippo past on his ride inland over the Highway 101 South area. Bill knew the type of car, as he said, by the "fins on the back." The two men checked all over the area, including searching the various mounds of trucks and cars piled on land. Whippo never found the car or its driver.

People drove up and down the coast all the time, looking for a job or visiting friends from Seattle to Los Angeles. When someone disappears without a trace, no one would know how or when that specifically took place. Some investigators believe that is what happened in Crescent City with several "unofficial" deaths, especially given this event's calamity and power.

A twelve-year-old boy, Michael Stevens, told Governor Brown what he had seen. Michael was staying with his parents at an ocean-front motel as the family drove home to Redmond, Washington. After the high waters had driven them to an upper floor, the boy watched "an elderly man and his wife" struggle through the swirling waters below. The woman fell, as the man tried to pick her up. The governor quoted the boy as saying, "Then a car came along with nobody in it and hit them. I never saw them again."

The official list was pared down over several days to fifteen, and one man listed in the newspapers as missing did eventually return. Sheriff's deputies were tipped off and subsequently located Frank D. Sobrero, age forty-four, who was "missing." They arrested him on a warrant for failing to follow the terms of his probation.

The authorities finally narrowed its official list down to three missing persons, although this number is still contested. At that time, Tuttie Clark, Robert Mertz, and Erick Lundberg (believed to be driving a 1956 Ford station wagon with Oregon plates) were listed as missing. Some residents say they aren't missing; others maintain that more than three people passed through from other states, the ocean quickly sweeping away their cars or tents and forever washing away all the evidence out to sea.

People jammed into Seaside Hospital. Twenty-five injured tsunami victims initially were brought in, joined by others desperately trying to locate missing family members or friends. The injured had severe cuts and bleeding, broken legs and limbs, concussions, broken backs, shock, and other severe injuries. The hospital tried to get its staff back in, but all of its telephone lines were out. The people on duty could only try and comfort those who were searching for others and refer them to the sheriff's department.

No business was conducted that morning, as the tsunami had destroyed or caused major damage to 150 businesses. Just twenty-nine commercial operations incurred only minor damage, and two thirds of the businesses in the city had been wiped out completely or weren't able to operate. A combined total of 290 businesses and homes had been destroyed or damaged, including ninety-one homes and nineteen trailers.

The tidal waves had severed or ripped out telephone, sewer, water, and gas lines in numbers of areas, including downtown and Highway 101 South, and over four hundred people were homeless with another 150 temporarily forced out. The bodies of dead animals, from cats and dogs to horses and cows, were scattered over land and sea. The Greyhound bus station was destroyed, leaving just an outer shell and its cement floor lifted three feet higher.

There were no food, clothing, or transportation centers available within close-by parts of the city, as no restaurants, grocery stores, bus stations, or even barbershops could open inside the inundation area. In fact, Safeway and all other markets had to throw away all of the food they had on stock, given the extent of destruction to their facilities and state regulations.

Barreling inland one to two miles over a twelve-mile swatch of the city and its surroundings, the retreating waves left behind a huge amount of debris, including 2.5 million board feet of lumber widely scattered around, one thousand wrecked cars, numerous shattered buildings, and thousands and thousands of fish from the ocean. Fish were everywhere, in hanging flower baskets, rafters, drawers, walls, trees, and clumped in large piles. When Dale Long opened his car trunk, some distance from where he had parked it, he found it loaded down with fish.

The tidal waves had splintered numbers of houses or spun them from their foundations, and the remnants littered the streets at crazy angles. Huge four-foot wide or wider redwood logs had slammed completely through entire buildings; some smashed through walls in one place, then crashed through another portion when the seas receded. The walls of hotels, motels, and other buildings bulged out, showing the ocean's force when it receded back so powerfully. Land where apartment buildings once stood now looked like trashed parking lots.

Boats, logs, smashed houses, overturned trailers, merchandise, cars, and debris littered the land and ocean for miles. Parking lots, streets, sidewalks, and streetlights had been swept away. The seawall on Front Street was gouged out in wide stretches with deep canyons left behind. Nearly all the trees were uprooted, houses and trailers washed completely away for long distances, and the asphalt topping on streets sheared off. Mud, silt, sand, and seaweed were heaped around and over the driftwood, lumber, wrecked cars, and huge logs left in heaps and elephant-graveyard depositories. A stench of salt water, decaying seaweed, dead fish, and burning gasoline pervaded the air.

The surges trashed automobiles and dumped several on top of one another in high heaps. Cars were stacked three, even four high, with the lighter trunks of some washed over and slammed onto the heavier fronts of others. Vehicles had been slammed through storefront windows and buildings, jammed upside down, wrapped around telephone poles, propped up on parking meters, rolled over and over into twisted metal shells, or swept out to sea. Buckner's Used Car lot looked like its cars had been stirred with a giant mixing spoon, the currents leaving five cars stacked against one light pole at its front. Sand was left behind, sometimes up to two inches, but less than expected due to the tsunami's strong receding power.

AT THE HARBOR, the tidal waves sank or capsized fifteen commercial fishing vessels that were thirty feet long or more; three ships were never found and seven destroyed in the supposedly protected moorage area between the sand barrier and Citizen's Dock, when the tidal waves turned 180 degrees around and powered their way into that secluded area. These surges slammed the vessels against one another and the inside jetty. The ocean washed one boat completely over the fuel dock, lodging this one between the dock and an inner sea wall, while smashing others over the beach and inland areas.

The tsunami's actions had capsized, destroyed, or sunk a total of twenty-five commercial fishing boats, due in part to their being moored at both ends while the ocean surged forward, then sucked back to leave the boats wallowing in mud. Boats weren't in the harbor as they should be, but instead far inland, smashed against buildings, or capsized miles away in the ocean. Numbers of pleasure boats and smaller craft had disappeared forever, and the coastal waters were a deep, murderous brown in place of the usual blues. The bay was littered at its bottom and nearly solid in places with destroyed cars, boats, appliances, logs, and lumber. Carried down from the logging camps of Washington and Oregon, tens upon tens of thousands of logs covered the beaches and coastal waters for miles in both directions.

The wave actions hit Citizen's Dock particularly hard. In 1950, Del Norte County citizens had raised 250,000 dollars in cash and materials, then donated the time to build this vital commercial wharf. They had added improvements to the dock over time, such as a small-boat launching facility, fish wing, commercial fish-unloading facility, and various buildings. The facilities included a small boat basin, floats, and docking areas.

The ocean's sudden draining and surging back numbers of times battered and twisted the dock out of shape, including damaging beyond repair or washing out over one-half of its support pilings. A huge lumber barge was tethered to the dock; it was 210 feet long with a fifty-five-foot beam and drew fifteen feet of water. A similar but empty lumber barge was floated out to sea from Brookings harbor as a precautionary measure. Unlike those circumstances, the Crescent City boat was not only fully loaded with over a million board feet of lumber, but also securely tied to its dock. The violent waters forced this heavy vessel up, over, down, and under the dock, and the barge smashed every part of the pier that it rammed into. The currents also swept over the barge, carrying lumber away and scattering it over the bay, city, and surrounding coastline.

After the tsunami passed, Citizen's Dock had buckled and the Coast Guard Station and Harbor Commission Building had washed out to sea, along with the boats, cars, and fishing boats. Located across the street from the Harbor Grotto, the Dock Cafe and Sea Scout Building were both washed into the Olson Shipping Company's lumberyards. They were smashed beyond repair and wedged against other shops, mounds of fish, and overturned boats.

The wave actions scattered lumber from Citizen's Dock, the Olson and Pacific Inland Navigation shipping companies, and other nearby lumber companies over the ocean, Crescent City, and Highway 101. The tidal waves tossed other smaller buildings and shops around like the boats, easily destroying or sweeping them into the bay. Numbers of cars and trucks bobbed up and down in the harbor, along with the capsized vessels and other debris.

Cranes, winches, forklifts, and other heavy equipment were also sucked into the sea. The concrete wave barrier protecting the small boat area by Citizen's Dock had been broken up, and deep channels gouged through beach areas when the tidal waves receded. The savage runoffs tore streetlights and parking meters from their concrete foundations or bent them at right angles, dug out and laid bare corrugated steel drainage culverts, and cut away a deep section of Front Street that was 150 feet long, ten feet wide, and five feet deep.

Dutton Dock on the other side of the Harbor survived, as the tidal surges weren't as strong there. This private lumber dock was also well engineered with steel straps, cross-bracing, and bolted connections between the decking and supporting piles. The Sause Dock was adjacent to the Dutton pier. It had been abandoned for several years and was in a state of decay. The surges cleanly lifted away all of the remaining decking and tossed this around the harbor.

The tsunami tore away nearly all of the channel buoys and carried them far out to sea. The harbor would need to be dredged and cleaned up, as sunken debris now littered its bottom. Sand silted the bay in wide areas and required substantial dredging. The receding ocean scoured away new channels, including one that was eighty feet wide and stopped in deep ocean.

Constructed with 1,975 twenty-five-ton, concrete tetrapods (huge, four-pronged structures that look like giant jacks and fit together), the outer breakwater by the Lighthouse still stood. To keep the heavy seas from destroying this important barrier, in 1956–1957 the Army Corp of Engineers had interlaced the tetrapods on the seaward side of the outer breakwater. The tetrapods remained basically intact, despite the savage flows that ran back and forth. However, even on this jetty, repair work would need to be completed.

When daylight finally came, Peggy Coons and her husband saw that the commercial fishing boats that had found safety rode in the offshore swells. Bouncing over the sea during the night, one of the fishing shacks had finally sunk. The boat that had magically slid up

Elk Creek was now on land, inside the destroyed Olympic Pool by the beach. Peggy observed:

> The whole beachfront was a mass of destruction. Logs, boats, furniture, cars, along with buildings were tossed helter-skelter. The lumber from three big yards was high on the beach or floating around in the water. The two small buildings, along with cars that had washed off the dock, had faded from sight. Some of the boat landings and small crafts were sailing around on top of the ocean in a dizzying pattern.
>
> At midday, the tide flowed in and filled the basin so full that it ran back over the breakwater. The big tug returned, hooked onto the lumber barge, and pulled it back out to sea. The other boats came in, hovering around the Coast Guard cutter. The silent killer, after taking its toll of life and property had left. Isolated on the island, we watched the search begin the next morning along Elk Creek for bodies. . . . It was hard to believe that, of all the things that floated by, the only bit of salvage to reach the island was one spool of lavender thread!

As the violent ocean surges around the Battery Point Lighthouse were continual over this time, they kept the captured objects and debris in constant motion. These ended up either inland or in the ocean, but could never come to a rest at this place.

The oil tanks at the Hussey-Texaco bulk-oil plant continued to burn out of control with dense smoke billowing over the area. Adjacent structures such as Nichol's Pontiac, service stations, and adjoining shops had burned to the ground or were severely damaged. Other fires followed these, including a home in a housing tract that caught fire at 2:00 A.M. on Sunday morning, twenty-four hours after the last tidal-wave action. Fortunately, the husband and wife had led their six children to safety from the house, so no deaths or injuries occurred there.

Neither the owners nor their neighbors had been able to telephone this fire disaster in, since phone service was still cut to this area. The alarm couldn't be given to any authorities until one neighbor drove away and finally located a California Highway Patrolman, then directing traffic around the disaster area. The patrolman radioed in the alarm. By the time the seventeen firemen and volunteers arrived, the flames had consumed the entire structure.

The experiences of the Crescent City fire department and others are very typical as to what happens with tsunamis. Fires are a natural, terrifying outgrowth of tidal waves. The powerful currents hurl debris against gasoline storage tanks, butane or propane tanks, gas tanks, gas lines—anything storing flammable liquids or gases—easily puncturing or ripping them apart. The volatile fluids and gases are quickly ignited when tanks collide, sparks shower from shorted electrical wires, power poles topple into gasoline pools, or any number of other ways.

Fire crews are hamstrung in their firefighting efforts, and confusion reigns with wrong decisions made. The tidal waves can inundate or earthquakes destroy fire department vehicles with their drivers. Street damage and obstacles hinder firemen from getting to the conflagrations. Communication systems are down or very badly damaged, thus adding more delays to response times. Even when equipment and fire personnel are in place, everyone must be continually on guard so that they don't become victims of another towering surge. All of these risks and problems occurred in Crescent City.

Only the courageous efforts by the firefighters prevented the flames from spreading to the entire city, even though they couldn't do much about what had already happened. That by itself was a major accomplishment.

ALTHOUGH THE SUN had come out, the land and streets were just one color that day: a dirty gray from the tons of mud and silt left behind. There were no birds at the beaches. There were no dogs or cats playing with children, just mud and debris and destruction. People cried out and searched frantically for the missing—and wreckage from Crescent City had been strewn down the California coastline as far south as San Diego and Mexico.

Unsuspecting officials were crestfallen when they learned that morning about the extent of the destruction. Serving years later as the Mayor of Crescent City, Bob Seligman, recalled, "I came home and went to bed. I didn't know anything had happened." Seligman lived on the far west side of town, which is high above the low-lying areas. A friend called him up the next morning and asked if his business had survived the tidal wave. "What tidal wave?" replied Seligman with bewilderment. Later that day, he worked his way downtown and viewed the destruction. He couldn't believe what he saw.

Bernie McClendon heard the news about the impending tidal wave on television. A realtor, commander of the local National Guard unit, and a County Supervisor, Bernie raced downtown to meet the Chief of Police, Andy Keyzers. McClendon rode around with Andy and helped alert people about the possible danger, telling them to evacuate at least to Fifth Street. While they were making their rounds, another surge brought water and debris over the Front Street curb past Second Street. As the damage to structures appeared limited, even Bernie headed back home to watch television. He learned later about the last large waves when the lights at his home blacked out and he heard the fire alarms wailing. His wall clock showed that the time of the blackout was 1:46 A.M. Then, Norman Wier of Wier Mortuary knocked on his door and told him that most of the downtown had just been destroyed. Bernie toured the area later that day and wrote:

> I, as Company Commander, made an inspection and found that from the south city limits near the Breakers Motel on Highway 101, the highway was blocked by debris and displaced buildings. Within the tangle of building materials, logs of all description, and downed power and phone lines, only foot traffic was possible.
>
> Front Street was littered with debris of all kinds from partially demolished buildings to just about anything one could imagine. Our two office buildings and the house where Mrs. Mabel Martin lived had vanished and the concrete building at Front and M was standing but damaged. Further down the street toward the Seaside Hospital, the Royal Motel and Thunderbird Motel had endured severe damage. Cliff Moore's place was buckled and where the present B Street is, a trailer had been upended and was sticking high into the air.

On Second Street, going back easterly, I found the devastation even greater. Several buildings had been completely destroyed or badly damaged, and even the two-story Odd Fellows' Masonic Temple had been torn lose from its foundation and moved. Numbers of automobiles were tossed about and lodged against power poles, buildings, or stacked one on top of another.

The old Ford Agency building, leased by Harold Thoreson, was blocking Second Street, and around all of it was scattered merchandise and slime from the ocean. To the best of my recollection, every building along Second Street, and those between Front and Second Street, were destroyed or suffered extensive damage—such as at the Tides. Trehearne's building had buckled so that the sides were bulged, and Hiller's Service Station was completely missing. The old Piggly Wiggly building (occupied by Bob Ames) was standing, as was Glen's Bakery, but both had suffered extensive damage. Several automobiles were twisted around a power pole in front of Ames's Store. At the corner of Second and N, Crescent City Lumber Company's building had moved and stacks of lumber that had been decked were no longer visible.

On Third Street, the damage was obvious. G&G Liquor store took a beating with considerable merchandise floating with the tide. The same held true with the Ben Franklin store and the old Safeway, now where Beno's located. Daly's and First Western Bank were badly damaged, along with houses and homes clear up to Fifth Street.

Damage along Highway 101 south of town was equally depressing, and at the harbor, the Grotto and other buildings had taken a devastating beating. As the water in the bay receded before surges, fishing boats and crafts in the bay settled on the sand. Those that remained upright floated clear as the water came back, but those boats and crafts that had turned on their sides filled with water and were inundated, creating serious salvage problems for their owners.

13

Restoring a City's Life

Early Saturday morning, sheriff deputies, California Highway Patrol, Coast Guard, and other authorities were too busy escaping the last big surges or trying to rescue people to assess or report how much damage had in fact occurred. They discovered the extent at daybreak.

After Bernie McClendon learned how bad the devastation was, he told the first sergeant and company clerk in his National Guard unit to alert all other reserve members to meet as soon as possible at the Sheriff's Office. By word of mouth, knocking on doors, and using combat mobile telephones, nearly everyone in that National Guard company was contacted. The sun hadn't yet risen when personnel began pouring into the disaster office headquarters. McClendon gave orders to immediately start patrolling the disaster areas and safeguard lives and property. The authorities were handicapped in their communications at first due to the downed telephone lines. They used messengers and mobile phones as alternatives to communicate until communications lines were restored and a grid established.

Local, state, and federal authorities sent personnel to the aid of the stricken city, including the U.S. Agriculture Department, which at that time oversaw the national forests. Government officials from nearby cities such as Gasquet (close to Jedediah Smith State Park), Smith River, Fort Dick, and Klamath to Eureka farther away, also came to offer their support. Crescent City and Del Norte County department heads—from road, engineering, building, and sanitation to health and civil defense—quickly reported to pre-set meeting places. All had to show proper identification at the checkpoints being established around the areas of destruction.

While authorities were conferring, the fire department was fighting the fires, telephone and power companies inspecting to see how to restore service, ambulances were taking the injured to hospitals, and Seaside Hospital began treating those first waves of the injured. A control center was set up at the new jail building to coordinate the overall emergency response.

Bill Parker telephoned an aide to Governor Edmund G. "Pat" Brown of California, who worked at the state's Disaster Office and with whom he had talked earlier that night. Bill simply said, "Crescent City is wiped out." Stunned, the man replied, "But you told me that there was only minor flooding. How can I tell the governor that?" Parker calmly answered that with the coming of daylight, he saw that the destruction was beyond all comprehension. The state office quickly called Governor Brown, who made immediate plans to fly to Crescent City.

As the Del Norte Civilian Defense Director, Parker declared a state of extreme emergency at 5:00 A.M. after his conferences. An emergency meeting of the Del Norte County Board of Supervisors and the City Council of Crescent City was held later that morning at 8:00 A.M. They confirmed the emergency declaration, and Bill Parker sent a request to Governor Brown to declare Del Norte County as a disaster area, in order to start the process to receive state moneys and assistance. At the same time, Crescent City officials were making the required assessments so that they could request President Lyndon Johnson to declare the location as a national disaster area, thus making available federal program assistance. The authorities also contacted the regional Red Cross center in San Francisco for help.

Countless numbers of people immediately needed food, housing, dental, and medical help. There was the fear and danger of disease, typhoid, and an epidemic of rats, and the area needed to be safeguarded from looters and lawlessness. Services that people took for granted, such as electricity, water, sanitation, heat, eating, and even banking had to be restored. Streets and roads had to become passable again, and transportation functions reinstated. Law and order had to be put back in place.

At 9:30 A.M. that day, Governor Brown arrived by plane for an on-the-spot inspection. He had spent the night in nearby Eureka in Humboldt County, after inspecting a controversial highway path through a particularly beautiful section of redwoods in a state park. When his aide told him that early morning about the news of the destruction, he canceled any further plans in Humboldt County and flew north to Crescent City.

Governor Brown toured the tsunami-damaged area, nearly becoming another headline. During the first hours of the cleanup, a cousin of Ruth Long had started his bulldozer. He had just put his heavy equipment into reverse and was not watching where it was moving. The governor was then making his tour of the same disaster area as the bulldozer bore down on him. At the very last moment, Brown saw the heavy equipment heading his way and was forced to dive out of harm's way.

After touring the inundation area, Governor Brown was visibly shaken by what he had seen. He said in muddy shoes and dirty trousers later at the airport, "It was terrible. The people don't know what hit them, yet." His deepest impression of the trip came from his conversation with the boy, Michael Stevens, who described the older couple that had disappeared underneath the raging waters. The Governor wasted no time declaring Crescent City a disaster area, and he ordered the California Disaster Office Director, John Gaffney, to take personal charge in arranging all necessary and allowable state aid to the stricken city.

CIVILIAN DEFENSE personnel, Sheriff O. E. Hovgaard and his deputies, Police Chief Andrew Keyzers and his Crescent City policemen, national guardsmen under Bernard McClendon, and many deputized volunteers rolled up their sleeves to search for the injured, keep the peace, secure the cordoned-off area, and aid in the general cleanup efforts that started that very day. Every one knew that the city was paralyzed and restoring essential services a prime objective.

Long hours were put in by both residents and authorities. Policeman Johann Jochimsen said, "We worked twenty hours a day at first, then cut down to twelve-hour shifts." The entire downtown and Highway 101 South areas were cordoned off to prevent looting, and people could only enter by showing proper identification and a pass. Police Chief Keyzers said, "These closed-off sections are limited to people who have business establishments in the area or other authorized people. However, everyone who enters does so at their own risk."

California State Highway Patrol (CHP) units established roadblocks both north and south of Crescent City that Saturday, routing traffic around the devastated city. Commanders sent extra units over from Yreka to aid in this work. Units of the California State Fish and Game Commission and the Sheriff's Marine Posse from Humboldt County joined local city and county police units to patrol the streets and aid in the search for the injured and missing. The California State Military Reserve sent in thirty-seven troops on Saturday night alone to aid in patrolling and protecting the city's residents. This additional manpower was essential not only for law and order, but also because sightseers from outside the area were clogging the highways and interfering with the cleanup operations.

Sheriff Hovgaard and his patrolmen handled law enforcement in town, while the CHP took over the traffic problems. The CHP Commissioner called personally and offered as many men, vehicles, and equipment as the county required for law enforcement.

Although the police station was normally closed from 6:00 P.M. to 6:00 A.M., the Police Chief called in reserves, deputized volunteers, and accepted volunteer help to man the station 24/7. Their duties extended beyond normal law enforcement functions, now including prevention of looting, control of disaster areas, and even later guarding disabled cars until insurance companies could tow them away. They also helped other agencies such as California Fish & Game reconstruct records lost or damaged when the tsunami wrecked their offices.

After the last large tidal wave receded, the fire department received numerous emergency requests concerning electrical shorts, gas leaks, and fires. They couldn't handle all of the problems at first and tried to concentrate on what appeared to be the most serious situations, even though many had a high-risk potential. It was almost too difficult to contain those fires that were already blazing, not to mention the serious risk of others occurring—especially after one house burned to the ground due to the lack of telephone service. Later that day, the department opened its station doors so volunteers could pass out food and coffee to people working on the cleanup. After the fire danger passed, firemen washed down streets and parking lots, pumped seawater from buildings, and supervised the burning of the mountains of debris and wrecked structures.

Local ham operators filled a void by reestablishing communications, a high priority. Their ability to get messages in and out of the area took pressure off the Sheriff's Department, especially in answering the crush of desperate questions being asked by people searching for lost ones or relatives who lived in Crescent City. Fire personnel also monitored the numerous offers of aid that came pouring in from around the country.

Using their mobile radio equipment, Bill Beard (then President of the Amateur Radio Association) and other ham personnel established a grid of operators in different areas, ranging from U.S. Highway 101 North down to Eureka and Arcata. Early that Saturday morning, they delegated responsibilities on who would handle military messages, connect with telephone operators outside the stricken city, or communicate with civil defense headquarters and the Red Cross. Two former ship operators with knowledge of U.S. Navy procedures talked with officers on board the U.S.S. *Bennington*—a 27,100-ton Essex class aircraft carrier—which eventually took over all traffic control and became the network control station. The ham network logged over 3,200 messages in twenty-four hours and then shut down, its mission fulfilled. This ad-hoc network took a sizeable load off the law enforcement agencies during this important time period by its handling of many non-emergency calls.

The tsunami had severed a Second Street telephone cable, the prime reason behind the downtown area's loss of service. When this line carrying southbound traffic became lost, operators were forced to reroute calls to the north. Telephone lines were also down in other areas due to destroyed and damaged poles with spotty service from the worsening corrosion caused by the ever-present saltwater.

Replacing telephone service in downtown areas was further delayed when the telephone company had to wait for a city council decision whether utilities would be buried underground: this idea eventually was approved. The telephone company strung temporary wiring to Seaside Hospital, but many other areas didn't have telephone service for months. Outside the disaster area, over 10,000 telephone calls (of which 7,500 were long distance) were handled between midnight Friday and midnight Saturday—a remarkable statistic, given that parts of the service were out and only 3,000 people lived in the city.

Still-working power lines had to be shut off during the night so workers could repair the destroyed ones. This reconstruction process would take nearly two months before underground electrical cables could be laid and full service finally restored. Until then, people had to rely on portable generators for their electricity. Emergency crews worked overtime to shut off damaged propane and butane tanks. The restoration of heating was easier since new propane tanks could be installed more quickly with new piping and heaters, whereas entire systems needed to be reconstructed for utilities such as telephone, sewer, and power.

Until new sewer and sanitation facilities could be built, police kept people out of the cordoned-off area for security and sanitation reasons—unless they had a valid pass and reason for being there. The permits were valid only for the specific address where one was working, and didn't allow any moving about the general area. Two local residents decided to test this and wandered off from their specifically assigned store location to look around. A policeman quickly stopped both of the women and told them in no uncertain terms to get back to where they were supposed to be or they would be "put where they belonged."

Buildings had to be demolished and removed from the area, especially where sewage was leaking from ruptured sewers or septic tanks. Many structures were unsafe. When Ruth and Dale Long inspected their apartment on top of G&G Liquors, the couple knew that they had to be very careful. They discovered that the raging waters had torn away the supports for the upper floor, having hurled a huge redwood tree, long branches and trailing roots intact, through the lower portions. The floor now rested on that tree as its main support.

Huge logs, nine feet of ocean, and heavy waterlogged rolls of newsprint devastated the *Del Norte Triplicate*'s building at Third and J Street. Mud oozed everywhere, and the offices smelled of kelp and fish. The main newspaper offices were temporarily moved to publisher Jim Yarborough's home, and the printing completed at a sister publication's facilities in Arcata—a two-hour's drive south of Crescent City.

That Saturday afternoon, Wally Griffin in an extraordinary effort published a special edition of his *Crescent City American*. With the city's other lead newspaper, the *Del Norte Triplicate*, severely disabled, Wally knew he had to record what had happened and tell the city. Fortunately, his facilities were located one block from where the ocean's surges finally stopped.

After a neighbor, Elaine Cherny, warned him by telephone that a tidal wave had just washed into the Tides, at Front and I Street, where she worked, Wally grabbed his camera and started taking pictures, having to run and drive for his life when the third wave hit. By driving the back roads behind the city to Highway 199 and then back into town, he managed to avoid the monster fourth wave. While an editor and reporters worked on interviews, Wally took pictures and assessed what had happened, including spending time on Saturday in an airplane inspecting the damage and taking aerial photographs.

Griffin then knit together all of the information and pictures and went to press. The lead, front-page and other disaster stories were accurate, and the columns gave vital information on emergency measures, as well as where people could be fed, housed, and clothed. In hindsight, it is remarkable that this edition came out as well and fast as it did on the day of such a disaster. It would be two-and-a-half days later before Wally Griffin would finally be able to get to bed and sleep after first receiving the disaster news.

Nearly six feet of water had covered the U.S. Post Office on Third Street. The currents knocked over letter cases; a big log had skewered the walls; and when the wave receded, it sucked out letters like a vacuum cleaner. Postal workers later discovered much of the mail in a rear parking lot and adjacent hedges. Employees picked up the wet mail, trucked it to the U.S. Agricultural Building by the airport, then cleaned and dried it, so that the mail could be delivered the next day. Over 95 percent of the mail was delivered, even though the tidal waves had ripped mailboxes from their cement anchors and carried them away for blocks, including one that was discovered in the McNamara-and-Peepe graveyard. The old high school was used as a processing postal center until a new location could be set up. The Eureka post office sent up equipment so that by Monday morning Crescent City's post office even had a window open for service.

The manager of the Well's Fargo bank branch opened that Saturday at a temporary location. Its original place at Second and K Streets was part of the most devastated portions of the city. The sea had carried away all of the furnishings except for the heavy iron vault. Workmen hastily nailed up large plywood sheets over the gaping holes in the brick building.

United California Bank trucked up a temporary facility from San Francisco. With weekend help from their employees, the bank opened the next Monday at 10:00 A.M. from a small building behind the Redlands Cafe. This facility came complete with an operating bank alarm system. Both banks were back in their respective facilities within forty-five days. Crescent City's sagging economy yielded one benefit: ample vacancies for leased space existed away from the devastated downtown area.

The tidal waves had flooded nearly all of the service stations in or near town, and the danger of explosion was still a real risk. One Signal Oil service station, however, was open that night at Ninth and L Streets. The operator was forced to limit gasoline purchases when people started to arrive in numbers to "top off" their gas tanks.

Housing for the victims seemed to be fairly and quickly solved by offers that came pouring in from church groups, private citizens, the Red Cross, American Legion, Lions Club, and others. Residents who were fortunate to have relatives or summer cabins around the city, as in nearby Gasquet in the mountains, quickly left for those places. Through arrangements later made by the Civil Defense and Red Cross agencies, people were taken to motels in outlying areas and housed. Many locals volunteered their homes, and acting Welfare Director Gertrude McNamara set up emergency facilities in the Del Norte Fairgrounds.

County Sanitarian Joe Creisler was in charge of ensuring that adequate sanitation facilities were established that day. He arranged for "porta-potties" to be trucked in and municipal buildings made available under controlled situations. Except for passes, the cordoned-off areas were now off limits, as the spread of disease was a distinct risk. Many houses and buildings swept away or shredded had been hooked to septic tanks, and those tanks were now ripped open or ruptured underground with leaking refuse.

Whether from the city or outside its boundaries, doctors and nurses came in full force that day to Seaside Hospital, and the hearses of both Wier's and Roeder's Mortuaries were also in full use. Road Commissioner Harkey Forkner and his crew were in charge of clearing the log-jammed and debris-ridden roads and streets. Del Norte County Building Inspector Walter Davis was in charge of condemning the multitudes of unsafe homes and buildings. Volunteers worked alongside the police, road crews, and forest crews to help clear streets, remove debris, and tear down impeding or unsafe structures.

The U.S. Corps of Army Engineers, more California National Guard, and other policing units were quickly speeding into the area. Plans were made to bring in food, electrical generators, and portable sanitation devices. The authorities and charities trucked in potable water, along with donated clothing and canned food. Contacts were made to mobilize the equipment necessary to begin the massive cleanup.

Saturday was cloudy and the temperature in the cool, high 40s. An engulfing fog rolled in from the sea at 5:00 P.M., dampening spirits. Dressed in blue jeans and rubber boots, workers and store owners filled the town with their cleanup activities, the sounds of hammers, trucks carting away debris, and sledgehammer cracks cutting the air. Clothing stores, drugstores, supermarkets, hardware businesses, and nearly all other retail stores had to throw out countless tons of salt-waterlogged, once-valuable merchandise with little hope of salvaging anything.

At the same time, rescuers continued the search for victims buried beneath the rubble. Over the weekend, residents who had fled the quarantined area picked up passes from the Sheriff's Office, so that they could return to their home or work. But despite all this, people came to their churches or synagogue to pray at all hours. Residents joked, "we had as many churches as we had bars," and they stayed open longer for their parishioners now.

Attendance for Sunday's Easter services at the city's eleven churches was lower than normal with people trying to dig out of the tsunami's rubble. Although the children enjoyed a traditional Easter egg hunt on Good Friday, every other Easter activity other than church services was cancelled. Residents attended church, prayed hard, and then went back to salvaging possessions or searching for the injured or dead. There were no services at the Nazarene Church, however, which was the only church located near the beach. A seven-foot high tidal surge had pounded the building, leaving behind overturned pews, driftwood, and debris piled high.

HELP CAME FROM others and people pitched in, even before the tsunami withdrew from the area. Jo Anna McRoberts co-owned the Pizza King north of Highway 101. When she received word about the tidal waves, she knew they would need extra food for the locals and tourists. Jo Anna called up her husband, Curt, and asked him to bring down everything in the house that could make sandwiches, including a lot more coffee.

The tiny place soon became crowded with people, and according to Curt, "everyone seemed to be cold, scared, and confused." A wood fire was kept constantly burning to help people warm up. Two schoolteachers were still somewhat dazed after being rousted from their beachfront motel; they discovered the next morning that their motel had been reduced to "boards and debris." Forced from his radio station by the flooding high waves and severing of the building's power, KPOD's Bill Stamps came in to keep up with the news. Although usually closed by midnight, the McRoberts's store stayed open until five in the morning—and there was no charge for anything eaten or drunk during that time.

When the extent of the damage became apparent, the people of Crescent City seemed to know just what to do. They had been through storms and floods before. The owners of two large markets on the upper end of town, Louis Tosio of the Pacific Market and the Skeels of Ray's Market, spent the night running coffee and sandwiches down to the night patrols. People took in friends and strangers alike, when they had no other place to go.

Before anyone could arrive to help from out of town, a group of Seventh Day Adventists provided breakfast that morning, along with blankets and clothing at their school located above the inundation zone. When their regular stock of clothing became exhausted that Saturday, KPLY put the call out for more donations. The Seventh Day Adventists soon received so much clothing from residents that they had no place to store it. During the next few days, disaster victims poured into the school to get the clothing that they needed.

Just hours after the last surge receded, a Salvation Army truck from Eureka drove to Crescent City and arrived there that Saturday morning. By 10:00 A.M., their volunteers were passing out hot chocolate, coffee, and doughnuts to people working on the cleanup. The Smith River American Legion Post served workers with coffee and hot dogs, staying on the job until the Red Cross could set up their facilities and take over this task.

The Red Cross quickly flew in disaster experts from throughout California and the West Coast that morning who set up facilities that fed, housed, or clothed over five hundred people. It established headquarters at the Memorial Building just outside the devastated area; cots with blankets were set up for the homeless. Two nurses attended to those in shock or who were emotionally distraught, and sandwiches and coffee were fed to the hungry. By Sunday, complete meals with meat loaf or hot chili were served, along with coffee and food for the National Guardsmen and anyone else who needed it.

This agency by itself placed over two hundred people in rented apartments, motel units, and private homes. It gave direct financial aid, so that the homeless could pay for a place to stay and buy needed food, clothing, and medical services. The only condition on the cash payments was that the people should buy whatever they needed from local area businesses.

The Red Cross provided nearly sixty thousand dollars—the equivalent of half a million dollars today—in outright financial aid, mostly for rebuilding housing, restocking small businesses, and buying food, clothing, and shelter. All that people had to do was show up and apply. The agency also helped with burial expenses, so that everyone who died had a proper service and burial. The Red Cross later expanded its payments to include permanent housing, its stated objective being to help people so that they could help themselves.

One couple applied for and received moneys to buy a lot and the lumber for them to build a house. The Red Cross gave them half the funds, asking only that they help serve coffee and food if another disaster occurred. The agency quickly received all of the volunteer help needed, and even ended up with a surplus of clothing. The Red Cross later applauded the community's response to its calls for help.

The American Legion, Lions Club, churches, and other volunteer groups joined the efforts of the Red Cross to provide victims with temporary shelter, food, and clothing. The American Legion of Yuba City-Marysville, over three hundred miles away near Sacramento, California, sent two trucks and a trailerload of supplies to the city. They remembered the bad flood in their towns during 1955 and the generosity of Crescent City during their time of need. Money donations were sent to Crescent City from around the country and world, including from such faraway places as Nicaragua.

The Lions Club sponsored the Sea Explorer Scouts in town. When the Sea Scouts lost their meeting hall at Citizen's Dock, Lions Clubs from across the nation sent 3,500 dollars and the Texas clubs donated two large vans of clothing and food. Operating from a vacant store on Second Street, the Crescent City Lions distributed the cash, food, and clothing to the needy, giving what was left over to the Red Cross. The young Sea Scouts helped with the cleanup of the dock area, the repair of fishermen's boats, and the removal of debris from the harbor.

Similarly, residents helped out one another. Ruth and Dale Long spent the next days cleaning up and repairing their shop, until a heavy sheet of steel smashed down on Dale's foot, fracturing it badly. They didn't know then how they would pay for the doctor. The Elks Club, however, gave each of their members one hundred dollars to help in the recovery. The doctor sent them a bill for exactly one hundred dollars.

UPWARDS OF two-hundred volunteers turned up in the devastated downtown and Highway 101 South sections with their pick-ups, dump trucks, Caterpillar tractors, chain saws, and bare hands. No one had asked them to come down and help—they just did. They immediately began clearing off highways and streets—starting that first early Saturday morning—before most of the country even knew that a tidal wave had destroyed wide areas of Crescent City. Working alongside the police and CHP, these volunteers searched for the injured and missing. Friends, foes, customers, and strangers alike rolled up their sleeves to help the shopkeepers and homeowners clean out their soiled and destroyed structures. They did this for days, without expecting or receiving any payment.

Hundreds of thousands of tons of rubble and wreckage needed to be cleared away and disposed. From all over California, scoop shovels, bulldozers, bucket and claw cranes, dump trucks, vehicles with chains, flatbed trucks, tow trucks, and equipment of every size and shape were placed into operation. The California Division of Forestry Redwood Parks system sent eighty-two men, two bulldozers, and four fire trucks to assist in these efforts. The Department of Correction's Alder Forestry Conservation Camp near Klamath brought in sixty-four minimum-security inmates to help clear and repair the damaged roads. Scores of city, county, and volunteer crews began pulling down the homes and buildings that couldn't be salvaged—and that was nearly all of them. Major cleanup work, such as the docks and large buildings, were contracted to commercial firms.

Individuals made their own arrangements to wash off furniture and store items with friends. Business owners began tracking down salvageable inventory, some of it floating in the bay and others deposited inland miles away. People dried out their cash at home, or clipped them on clotheslines; in 1964 few safes were used, credit cards were uncommon, and checks weren't preferred in this city.

The corrosive action from the saltwater soon became evident. The brackish water already had rusted the *Triplicate*'s presses and printing machinery into a deep-red color before they could be moved. Daly's Department Store needed to discard all of its clothing and fabrics, as the metal tags quickly rusted and ruined the merchandise. The ocean had sand-logged and stiffened the shoes at Del Ponte Shoes on Third Street. The store had to throw 90 percent of its inventory away, opting to sell some of it off in a huge "tidal wave" sale where shoes went for fifty cents or a dollar a pair, depending on their condition.

A twenty-foot log pounded into Baker and Stanton's appliance store on Third Street, tearing out windows and a portion of the back wall; this store lost 95 percent of its stock. Burtshell's Paints was fortunate, losing only one-half of its inventory. There was one additional problem: the ocean had lifted their large counter on top of an aerosol paint can, which had sprayed white paint over everything. Gordon Johnson's Men's Store lost two-thirds of his inventory, finding shoeboxes that were wet on the outside but dry and sandy inside.

The surges ransacked The Coin Shop on Second Street, sweeping away most of its valuable coins. At the Safeway store, clerks shoveled goods into wheelbarrows and dumped them outside in huge piles. G&G Liquors lost its entire liquor inventory, even when the bottles were still good, but with the labels washed off. Under state law, all "contaminated" food and liquids had to be destroyed, regardless of whether the container was broken—not having labels qualified.

In the morning, National Guard troops had marched up and relieved Don Mather and his friends of their duties. Like nearly all of the businesses in that disaster area, Bay City Market would not be operational for some time. Over 90 percent of its produce and milk products already had gone bad or soured in the saltwater, and under that state law all of their non-perishable, canned goods had to be also destroyed.

Insurance covered none of these losses. Only the Ben Franklin and the Union bulk-oil facilities, covered by their company's national tidal wave coverage, were fortunate enough to receive compensation. All of the other 150 businesses took their losses right on the chin without any hope of reimbursement—and they didn't sue over this at that time either.

Cleanup crews bulldozed debris into huge piles near or on the beach. Under the watchful eyes of the fire department, the mountains of materials were set ablaze. The bonfires started that day and continued for weeks. These blazes were described as being the largest deliberate ones set since the San Francisco earthquake and fire of 1906.

In fact, by the time Joe and Eleanor McKay returned on Sunday to search for their possessions at the motel's new site (the tsunami had moved it far from its original location), they discovered that the units had already been bulldozed into rubble, the debris stacked up, and were now burning up in a blazing pile. Where the first settlers had camped over two centuries ago, the downtown remains of their built city were now ablaze.

Workers quickly moved debris to the sides of streets so that the roads could open. From there, it was trucked to the burn sites. Weeks would pass before all of the wrecked houses, trailers, huge redwood logs, damaged cars, merchandise, and other debris was picked up and disposed. It would take months before new houses and buildings could even begin to be built, as this depended on an urban renewal process that needed to be created.

The cleanup wasn't just limited to land. Skindivers began their salvage work in the harbor on Sunday, clearing away debris that had sunk or now bobbed on the surface. They searched the bottom to see which if any boats could be raised. Sunken boats that had swamped, but still in good condition, were towed toward land so that their owners could pump out the water and right the vessels.

Aiding in the recovery efforts, Coast Guard boats motored around the harbor. Stationed in Crescent City, the ninety-five-foot-long Coast Guard Cutter *Cape Carter* patrolled outside the harbor and searched for bodies and salvageable equipment. The Coast Guard tender *Magnolia* from Humboldt Bay retrieved the huge channel buoys that had swept out to sea. Smaller vessels began towing back to land half-sunk cars and appliances previously littering the bay.

When the damage in Crescent City became known, a Brookings-based Coast Guard cutter soon departed for the area. However, when leaving the port, the boat struck rocks from the jetty and bent a propeller shaft. Despite the damage, the boat continued down towards the city. It then discovered the Crescent City Coast Guard building floating three miles offshore. The boat towed the building to Brookings, then cruised back to Crescent City and joined the *Cape Carter* in the search and tow efforts. At the same time, the fifty-two-foot *Coos Bay* motorized lifeboat with its crew of four sailed to Brookings to take its place.

Unlike what would happen today, few lawsuits were filed over this tsunami—and those were brought by the redevelopment agency to condemn, or acquire, the land it wanted. Lawyers and their clients now would be suing insurance agents for "failing to disclose" potential non-coverage, the city for not taking adequate precautions or responses during the emergency, the police for not moving fast enough to protect persons and property, and any number of negligence actions designed to receive compensation. Class-action lawyers would be speeding into the disaster zone to sign up clients. It would be a legal haven—but a nightmare for everyone else. This didn't happen in those days. People instead focused on how they could rebuild their businesses and lives through their own efforts, rather than relying on the courts.

The Crescent City disaster became a national story. Once producers looked up where the city was located, journalists and television and radio producers flooded the area. Television newscasters Harry Reasoner, Ted Koppel, and Peter Jennings filed major stories. Walter

Cronkite later picked up the story of the "Comeback Town" and gave Crescent City another national story.

Monday brought some good news when the time locks of the city's three shattered banks clicked open early that morning. The bankers further discovered that the tidal waves had not damaged the money or records in those waterproof vaults. And by Monday night, eight of the fifteen townspeople who had been listed as "officially" missing showed up. They were unaware that they had even been the objects of a search.

SURVIVORS WERE cleaning up, trying to put their lives back together, and attending funerals. Juanita Wright found the inner strength to attend the joint services for her three-year-old daughter and ten-month-old son, placed quietly to rest and buried together in the same casket. No surviving relatives attended the services for Adolph Arrigoni and James Parks. The Red Cross assisted financially in arranging most of the funeral services that took place in the city, including for Arrigoni and Parks. Later in April, fishermen recovered the body of Sergeant Donald McClure from the ocean, and those services then took place.

Three days after the tsunami hit, Gary Clawson presided over the funeral services for his mother and father, then twenty minutes later did the same for his lost fiancée, Joanie Fields. Understandably, it would be a long time before he could overcome his feelings of numbness and grief. Adding to it all, Gary even read about his own death in the obituary columns—at least four times—including one printed in a Sacramento newspaper. Both the son's and father's first names were William, Gary being "William Gary Clawson," his dad "William Eben Clawson." These reporters had not confirmed their information, listing his death along with the actual ones of his parents, fiancée, and friends.

Mac McGuire continued searching for his old 1940 Ford truck that had been parked outside the tavern and washed away. He wanted to know what had happened to it. Months later, he located the vehicle buried on a beach several miles away. Part of the door and one headlight stuck out from a pile of driftwood and sand. Mac eventually dug his truck from the debris. He cleaned it up and the beat-up flatbed ran fine, although it was missing its hood.

The McKenzies, whose four young children were washed away by the tsunami on the Oregon coast, had met tragedy before—and recently—having lost their nine-year-old daughter, Susan, that previous August. Susan's clothing had caught fire as she tried to start a campfire, and the little girl died from the severe burns she suffered.

Marion Teal, a seasoned reporter with the *Corvallis Gazette-Times*, interviewed Rita McKenzie that Easter weekend in the hospital, as she recuperated from the injuries she received. Mrs. Teal said that doing this interview was the hardest thing she ever had to do as a reporter, and she "cried the entire time" she interviewed Mrs. McKenzie. Rita McKenzie seemed to be "quite stoic," probably because she was "totally disbelieving what had happened." Rita said that the family had been extremely close, enjoying many activities together such as camping, boating, and swimming. "All our children had full lives," she had said. "The only answer now is for my husband and me to start all over and have a new family." The *Oregonian* of April 1 carried Marion Teal's story. The headline read: "Tacoma Couple To Start Again As Sea Robs Them Of Children." The McKenzies began looking to adopt children to start a new family.

That same week, Congressman Don Clausen visited those who were still hospitalized in Seaside Hospital, including Mabel Martin. As Mabel told him about her ordeal, she said, "My nerves are much better now, but for a while I would scream when I heard a noise." On the day that Representative Clausen visited, Mabel asked him, "So you know what day this is?" When he said he didn't know, she answered with a smile: "This is my birthday."

She commented later, "For the second time in my seventy-five years on earth, I was left without my home and personal possessions. In 1921, my home burned and now, due to an act of God, I have once again lost everything." However, Mabel Martin knew she was lucky to still be alive. Three years later, she died peacefully in her sleep.

Diane Anderson had watched the tsunami and its destruction from her parents' home close to Seaside Hospital, then volunteered her services late that night to help out at the hospital. After getting over the shock of that disaster, her thoughts turned to her impending wedding set for April 4th—one week later. Diane decided it was too late to reset the wedding reception, as the invitations had already been mailed. The U.S. Post Office came through and delivered the wedding cards, although they were still soggy. The first problem was that the reception was to be held at the Surf Hotel. As this hotel was located in the cordoned-off area, the reception was changed to her parents' home. Since Diane's wedding shoes were buried under the sand and debris at Trehearne's Department Store, she decided to wear an old pair of white shoes. The bridal shop's owner still created Diane's wedding bouquet, even though her store lay in total ruins.

Since the tidal wave demolished the local bakery, a family friend baked and put together her wedding cake. Diane's wedding gifts had been stored in the back room of Nielsen's Hardware Store. Despite the extensive damage to the store when cars washed through the front windows, the table holding the wrapped gifts floated around and settled back to the ground without breaking a dish or denting a pan.

Diane's wedding was beautiful and the reception well attended. It was the first break for many of her guests from their hard work of cleaning up and rebuilding. While on their honeymoon, people continually questioned the newlyweds after discovering that they were from Crescent City. "Most thought that our town had been completely washed away," she said.

"As a child, I remembered other tidal-wave alerts which emptied the town of all its citizens," Diane Anderson wrote, "and we would stand on the hill overlooking Crescent City waiting for the wave that never arrived. Never in my wildest dreams did I ever think that this wave would come rolling in the middle of the night, unseen and unexpected. Now, I am unlikely to forget this—especially when my wedding anniversary serves as a constant reminder."

ALTHOUGH THE CLEANUP was under way in full force by the end of the first weekend, it would take months to complete, leaving huge gaps on the land where buildings used to be. The Small Business Administration (SBA) sent a representative within days to process small business, low-interest loans for operations hurt by the tsunami. The Army Corps of Engineers was analyzing what needed to be done to repair the harbor and dock areas, as well as contacting private contractors on the demolition of the unsafe buildings. Informal and formal meetings between residents and civic leaders alike over rebuilding the area already had started in their "free" time after cleaning up, repairing, and trying to re-establish livelihoods.

Six days after the tsunami's devastation, President Johnson on April 2 declared the area to be a national disaster area, paving the way for federal assistance and low-interest loans. Regardless of party leanings or affiliations, Congressman Don Clausen, Senators Thomas Kuchel and Randolph Collier, and Governor Pat Brown joined together to get the information about the disaster into the right people's hands, so that the declaration was made quickly by the President. The declaration allowed Crescent City taxpayers to take advantage also of a special tax provision. Taxpayers who incurred financial losses in 1964 because of the tidal wave could take the losses as a deduction on their 1963 federal income tax filing, now due in two weeks. The accelerated deduction meant that they would be able to receive a cash refund from previously paid federal taxes. Any refunds could also be used to help pay their current tax bill, although few residents were worrying now about paying their taxes on time.

California quickly followed with a conforming provision for its state income taxes. About 1½ months later, Governor Brown signed a bill authorizing the County Assessor to lower property values, based on the quite reduced values of those properties, and give residents a break on their property taxes.

Horsemen from Lyle Corliss's Horsemen's Association patrolled the beach area from Pozzi Ranch to the south of town all the way to Seaside Hospital, including up Elk Creek. Volunteer police patrolled the streets to guard against looters. Police arrested a total of three looters over the weekend, including one man who had tried to scoop up groceries for his Easter basket, as they washed down from a wrecked supermarket. As one resident observed, "There was very little looting. For the most part, people were there to help."

The heavy transfusion requirements for injured tsunami victims drastically reduced blood stocks in the Pacific Northwest. Accordingly, Red Cross blood drives were emphasized in several cities, and the Red Cross bloodmobile began scheduling visits to restock the quite low supplies. In Medford, Oregon, the people in two days donated 257 pints of precious blood.

With so many businesses no longer operating, Crescent City's newspapers were running into severe cash problems as advertising revenues dramatically declined. Accordingly, regional associations of merchants and banks placed institutional advertising so that the newspapers could stay in business. In further support, some firms took large advertisements—although presumably at reduced rates—to reassure the public about their products and commitment to the area.

For example, the Auto Mart dealership placed an advertisement in large, bold print that read: "WE GUARANTEE THAT: All vehicles damaged by water have been sold to an out-of-town salvage company. We will not wholesale or retail any of the damaged vehicles in this area. Forty (40) current model 1964 vehicles and late model used vehicles are now being shipped into our new lot on Highway 101 North. . . ."

The Pacific Market, which with Ray's was the only other market left intact in the area, ran an advertisement that read: "WE ARE OPEN TO SERVE YOU. We wish to express our sympathy to the stricken people and businesses of Crescent City, and also to assure you that we will do everything possible to supply your food needs. OUR PRICES WILL NOT BE RAISED." Whether located in Crescent City or in Del Norte County, businesses didn't take unfair advantage of this situation to raise prices, gouge customers, or line their pockets.

The U.S. Treasury announced that residents with lost or destroyed U.S. Savings Bonds due to the disaster could apply to have those bonds replaced or paid off in cash. If the owner clearly marked that the loss was due to the tidal wave (to help Alaskan residents, the Treasury advised using the words "Earthquake Emergency"), then that application was given a priority status to speed up its processing.

One week after the tsunami's destruction, a low-level magnitude earthquake hit Alaska. The authorities quickly spread the alarm to already-nervous residents. Although a full-scale evacuation wasn't called, some people moved to higher ground. In Oregon, highway and state park employees closed off roads to the beaches and urged visitors to find higher ground immediately. The alert was canceled when the feared high waves didn't materialize.

THE PEOPLE and press began reporting the oddities of this tidal wave, joining the other stories of tsunami lore. For example, one family returned to retrieve their possessions. The sea waves had washed their house four hundred yards across Highway 101 into a swamp with trees. Having had to run for their lives from their house, they were surprised to find their two pet goldfish unharmed, still swimming in a bowl on a chest in the living room where they had left them.

Another person ran away from her trailer with her husband, leaving behind a glass of ice water, cup of coffee, and some paper with a pencil where she had been working. Her trailer was later discovered one block away, bent and twisted out of shape. However, the glass of water, coffee, and paper and pencil were right where she had left them, not one drop spilled or an item out of place.

When Dick and Jackie Childs came home to their house on Front Street, they discovered that it had changed from a straight house to a bent one in the shape of an L. The waves had broken the cement floor in the family room into pieces and piled this up in the center of the room. Although the fireplace was completely destroyed, their fragile china hadn't been touched. A beautiful driftwood bowl of theirs was found on the beach, still with one orange in it.

A home on Front Street broke in half, and a portion of it swept away. The grass lawn at the site was untouched and not damaged. The Coin Shop on Second Street lost many coins, some still in their packages. The owner reported people picking them up and going out of their way to hand them back to him.

The following items floated into the *Triplicate*'s building: a coin vial from The Coin Shop, washers from Nielsen's Hardware, a twelve-foot redwood log, one blue dress from Daly's Department Store, a plastic plate from Nielsen's, two fishing poles and one dead flounder, two live fish in the press pit, and a few odd coffee pots, among other items. A fisherman came by Daly's to buy a wooden salad fork and spoon; he said it would go well with the salad bowl he had discovered floating three miles out to sea with the store's name on its bottom.

The main part of the cash register from Miller's Fountain on Second Street was located several blocks away in the Ben Franklin store on Third Street, while the top to it was on Front Street in the opposite direction. The currents carried away Helen Boone's shed with barrels of her fine old dishes; although the structure was left on its side one-half block away, all of her dishes were still undamaged.

The owner of the Del Norte Feed store found a witches' brew of slime on the floor where boxes of insecticides, fertilizers, and herbicides had broken and mixed in with the mud. He was able to save a little merchandise, several crates of baby chicks, fifty small turtles, and his mynah bird, but everything else was lost. Although the turtle aquarium was empty and filled with dirty seawater, employees discovered the small turtles in the toxic mud. They had dug into the layers during the ocean storms. After they washed off the tiny turtles, all of them were fine.

A deputy sheriff warned a man in a bar about the oncoming tidal wave, then jumped in his car to speed away. The drunk ran out of the bar with the tidal wave nipping at his heels. He grabbed the patrol car's rear bumper as the deputy sped away, and surfed behind while the car slid over the ocean.

Two cars swerved into the Shell station at Ninth and L Streets for gas after the tidal waves hit. This was one of the very few stations in the city still operable. One driver said, "Fill it up, I want to see this tidal wave." The other said even quicker, "Fill it up, I want to get the hell out of here."

GIVEN THE SEVERITY of the tidal waves, the question is why, thankfully, didn't this tragedy bring about more deaths? One reason is that the first two waves that rolled in were not as powerful and large as the last two; they did not cause any reported deaths while giving a non-fatal warning about the tsunami. This important fact allowed authorities to set up road blocks that many people did observe, prior to the huge rollers that surged in later. The problems then surfaced when police and other authorities allowed business-people that they knew personally to return and clean up their stores in the commercial district. Also, many Crescent City residents kept their curiosity at bay when they first heard the reports, deciding to stay where they were on safer, higher ground.

Had the first wave been as large as the monster fourth, the death total would have been much higher. An ocean surge that large would have caught many people unaware and trapped, such as those partying at the Tides, people asleep in their oceanfront motel rooms (before the managers could rush them onto roofs after the second surge), or those strolling around downtown. The landslide-induced sea waves that inundated Alaskan coastal towns were large and powerful at the very first, thundering down on people without advance warning as given by the first smaller surges at Crescent City.

When the third wave pummeled onto shore half an hour after the second one receded, some people took the message and raced away from the coastal area, as best they could. People trapped by the third wave on Highway 101 South, but who survived, definitely would not have survived the killer fourth roller. Although taking heavy damage, the buildings in the downtown area also buffered from injury people whom the third wave caught. The fourth "black mass" would have drowned them, especially those closest to the beachfront or trapped by low ceilings.

Another reason that kept death and injuries lower was that, since it was only March, the summer tourist season had not yet started. Had the tourist season been in full swing, the area's motels and hotels would have been full. Even though some students had returned to their families for the Easter vacation break, most would have been home anyway during the summer.

Lastly, Crescent City residents were used to the elements—numbers earned their livelihoods by fishing in the high seas or cutting down tall timber. Like Gary Clawson, people in this area scuba dived, fished, or boated in the ocean for fun and recreation. These people did not panic when they awoke immersed in chilling seawater or watched as the sea crashed towards them. They did not make bad decisions or freeze into inaction, as those not used to harsh conditions might have done, which would have increased the numbers of fatalities and serious injuries. Even so, the extent of the destruction caused was still extreme and the numbers of the confirmed dead, missing, and injured high.

14

Rebuilding to Reawaken

A few days afterwards, Mayor Bill Peepe and other civic leaders met to start officially planning the steps for the city's recovery and reconstruction. Bill's house wasn't affected like many others, being on Pacific Avenue above the inundation area. Since his sawmill was located at the higher end of town and away from the beach, only a "foot of water or so" crested through his building with the equipment being basically unaffected. The lighter damage occurred despite the general area becoming a large depositing ground for houses, people, and debris that the surges washed up. Situated on even higher ground, his yard was located past the prime dumping point. Needing to spend only two days on his business cleanup, Mayor Peepe quickly stepped in and helped lead the rebuilding process.

Bill Peepe had been a prisoner of war in World War II after Japanese troops captured him on Wake Island. He had spent twenty-two hard months in a Shanghai jail, and then the same amount of time in an even worse prison camp in Japan before the war ended. He took his Army backpay and used it to start up his lumber mill, McNamara & Peepe Lumber Company, with a partner in 1947. In the early sixties, Bill set up another lumber operation and mill on the Amazon River in Brazil. He flew back and forth for a time from the Amazon to Crescent City, overseeing both operations before eventually closing the overseas venture.

An old friend had approached him one day and said he was resigning from the City Council. "We've decided," the friend said, "that you take my place on the Council." Bill did and won that seat outright in later elections. Peepe then "found himself mayor" during this time. He was being modest with that statement, because from many accounts Bill Peepe was credited with being a very capable official during what was a very difficult time.

Some saw the disaster as an opportunity to replace the old, wooden buildings that previously had dotted the city's landscape and to completely remake the town into one with a modern infrastructure. Others weren't so sure about how much federal aid should be solicited, with its ensuing regulations. Before one week had passed, however, the City Council in a special session adopted an emergency-planning ordinance to clear the way for a federal urban renewal project within the disaster area.

This resolution freed up a 30,000 dollar federal grant to help pay for the 40,000 dollar planning job. Federal officials assured city council members that they could back out from the process at any time without penalty. As part of this, no building permits would be issued nor any rebuilding allowed in the disaster zone until the urban renewal construction plans had been officially formulated and approved. Planners from leading architectural companies flew to Crescent City from all over the country to make preliminary proposals.

Within two weeks, the major streets had been basically cleared and fifty-six condemned buildings had either been demolished or painted with the large "Red X" by the County Building Inspector to indicate they would soon be destroyed. This total didn't include downtown buildings not yet reached, structures condemned but contested by their owners, or the vast three-mile stretch along Highway 101 South. Some structures dating back to the 1800s had already been razed and fed into the huge crackling bonfires at the beach. These magnificent buildings included the Duffy House and Odd Fellows Hall.

Crescent City attorney Jim Hooper oversaw the establishment of the redevelopment agency and other reconstruction efforts. Although he had been the town's City Attorney for several years, Hooper had resigned just a few months earlier to spend more time on his growing private practice. He had also been fortunate in that his home and office were on high ground and not damaged, so like Bill Peepe, he was able to focus immediately on the general problems at hand.

These challenges were considerable. Although major portions of the town had been destroyed, Crescent City was bankrupt and had no funds with which to rebuild. City officials had to look to the state and federal governments for help, although "they didn't know what to do at first, were used to doing things by themselves, and didn't trust government," as Jim Hopper said. Bill Peepe and other City Council members were quick to realize that their city needed federal and state aid, because they had no other choice. They knew there would be many hearings and controversy when officials worked to set up the urban renewal area and procedures. Some people voiced strong opinions that they didn't want to rebuild, that they felt Crescent City was in a vulnerable coastal area and that what was rebuilt would only be destroyed again. They also did not believe government, with its seemingly endless regulations, could do a better job than they would.

The first challenge of the city's civic leaders was learning how to work with "big" government in such a way that the city and its residents wouldn't lose their local autonomy. To do this, they needed to learn what the redevelopment rules were, especially with this type of disaster. "It wasn't that easy at first," said Jim Hooper. "I started studying the volumes of urban renewal rules and regulations. I called up the federal Regional Director of what later came to be called the Department of Housing and Urban Development (HUD) that had jurisdiction over the urban renewal process and started to make the necessary contacts and inquiries."

Hooper located a provision of the HUD regulations that allowed Crescent City to apply for redevelopment dollars. Although these funds were designed for inner-city redevelopment projects, because Crescent City was then in the economic doldrums, Hooper correctly assessed that the city could apply for, qualify, and receive urban-renewal funds—even though the prime reason for their request was to rebuild from a natural disaster and not urban redevelopment.

This was the first time that the federal government allowed this approach to be so used.

At the same time the redevelopment process was starting, even community leaders had to reopen and run their own businesses, earn money, and pay their bills, like everyone else. This meant long hours at work, compounded by numerous committee meetings, conferences, traveling, and conversations, whether during the day or late at night. People put in countless unpaid hours to help rebuild their community. Jim Hooper worked "seventeen to eighteen hours a day, six to seven days a week, for the next several weeks on the city's redevelopment efforts plus earning my living by my general law practice." Mayor Peepe ran his saw mill during the day, then like the others, met during the night.

The important backing of political leaders such as Governor Brown and his offices, along with California Congressman Don Clausen and U.S. Senator Thomas Kuchel, was essential to any plan coming into reality—and they came through. First of all, these men were instrumental in bringing about President Johnson's declaration of the city as an emergency disaster area. State representatives such as State Senator Randolph Collier and Assemblyman Frank Belotti came to the aid of the stricken town, working to get special state legislation enacted that would help clear the way for Crescent City's urban renewal efforts.

Crescent City, Del Norte County, and the Harbor District formed the Tri-Agency Economic Development Authority (or the "Redevelopment Agency") as a joint venture to accomplish the redevelopment. The key people for the Redevelopment Agency included its Director, Pat Hanratty, who formerly had been the head of the City's Chamber of Commerce; Jim Hooper, who acted as General Council to the Redevelopment Agency (and Special Counsel to the City Council); and their planning consultant, George Gatter. As permitted under California law, governing board members of the Redevelopment Agency were the same as those on the City Council, although these were separate agencies. Everyone worked in his area of specialty to help forge the redevelopment plans and process.

After consulting with officials at all levels of the city and government, Hooper drafted the necessary legal documents to apply for the redevelopment dollars, and a redevelopment plan was quickly created. "Trying to know more than the regulators helped us," he said. "When they found out that we knew what we were talking about, they then respected us and started to help us. And we also took hard, no uncertain stands."

When federal urban renewal officials first traveled to Crescent City, they told the town's stunned representatives that it would take at least three months, if not six, to act on their redevelopment plan—if the federal government gave its approval at all—and that the entire evaluation process could only start *after* the appropriate agencies had received the city's approved redevelopment plan. The entire urban-renewal approval process would take at least one year with most taking two years from start to finish.

The indignant citizens said "no way." They argued that they hadn't applied for anything before, they had been very self-sufficient in the past, and that this was a disaster. One official after another, including their elected state and national representatives, told the federal personnel that they were not dealing with their money, but with the taxpayers' money. Hooper said pointedly to the federal officials: "We'll submit the plan to the City Council for approval, and then we're going to get your approval. We're not going to wait three to six months for any approval—you're going to give it to us in a few hours, after we submit it to you. And if you don't, then we're going to request a full Congressional hearing, which is our right under the law. And that will cost you bad publicity, time, and money."

Less than thirty days after the tsunami stormed in, the Redevelopment Agency made its application to HUD for an urban renewal redevelopment grant. An area of fifteen square blocks between Fourth Street and Front, from H to M Street, was designated as part of the urban renewal zone, along with the entire beachfront and its blocks from Front Street to the ocean. The plans were keyed around the construction of a mall on Second Street from H Street east to K, a covered walkway, no overhead utilities, and the elimination of all parking meters within the zone. Other conditions included prohibiting billboards in the project area, providing sufficient off-street parking, and constructing attractive landscaping.

The federal urban renewal agency gave its approval in twenty-four hours.

Five weeks after the tidal wave crested in, Hooper finished drafting the Redevelopment Procedures Manual. This thick manual detailed the numbers of steps and procedures necessary to build under the federal Urban Renewal Program, showing what applicants had to do to gain approval for their rebuilding projects. His manual also described the procedures that the Redevelopment Agency had to follow, as well as the special state legislation that made possible a speed-up of those procedures.

With support from their elected representatives inside the government, the leaders of Crescent City had completed an urban renewal application process that normally took one year—but took them little over one month. Given the bureaucratic red tape present with any government program, this was an amazing accomplishment. The city's great need, the tenacity of its leaders, backing of strong political representatives, and some luck had managed the seemingly impossible. It is doubtful that this feat will be duplicated again.

Another month was required to gain all of the necessary city, state, and federal agency approvals. On May 26, the Crescent City Urban Development Committee and its Planning Commission approved the city's Disaster Development Plan. Later that afternoon, the full City Council voted unanimously to adopt the emergency ordinance authorizing that plan and the forthcoming urban renewal process. It took an entire day of public hearings to gain that approval, as the plan centered on two aspects: what the agency would do, or its plan; and the scope of those efforts, or how big the redevelopment zone would be. Anticipating tough questions from residents, city officials conferred earlier that day with each other and Jim Hooper to determine what they could say honestly and to the point.

As great a problem in gaining the quick approval of the necessary authorities was gaining the trust of their own citizens. Used to their own independence and taking care of themselves, Crescent City residents generally didn't like government telling them what to do. It was hard at first to convince them that the town could keep local control without the federal government taking over. "We had to win on that point and we did," said Jim Hooper. "However, that task was almost as much of a challenge as it was to sell the federal and state agencies on working with us." With all the required authorizations in hand, the city's Redevelopment Agency became legally created and authorized to proceed. Preliminary building plans by any developer needed to be approved first by the newly created agency before it would authorize any land to be built on or purchased from it. Final development plans had to be submitted to the city's planning department for approval and architectural review, then to the Redevelopment Agency for its final approval.

As city officials debated, worked on, and finally gained government approval for the urban reconstruction, workers and crews were ripping down the damaged and collapsed structures. Thick smoke hung over the beach, this time not from the blazing bulk plant and gasoline stations on fire, but instead from the huge bonfires of old, splintered building remains. During the entire day and into the night, Skil saws buzzed, workers hammered, trucks groaned hauling heavy loads, and old buildings crashed to the ground. While the city began its long road to some semblance of recovery, its residents held bake or rummage sales for money earmarked to rebuilding community projects, as well as restarting up their lives.

Others like Peggy Sullivan and Mabel Martin were trying to heal from their severe injuries and condition. Seaside Hospital released both after one month. Due to the extensive nature of her injuries, Joyce London was hospitalized for three months, including having to undergo several surgeries and physical therapy, before she could be released. Despondent over the loss of his two young children, Billy Wright slashed his wrists one and a half months later as he was preparing food for the prisoners' evening meal. He was immediately rushed to Seaside Hospital, reported later to be in good condition, and eventually recovered from his attempted suicide. Later, Juanita

Wright and their one surviving child, Debbie Lee, left the area for parts unknown.

THE LOSSES suffered by individuals and businesses took many forms, including that their financial setbacks weren't covered by insurance. Tsunami or flood insurance was too expensive or not obtainable, and individual home insurance and liability policies didn't cover earthquakes, floods, tidal waves, or other "acts of God." These residents shouldered their losses—whether homes, furnishings, and cars or buildings, inventory, and fixtures at their business. Some insurance companies paid the claims of people for their destroyed or disabled cars, but this wasn't the general rule. And there was little evidence of threats made or lawsuits filed to gain compensation of any kind.

Federal disaster funds were available to repair and rebuild public facilities, without need to be paid back, but there were no similar disaster grants that could be used for an individual's home or business. Although the Red Cross made helpful outright assistance grants, these amounts were limited and more morale-boosting than anything else. This left only the federal Small Business Administration (SBA) program as a resource. The SBA quickly set up temporary offices at the old high school building to help people apply for its low-interest, 3 percent loan programs.

Small businesses, which also included commercial fishing fleet operators, could apply for these loans. However, the area's residents were wary that bureaucrats might be able to dictate what they could or couldn't do with their lives. No one initially applied. Although the SBA announcement was made within days of the disaster, only one homeowner consulted with them during the first two weeks. After conferring with local leaders, the SBA held a public meeting to actually appeal to the public to apply for its loan program.

The Chamber of Commerce worked with Mayor Peepe and Congressman Don Clausen to bring the residents together with SBA officials, local banks, and accountants who would assist them in the rebuilding process. Although people had lost all of the equity in their properties and businesses, they could still borrow the money to rebuild. Applications began to trickle in, as people decided that some regulation with loans was better than nothing at all. When the emergency SBA office closed in June, disaster loan applications totaling over one million dollars had been submitted, and about one-half of those requests were approved. Thirty small businesses (and two home-office businesses) qualified to receive loans under this program. Even so, most businesses and individuals didn't apply.

One week after the city's destruction, Congressman Clausen notified the *Crescent City American* that the city would receive 1.25 million dollars of disaster relief funds to pay for the work of the U.S. Army Corps of Engineers. This grant would cover the costs of repairing the ocean outlet for the sewer system, replacing part of the seawall washed from the harbor, and reconstructing the harbor facilities and Citizen's Dock, among other public facilities. After two weeks, Crescent City formally ceded the responsibility for the building demolition and the overall cleanup to the U.S. Army Corp of Engineers. Meanwhile, the public kept pitching in, whether it was pounding nails, battering down buildings, or helping their neighbors. Hour by hour, the town inched towards functioning again.

The first project the Army Corps of Engineers faced was rebuilding Citizen's Dock. This dock was crucial to Del Norte County's ability to ship lumber to Southern California, as well as to its fishing industry. What was left of the commercial fleet used the limited pleasure-craft facilities until another dock could be built, and only commercial-boating use was allowed until then. Reconstructing the dock was considered so important that its demolition began two days after the tidal wave and without any regard to "proper" procedures or government regulations.

The Army Engineers formally arranged for Citizen's Dock to be demolished within two weeks. It awarded the contract to local contractor, Dave Scott, who bid 253,000 dollars to tear the dock down and rebuild it. The project included demolishing what couldn't be rebuilt and building new pilings, lumber wing, the dock to the lumber wing, as well as repairing all of the damage to the fish wing. Federal disaster funds paid for all of this reconstruction, and out-of-work men could start working again, this time for money.

Onlookers watched silently in a drizzling rain while workers scurried over the remains of Citizen's Dock to complete its demolition. The crowd stared at the ripping and tearing away of the dock. Only fourteen years had elapsed since the people had worked so hard together to build the facility with their own hands. Now they watched the dock disappear into the ocean, the combined efforts of a tugboat, crane, and men with chainsaws finally completing its demise. Construction work continued for ten hours a day, six days a week, week after week, until the new dock was completed in mid-June, two months after beginning its construction.

While the city worked on formalizing urban renewal, the U.S. Army Corps of Engineers completed the town's demolition. The Corps cleared away the harbor debris, and arranged for private contractors to rip up and haul away the ruined structures on land. The curious again watched as bulldozers, steam shovels, clamshells, and other heavy equipment smashed through buildings long known and once an integral part of the city's history. Debris littered so much of the city's land and streets at first that six weeks passed before major portions were cleared off. By then, the city had huge, gaping holes in its landscape that were completely barren.

AT THE SAME TIME that urban renewal and reconstruction was under way, business owners rebuilt and reopened or gave up. Ruth and Dale Long soon reopened their welding business, due to Dale's efforts, a structurally strong building, and their structure being sheltered from some of the worst currents. Although the raging ocean had ripped the large, heavy metal doors from their building, carrying the weighted steel blocks to the McNamara and Peepe depositing grounds, the Longs were able to salvage them. They only had one functioning welding machine, however, in the beginning. Since the tsunami had nearly collapsed their apartment into the G&G Liquors store below, the Longs needed to find housing. They first spent several days with Ruth's aunt and uncle in Crescent City, later renting and moving to a house in Gasquet, located outside of Crescent City and its reconstruction activities.

With around-the-clock effort, Bob Ames reopened his appliance store in two months. Bob concluded that the location of the Thunderbird Lodge had saved the day for his family. The motel had been built one year before, straddling L Street between First and Second, and it received the brunt of the massive fourth wave with every ground-floor room destroyed. The structure diverted the ocean up L Street to circulate around the Ames and G&G Liquors stores, instead of pounding directly into his building with its full force.

Along with Bob Ames, Ruth Long was thankful that the Thunderbird Motel had taken the brunt of the ocean's force. "Otherwise, our building would also have been destroyed, but it certainly showed the damage from the force of those waves," Ruth said. Bud Pyke, Ernie's brother, had owned the local dry cleaner, but he left later for Seattle and opened a successful one there. Depending on the severity of the damage, some businesses reopened in weeks, others in months. Over one year elapsed before the Pykes could reopen their Ben Franklin store.

Daly's Department Store was one of the largest locally owned department store chains in Northern California. Based in Eureka, California, the chain of stores was run by four brothers, descendants of a pioneering Humboldt County family. Daly's gave a welcomed boost to Crescent City ten days after the tidal wave, when they announced that they were going to spend three hundred thousand dollars by June to completely rebuild their store.

Suppliers cooperated with their customers, the retail stores, enabling some businesses to reopen sooner. Daly's stated that many of its suppliers restocked the store at one-third to one-half off, and in one case, for free. The store had lost 165,000 dollars (nearly one million dollars now) in inventory, storefront improvements, and other losses. For the first two-and-one-half months, Daly's operated at two different locations, including the present site of the *Triplicate* on Fourth Street and a bar two doors down, before opening operations again at their pre-tsunami location.

Most businesses didn't have the size or standing of Daly's to get such support. The great majority of people needing help—business or otherwise—turned to their families, neighbors, creditors, and nonprofit agencies. The Red Cross, Lions Club, Salvation Army, and other nonprofits gave considerable assistance, and banks worked out payment plans and deferrals so that salvageable houses were spared foreclosure. In numbers of cases, people who owned battered structures beyond repair just handed the keys over to the bank.

Otherwise, people traded services, such as plumbing repairs for food or haircuts for gasoline. They lived and worked from a nearby relative's or friend's house. They bartered, gave credit (credit cards weren't in general use then), sold damaged goods at bargain-sale prices, and generally worked together. If a person couldn't afford food or pay some bill, another gave a helping hand in some way. People acted with each other as the close community they were, because they had to. There was no other choice. Going on welfare wasn't a strong program then or respected. And those who couldn't make it or didn't like the odds, simply moved away.

While the residents started rebuilding their structures and lives, Crescent City started its "Comeback Town, U.S.A." campaign. Bill Stamps, owner of radio station KPOD, is credited with making this concept become a reality. Business friends kept telling him, "We'll be back. . . . We're coming back." Stamps called Pitney-Bowes, the company that makes postage meters, and asked them to furnish two hundred "slugs" for postage meters with the slogan "Comeback Town, U.S.A." When these were delivered, red-white-and-blue nameplates and badges with the same slogan were manufactured with thousands sold. Billboards, radio jingles, and newspaper ads welcomed people with this slogan—still in use at the city and on a welcoming billboard today.

THE ARMY ENGINEERS contracted for more tetrapods to be built. These heavy, pronged objects were the key to the main harbor breakwater's ability to withstand most of the tsunami's barrages. First utilized in French-African ports, their use in these projects was the first in the Western Hemisphere. Tetrapods were invented in France, and royalties were paid on each one built. Workmen poured and formed the twenty-five ton concrete pods daily, and a total of eighty-six tetrapods were used to construct the protective port breakwater where the pleasure boats were moored.

As the tidal waves had gouged the beach and harbor floor, the SBA made seven hundred thousand dollars available for needed clearing and re-dredging. This project was also amazingly completed on time. HUD soon gave the welcome news to the Redevelopment Agency that three million dollars had been approved for their urban redevelopment efforts. The problem, however, was that the federal agency wanted Crescent City to put up matching funds—and the town had no money. The city's officials in turn asked the state legislature to borrow one million dollars. With the backing and support of Governor Brown, State Senator Randolph Collier, and Congressman Don Clausen, the legislature passed the enabling legislation and HUD approved. Jim Hooper and the city negotiated a provision into the legislation that if the town couldn't repay the loan—which at the time seemed a distinct possibility—the city could request that the loan be converted to an unconditional grant. This is what happened later. "Ronald Reagan was Governor of California, and a fiscal conservative when we asked them to convert the loan," said Hooper. "Despite this, he and the legislature finally agreed to the conversion."

The agency later received a 1.5 million-dollar grant as a revolving business loan fund to help existing and new businesses, along with a 500,000 dollar grant to build a cultural and convention center. Constructed near the beach, this is the modernistic Crescent City-Del Norte County Chamber of Commerce building located on Front Street.

Under the redevelopment program, the agency purchased property for resale to developers when the owners couldn't or didn't want to rebuild. It also acquired property from owners on which it would build the planned public facilities, such as the new shopping mall, streets, parking areas, and public walkways. The Redevelopment Agency negotiated to buy property within the redevelopment zone. It also had the legal right to acquire that land by right of eminent domain, a legal action allowing federal, state, or local governments and their agencies to force the sale of private property, but at "fair market" valuations. The Agency brought four such lawsuits against property owners when the parties couldn't agree on the purchase value. This litigation took place within one year after the tsunami hit, and another year would elapse before all of this litigation was either settled or decided.

After buying the "unwanted" property in the project area, the Redevelopment Agency then cleared and sold the land directly to whoever wanted to construct a new building, or held onto it until someone with such an interest came along later. Builders needed to gain the approval of various governmental agencies before they could start their construction.

Three-and-a-half months later, Glen's Bakery was the first business to receive a building permit under Crescent City's Redevelopment Plan. Its new building was to be built at Third and G Streets. Other permits were granted to build a new Turf Club, another Trehearne's Department Store, and a cocktail lounge. Other applications followed in turn the following year, and the building of new structures and houses in the disaster zone was under way. Outside the redevelopment district, rebuilding began as quickly as building permits could be issued—without red tape or long delays, but located outside the centralized downtown area.

Bill Peepe said, "There were meetings after meetings after meetings, including lots of public hearings. There were so many different agencies that had to give their approval, we wondered at times if achieving all of this was even possible. However, somehow everyone came to some sort of an agreement. We had to, we did it, and it was a lot of work."

Jim Hooper added, "One tragic fact is the slow, bureaucratic maze that the people and their representatives must get through before any real recovery work can get started. The long, complicated and burdensome documentation required by the federal government must be made much simpler and shorter."

The construction of public facilities in the urban renewal zone started, resulting in later years eventually in the "Tsunami Landing" mall that covers the area between Front to Third Streets and H to K Streets. At the corners of the enclosing streets, watermarks identify where the tsunami's height crested. Far from the beach and ocean, the first mark is six feet high over one mile inland in that particular downtown section.

Although the necessary approvals were gained and construction was now under way, every government project has its ups and downs. Later, HUD froze all of the funds for every redevelopment project in California, because the voters had approved a law permitting at the time discrimination in the sales of property (a law later overturned by the California Supreme Court). However, Crescent City was the only redevelopment agency in California whose funds were not actually cut off. Jim Hooper argued with HUD that under federal law these redevelopment funds could not be cut off again without first giving the town a formal Congressional hearing. Governor Brown and other state and federal California politicians made more arguments, including that the city would suffer irreparable harm with its immediate need to rebuild if those funds were cut off, and reiterated the demand for a full hearing before Congress. The U.S. Government reversed its policy for the town, and Crescent City didn't miss one disbursement or fall behind in its reconstruction timetable.

Even with a redevelopment zone in existence, city officials still had to find and convince businesses or governments to build there—otherwise, the ground stood vacant. When the Redwood National Park Service announced its intention to build a new headquarters the following year, every city in Northern California, from Darbenville to Eureka, wanted the park service to build in its locality. Without telling anyone in Crescent City—"which I had learned to do to get things done"—Jim Hooper and his wife flew to Washington, D.C., to lobby for the town. On the night before his meeting with the National Park Service, Jim's wife sketched out a possible design for the regional headquarters.

Hooper proposed that Crescent City would donate two blocks of land to the forest service if the agency would construct their building in the redevelopment zone, and then showed them the sketch that his wife had made. The service liked the idea and accepted the proposal, subject to local approval. The City Council and Redevelopment Agency later gave their approval to the proposed transaction.

To meet the requirements of the law, the Redevelopment Agency then conveyed two blocks of the project area to the city, which in turn donated this acreage to the National Park Service. In turn, the park service built its Redwood National Park Headquarters, still in use today. After it was constructed, Hooper said that the building looked much like his wife's sketch, with a drive-through street underneath a long contemporary structure, built, it is hoped, above a tidal wave's path. The large wooden rectangular building stretches between Front and Third Streets, with what used to be Second Street now a passageway underneath it, and lies within K and L Streets.

At times, different Crescent City officials would spearhead a particular project, sell its merits to the others, and then work to get it completed. Jim Hooper was one of them and a major force in the redevelopment. "To get the small boat harbor built," he said, "I arranged for the original harbor drawings to be completed at my own cost, then showed them to the City Council, Board of Supervisors, and Harbor Commission, sitting in joint session. With everything packaged, ready to go, and an explanation as to how we would get the funds to build it, the approval was given."

From funds earmarked for the purpose, over time the Redevelopment Agency built a convention center later as part of its new Beachfront Park. The agency arranged for the construction of the Northcoast Marine Mammal Center on the west side of the park near Battery Point, among other projects. These reconstruction efforts also had their critics. Various residents argued that Crescent City was losing its quaint, tourist-oriented shops and character for "boring" office buildings and a mall that needed tenants.

15

Time Moves On

Very few original buildings survived in the zone or devastated areas. Many structures savaged by the tsunami fell before the demolition crews, including a few whose old-time architecture and difficulty of repair made them demolition candidates. Others were condemned because they or their businesses were not compatible with the redevelopment plan. After reconstruction, just about the only building left standing in the downtown area was the once-grand, six-story Surf Hotel, located at the intersection of Front Street and H. Constructed with a strong structure of steel and concrete, this building survived the ocean's poundings. However, it stood empty for many years afterwards, then was bought and renovated in the late 1980s. It is currently being used as an apartment building.

The redevelopment approach taken is still a source of controversy with long-time Crescent City residents. Some like Jim Hooper argued that the old structures, many dating back to the late 1880s, were rickety and had to be rebuilt or replaced. If the owners didn't choose to do so, then Del Norte County had no choice but to demolish them and rebuild. Others, such as Wally Griffin and Bill Peepe, maintain that the destruction of those quaint, rustic structures contributed to the decline of tourism through the loss of the city's historical charm and look. Peepe remarked:

> The tidal wave was a bad thing. People left the area rather than rebuilding. The city lost some of its charm when its rustic look of downtown bars, restaurants, and tourist places were replaced

> by a municipal parking lot, the tsunami memorial, and one- and two-story modern-looking buildings. It was a bad thing, because the people never rebuilt in numbers of places. Even now some forty years later, there are jagged, saw-toothed parts of our city that still have vacant lots where buildings used to be. We had an old Pioneer-type of town with curio shops, museums, and even places where you could tie up a horse. People didn't tie up their horses then, but you could if you wanted to.

Since some destroyed buildings had been constructed of strong redwood and double walls, these residents believed that several of the historical structures could have been saved. Ruth Long didn't support the planning changes that occurred as part of this process.

> Our welding business had to be moved out of town, as the new planners felt that it was too "dirty" an operation to leave within town where it had been for some time. The problem was that they should have kept Second Street just like it had been with its attractive quaintness for the tourists. Instead, they plowed under all of those smaller shops and replaced it with what you see now. The city lost part of its identity and could never recover from that loss, no matter what later rebuilding occurred.

Jim Hooper, however, strongly believed that the city benefited over the long run from the urban renewal decisions and project.

> In one way, the disaster was a positive thing for Crescent City. Although no disaster is good, the deaths were tragic, and the property losses substantial, the city needed a lot of attention. It was then a rural lumber town with many old buildings. I don't believe for a moment that it had "rustic" charm, as some say. We needed to rebuild and we were given that opportunity. We constructed projects that would have otherwise never been started. The city built two seafood processing plants, a modern boat repair facility, small boat basin, community cultural and

convention center, completely rebuilt our aging water and sewer systems, and improved upon other public facilities.

Another issue raised involves the people. Helen M. Williams in *Yesteryears* wrote,

> The most curious aspect of the tidal wave's aftermath was the virtual disappearance of many of the City's most colorful and long-seen picturesque people, those on the benches, and the mysterious ones who looked from behind the lace curtains of the old buildings. Where did most of them go?

A way of life, once known, was now no more. Although the city lost its quaint, old-town charm and appearance due to the tsunami and redevelopment, the city's facilities and infrastructure were extensively improved and modernized. "Comeback Town, U.S.A." was a great slogan, but Crescent City had large challenges in front of it, even with the reconstruction activities.

Estimates at the time placed the total loss at between thirty and fifty million dollars, including the destroyed and damaged houses, buildings, public facilities such as docks and piers, harbor, fishing boats, inventory, lost income, wages, and other losses. One year later, some estimates were that the property losses alone were in the neighborhood of twenty million dollars.

If we assume the total damages were thirty million dollars, then the losses in today's dollars (rather than 1964 dollars) would have been over two hundred million. At an estimate of fifty million, including allowances for the lost income, wages, and adverse economic effects, this would translate to one-third of a billion dollars.

This sum doesn't include any allowance for lawsuits, attorney fees, defense costs, court and expert witness expenses, damage awards, or punitive damage assessments. If this tsunami had happened in today's legalistic environment, it's conceivable that the countless lawsuits filed and legal demands made would have aggregated in multiples of the actual value or today's present worth of what was actually lost then, and this would be in the billions of dollars.

But this wasn't the way people solved their problems then. Crescent City's officials handled problems the "old fashioned way." For example, with the destroyed municipal swimming pool, the contractor had spent fifty thousand dollars of public funds to build what he had, and the tidal wave then ripped it away in minutes. There were no lawsuits over the later disagreement concerning who should assume the financial cost of rebuilding the pool. The City Council and Bill Peepe simply said, "Hey, there were delays and not protecting what you had built was your fault. Let's split the difference." The contractor put up 25,000 dollars of his own funds into the rebuilding of the swimming pool. It was quickly rebuilt.

Bill Parker reflected:

> Many buildings and various homes were on septic tanks, so these had to be destroyed when the structures floated away, even if there was some salvage value. It was particularly hard for people to have their homes and buildings condemned and burned up, especially when they had owned them free and clear before. Without insurance in effect, even after rebuilding with low-interest loans, people had debt payments to make in an already economically depressed area. Some folks just left their destroyed businesses and homes and moved away, never to return.

Despite the ups and downs of the timber industry, Crescent City enjoyed somewhat better economic times afterwards with the bolstering by the reconstruction dollars now flowing in. However, nature soon conspired against these residents with its second disaster in nine months. Severe winter storms in 1964 caused the Klamath and Smith Rivers to flood wildly and cause extensive damage. The Klamath River in particular brought about widespread destruction, including wiping out the tiny town of Klamath that was later relocated when it had to be rebuilt. Over one mile of Highway 199—the main road tying Crescent City in Northern California to Medford, Oregon in Southern Oregon—slid into the Smith River. Once again, the Red Cross came to the rescue of the homeless and hungry, this time in the outlying areas of Del Norte County.

On the one-year anniversary of the tsunami, city officials held a "Tidal Wave Days" celebration to commemorate the "hardiness" of its residents and the rebuilding—as would be fitting of Crescent City. The town held a parade on Saturday morning, March 27, under clear and sunny skies. The County Sheriff, Crescent City Sheriff, Fish and Game, Fire Department, and other agencies paraded their washed and polished vehicles downtown. Marching as if this were a Fourth of July parade, high school bands, precision drill teams, politicians, veterans, and horsemen proceeded through the city and down Highway 101 to the refurbished Safeway parking lot.

Following the parade, the procession held groundbreaking ceremonies at Third and J Streets to celebrate the start of construction of the "Tsunami Landing" mall (which would be completed much later). Anonymous judges circulated through the crowd to award prizes, including cash, a one-hundred-dollar diamond ring, and merchandise, to those people judged as wearing the "craziest" garb based on a tidal wave or ocean theme. The next day, Sunday services were held in memory of those who had died in the disaster.

Although residents never forgot what had happened to them that day, later anniversaries of this date were not nearly as grand as the first one. Brief articles in the local newspapers did commemorate the dates of the second and third anniversaries, as well as later ones, but the festivities slimmed down. Because of the area's declining economy, rebuilding activities slowed down dramatically. And people moved away.

WHILE CRESCENT CITY worked with its rebuilding and urban renewal activities, people who were scarred by the tsunami tried to reconstruct their lives. Rita and Monte McKenzie found four young children that they intended to adopt and started caring for them. They filed adoption papers just months after losing their entire family. However, the McKenzies again had more marital and other problems, and the adoption proceedings were withdrawn. In June 1965, Monte McKenzie filed for divorce in Kings County, Washington. Both he and Rita soon moved out of the area. Monte McKenzie remarried and declined later interview requests from reporters. In

2000, Monte's wife reportedly told one reporter to just leave him alone. Several efforts to contact Rita McKenzie have been unsuccessful. The McKenzie family's tragedy is nearly beyond words.

Immediately following Stuart Harrington's report of his missing friend, a watch was maintained for days afterwards from the cliff at the mouth of the Klamath River. Nearly one month after the tsunami, fishermen on board the drag-boat *Sally*, from Trinidad harbor to the south, recovered the body of thirty-six-year-old Sergeant Donald McClure from the ocean. The men were working the boat's fishing net deeper than three hundred feet at the time of the discovery. Following the tidal wave's course down the California coast, McClure's remains drifted twenty miles south from where the Klamath River empties into the ocean. The condition of the corpse indicated that it had been buried in the sand and had probably surfaced a day or two prior to its discovery. Sergeant McClure was buried with full military honors at the National Cemetery in San Bruno, California.

Later, Stuart Harrington nominated Donald McClure for the Airman's Medal. The U.S. Air Force awards this medal as its highest recognition for bravery under peacetime conditions. Sergeant Harrington wrote:

> In looking back, it is apparent to me that Sergeant McClure was much more concerned about my safety than he was about his own. I know that if he hadn't removed my jacket and shirt, I never would have been able to swim the distance that I did to reach safety. If that heavy soggy clothing had stayed on, I would have surely drowned.
>
> He got me onto the log, despite the conditions; he explained to me what happened; he gave me good advice on when and how to leave the log. Without Sergeant McClure's assistance and help, I would not be alive to tell the facts of this unfortunate freak happening. I highly recommend and request that Sergeant McClure be awarded the Airman's Medal posthumously for his altruistic behavior involving voluntary risk of losing life under conditions other than those of a conflict with

an armed enemy of the United States, all while serving as a member of the United States Air Force.

Six months after his death, the U.S. Air Force awarded Sergeant Donald McClure the Airman's Medal for bravery in saving the life of Stuart Harrington. In a ceremony at nearby Del Norte County Airport, officials presented the medal to his widow, Mrs. Hisako McClure, and their three young children, Dorris (then age eleven), Shirley (age ten), and Jackie (seven months). Fellow U.S. Air Force officers and airmen of the 777th Radar Squad at Requa attended the solemn ceremonies, along with his best friend, Stuart Harrington.

By two years after the disaster, the agency had purchased eight hundred thousand dollars of land and resold another four hundred thousand dollars for development. Plans had been devised for new or present stores to cover about two-thirds of the downtown project, but not all of these would immediately be built. Four firms held grand openings or open houses at the two-year mark: Crescent City Lumber, the Crescent City Credit Bureau, the *Del Norte Triplicate*, and the Cardinet Florist (also located in the Triplicate building). A few other businesses had opened sooner.

When a national building slump occurred that particularly affected California, the local economy started to skid once more. The folding of the large California-Northern Plywood Company operations in the county in 1967 marked these hard times. Other lumbering and milling businesses closed their doors and never reopened again, and residents left Del Norte County and Crescent City in droves. In fact, Del Norte's population of 18,000 at the time dropped by more than one thousand in a matter of months following the closing of California-Northern Plywood.

Various citizens looked at the progress of urban renewal then and weren't very happy with what they saw. Although its Redevelopment Agency was one of the fastest-moving projects in HUD's eyes, the agency planners continued to underestimate the time it would take to complete their projects. The original plan called for spending 2.1 million dollars in thirty months to build new streets, parking lots, sewer mains, water mains, and a new civic center mall. Three years later, only the planned sewer and water mains and one block of the mall had been constructed. A block-and-a-half of the mall still needed to be started, and the streets and parking lots hadn't yet been paved. It would take much more time than initially thought, especially considering the cold, rainy weather that delayed construction during the winter months.

In 1967, the Federal Housing Administration (FHA) then became so concerned about future tidal waves that they wouldn't participate in any further local lending programs to public or individual borrowers in Crescent City until a protective seawall had been constructed. The Army Corps of Engineers initially wanted a twenty-five-foot-high seawall built; this structure would have made Crescent City the only city in the United States with such a tsunami wall. (Japan is notable for constructing them around their coastal cities.) Meanwhile, several building projects were put on hold until this problem was resolved.

The Army Engineers eventually built Beachfront Park by filling a three-block by ten-block area with landfill, bringing the oceanfront nearly ten feet above where sea level used to be and leveling this at the old concrete two-foot-high barrier by Front Street (then three blocks to the ocean). It built a rock base and higher mound of earth ringing the ocean to an approximate twelve- to fifteen-foot high barrier in places. The fill was composed of material dredged up previously from Crescent City Harbor in the wave's aftermath, along with the rubble of the streets and sidewalks left behind in the destruction. The city's ripped-up gutters, sidewalks, and streets were also used to construct the protecting barrier. Notwithstanding this construction, the last largest wave would have hurdled this barrier by ten feet.

The city constructed a new swimming pool in that beach park, basically in the same place as the partially built one that the tsunami destroyed. Named the Fred Endert Municipal Swimming Pool, this facility is an indoor, year-round public pool, complete with a curving water slide. "Tsunami-resistant" trees, which are deep-rooted and grow with high branches, were planted. If the powerful waves don't uproot them, these types of trees can become protective barriers, partially dissipating the destructive currents while catching some of the debris being carried inland.

Since surge-carried debris is a major cause of tsunami damage on land, coastal cities consider installing seawalls, dikes, and breakwaters. Crescent City eventually installed large cement tetrapod bumpers on land to channel future tidal flows into a predetermined route. Later, it reconstructed its breakwaters to be stronger and offer more protection for the newly built docks.

The fires at Highway 101 South took longer to remedy. To reduce that danger, the experts recommended that the shoreline bulk-oil tank farms be eliminated. Although this took time, the last of the bulk-oil tanks in that area finally closed in the 1980s. Such storage facilities are still present on the Seaside Hospital (A Street) side of town. The hospital was recently torn down and a new hotel complex constructed in its place after a new medical facility opened north of town.

CRESCENT CITY'S local economy showed little growth during the 1970s, then declined during the general boom times of the 1980s. Most of the economic development projects were completed or halted in the late 1970s. The area's timber and fishing economies declined precipitously to where the county's unemployment was 25 percent before the Pelican Bay prison was built.

Del Norte County moved in excess of three hundred million board feet of lumber from the early 1960s until 1980. Due to the economy, logging restrictions, import competition, and the carving out of Redwood National Park, this production fell to 210 million feet by 1980. By the 1990s, the output had declined to less than one hundred million board feet per year. The population of both the city and county also declined over this time period, which is not surprising, given the heavy dependence of the area's employment on the fortunes of its lumber industry. It took the construction of Pelican Bay State Prison to change both the economy and Crescent City.

Located to the northwest, the prison was constructed on 275 acres of land in the late 1980s and opened in December 1989. It imprisons California's most serious criminal offenders, about one-half secured in two Security Housing Units (SHU) for problem offenders, the rest housed in a general population setting. The SHU is a state-of-the-art design and construction for offenders who are habitual criminals, problem cases, prison gang members, and violence-oriented inmates. It is a tough, tough prison.

The facilities employee some 1,400 people, nearly 1,000 who are guards and on the custodial staff, the rest handling support services and administration. Its fully staffed capacity is 3,500 and currently there are around 3,300 inmates incarcerated in a year—the toughest and most incorrigible in California. Violence just among the inmates occurs on almost a daily basis.

Pelican Bay has had good and bad effects on Crescent City. As the economy nosedived, unemployed residents became certified as guards and took jobs at the prison. The penitentiary brought a stable employment base with more jobs, cutting the unemployment rate in half, and gaining extra revenues for the city and county, the prison's operating budget alone being nearly 125 million dollars. This added employment, however, also brought about large demands for additional schools, police, water, and utility services that had to be financed and built. According to some residents, Pelican Bay also brought about a lessening of the community spirit and closeness that had been so characteristic of the city. Working in a prison is a stressful job, and the average employee lasts only five years. When a job at Pelican Bay becomes too stressful, people generally leave the area for a less problematic prison or other employment. Owing to their long hours and nature of their jobs, employees and administrators at any prison also tend to stay in their own tight-knit group and not blend into the larger community. The psychological impact on any area of a maximum-security prison like this one clearly isn't the same as building a deep-sea harbor, a theater complex, or an international airport.

Even with the positive economic impact of Pelican Bay, Crescent City's population is currently just 5,000 (not including the prison population). Del Norte County's residents number a low 26,000, and the area is still considered to be a small, basically rural area with average-per-capita income lower than the California state average.

Jim Hooper echoed what many of the tidal-wave generation felt about Pelican Bay Prison. "The quality of life here in Crescent City did change, although the prison provided jobs for our people. However, I have always preferred private enterprise versus more and more government involvement in creating jobs. We should use government help only when we really need it and have no other practical choice."

Wal-Mart and Kmart later built large shopping centers on the town's outskirts, carving more business away from the local downtown merchants. The town's downtown business area still appears to be in the doldrums for the forseeable future and even Kmart stopped operating its facility in 2004 as part of a nationwide corporate reorganization. Although there are many more motels and tourist-oriented activities today, the tourist trade never seemed to make its comeback, whatever the reasons. Lots leveled back in the 1960s after the tsunami's destruction still lie vacant.

The regional hard decline of the timber industry in Northern California has been followed by more recent declines in the area's fishing industries. Both have occurred due to a combination of federal environmental regulations and worldwide economic trends, and have been hard on the local economies. Although the construction and operation of the Pelican Bay prison helped, this did not offset the overall trend. As retirees relocate to this area and service industries continue to grow, perhaps this trend can be reversed.

WITH THE LOCAL ECONOMY being so difficult over this long period, reopening didn't mean that business owners always stayed open. Ernie Pyke didn't borrow any money to reopen their Ben Franklin, feeling that it was "just a mess to borrow anything, given all that red tape." As one year elapsed before they could reconstruct their store, a new shopping center opened up first. Before then, Crescent City didn't have such centers with stores, both specialty and supermarket, offering such a variety of low-priced goods. Grocery stores only carried groceries and the Pyke family Ben Franklin store was a general variety store, carrying clothing, hardware, shoes, and a little bit of everything.

When the shopping center added product lines that competed against the Ben Franklin just as the mills began to close down, the already limited customer dollars shrank. "As I could see the handwriting on the wall," Ernie said later, "I sold the business for just what we had in it. Some guy from San Francisco bought it and got a good price, and I then looked for another job."

Ernie Pyke worked several jobs after owning the Ben Franklin. He first sold cars, becoming the top salesman in a couple of months, then was a shoe salesman and even worked for Safeway. Betty and Ernie divorced a few years after the tidal wave, and Ernie then married Mary Lou, his employee that the tsunami had trapped with the family in their Ben Franklin store.

One day, Ernie was down by the docks and saw a boat. "Right then and there," he decided to go into the commercial fishing business. Ernie asked his sons if they wanted to join him and they quickly said "yes." The family bought a forty-footer called the *Banshee*, or the "Screaming Ghost," and the family fished commercially since then for over thirty years, fishing for tuna, salmon, crab, and bottom fish, depending on what was selling best at the time. Ernie said:

> We've done well in the fishing business over the years, but you're risking your life everyday in this business. My sons have nearly drowned in the storms, or when one or the other has been tossed into the ocean during a bad storm, and I've seen a lot myself. I've been in eighteen-foot waves when the wind blows one-hundred miles per hour. Once the boat nearly rolled over with half of the tuna washing off its deck, but the boat made it and didn't catch on the waves to flip over. Further, in the fishing business, you never know how well you'll do, because you never know what price you're going to get.
>
> The fishing has been bad the last several years, but I'm no longer doing that, as my sons are running the business. . . . But this business is all we know, even with the problems. Sometimes you just skim by, but like after the tidal wave, you just keep smiling. It's all you can do. You just keep hacking away at it.

Ernie has since passed away. His twin sons, Doug and Steve, were sixteen when the tidal waves struck. After graduating from high school, they worked for the mills and later joined their father in the commercial fishing business. With over thirty years' experience, they underscored their father's assessment of fishing being a risky business. "I've been thrown into the high seas by a bad storm, where I was lucky to catch a rope when the boat even luckier was able to turn around and come back for me in heavy, heavy waves," said Doug. "But I'll never forget that tidal wave and what it did to everyone, not to mention this city and area."

Virtually all of the *Triplicate*'s printing equipment was beyond salvage due to the sand, saltwater damage to bearings, and ocean pummeling. The newspaper soon converted to offset printing and cold-type composition, and a new building was constructed two years later at Third and H Streets, where its operations are still housed today. The *Triplicate* became the only newspaper in town when it purchased Wally Griffin's *Crescent City American* a few years after the tsunami hit. Steve Yarborough later became the publisher, following in the footsteps of his father.

Bob Ames found reopening to be tough, but he, his wife Mary Jean, and his family were able to accomplish this in two months. They applied for and received a small business loan, paying it off in half the time. Six years later, they stopped selling appliances and began selling furniture with stores located in both Crescent City and nearby Brookings, Oregon. Over time, Bob was in another business or two, including now doing electrician's work—long after his "retirement." Bob's two sons, Guy and Brad, both graduated from college and left the area. Brad is teaching school, while Guy is a pension investment consultant.

After renting a house in the beautiful and nearby mountain area of Gasquet on Route 199 toward Medford, Oregon, Ruth and Dale Long returned one year later to buy a house in Crescent City, as their welding shop continued its commercial success. However, when the economy slowed down, their welding business also fell off. They decided to enter the boat-building business. Again due to governmental restrictions, that business slowed down years later. Ruth and Dale then started a successful boat and tug repair and "enlarging" business whose excellent reputation extends up and down the Pacific Coast.

Like everyone else, Ray Schach didn't have insurance that covered his tidal-wave losses, but he did carry some liability coverage on the equipment that helped him with that repair. He applied for a SBA loan, although it took him "nearly a year" to get it and an interest rate of 3¾ percent. The loan allowed Ray to get his mill running again, but he couldn't recover anything for his lost lumber and mill inventory. As other lumberyards experienced in the inundation zone, all of the lumber became salt-damaged and couldn't be used or salvaged. When the planning committee wouldn't let him rebuild at his old site on Second Street, Ray moved into another building. He bought land at Fourth and L, rebuilt, and started up again. "It took a lot of long hours and we had to cut back," Ray said, "but we were able to get going again." He ran that operation up to his retirement.

Roy Magnuson retired as a teacher. "I didn't even get my feet wet that night, although I must tell you that they were moving very fast. We weren't afraid or scared. You do just what you need to do to get through it all. I've got two kids, four grandkids, and I've been married to my wife for forty-five years now (at the time of this interview). The secret? . . ." He said laughingly, "Well, if we can live through a tidal wave, then we can live through just about anything."

After working those long hours on duty, Bud Clark stayed with the Sheriff's Office for one more year, then worked as a meat cutter. After that, he became the jailer at the county jail for "seven to eight" years. Bud then quit that job to drive an "eighteen-wheeler," hauling lumber and plywood to Merlin, Oregon, Merced, California, and Eureka. He then retired at age sixty-two and tends to his two-acre property.

Jim Hooper was politically connected and continued his law practice for years. He represented businesses, lumber companies, and public agencies, as a transactional or deal attorney. After many years of marriage, his first wife died and Jim later married his second wife, Sophia. They wintered in Sun City, Arizona, spending the summers in cooler Crescent City. Jim practiced law almost until his death in December, 2003, although on a reduced basis. A very active man, Jim took up golf after his "retirement," playing in the low 80s and better "than many people half my age." He bought a Harley-Davidson to ride a few years prior to his death, because he "just always wanted to do that."

Bill Parker later started working for the Del Norte County School System. He rose to the position of Director of Classified Employees and School Operations of the county school system. In addition to other civic activities, Bill also has been active for years on the Del Norte County Board of Education and has run other businesses, including his own janitorial company—also after his "retirement." The community has awarded Bill its "Man of the Year" Award for his years of community service and disaster preparedness, as well as he received a special Governor's award for his forty years of outstanding service as an emergency director. He was responsible for obtaining the city's tsunami-warning sirens, being included in the National Warning System, and installing the remote tide-sensing gauge in its harbor, among other instituted changes.

OF THE EIGHT PEOPLE at the Long Branch, only Mac, Bruce, and Gary survived. Mac is still happily married to Margot, his wife of over fifty years. They live in Crescent City and have three grown children and eight grandchildren.

Bruce Garden left the area and died much later of a heart attack. Gary Clawson said:

> He died on the doctor's examination table. This was incredible, as Bruce was the proverbial cat with nine lives. He had so many accidents and brushes with death, as with the Long Branch's destruction, but Bruce survived every one of them. One day he had a pain in his chest and went to see a doctor. He died, right then and there in the doctor's office.

Gary Clawson left Crescent City a few months later, the memories understandably too hard to continually be reminded about. After selling his grocery store and home in Crescent City, he headed north near Gold Hill in Oregon, located fifteen miles up Interstate 5 from Medford in Southern Oregon. Later that same year on December 1, he opened the Rogue Riviera Supper Club in Gold Hill, Oregon, a few miles from his new home. Set one-hundred yards back from the banks of the Rogue River at the top of a gently sloping incline, the restaurant enjoyed beautiful views of the river and a rural setting. Gary Clawson was back in business. Just one week later, however, the Rogue River flooded over its banks in a "one hundred year's flood." With five feet of swollen muddy water, broken trees, and debris surging through the first floor of his restaurant, Gary Clawson again had lost everything.

Twice snake bit, he found it difficult to answer the "Why me?" questions. But while waiting to talk to his attorney about filing for bankruptcy, he told his story about the Long Branch Tavern and the Rogue Riviera Supper Club to an older woman who sat next to him, waiting to meet with the same attorney. After hearing Gary's tales of surviving among death and sadness, Jennieve Briggs immediately bought up the mortgage on the place and lent him the money that he needed to repair the restaurant and start over again. The Rogue Riviera Supper Club reopened and became a very successful operation. In fact, although Gary sold the business three years later, the red-painted restaurant with some of the "best steaks in town" operates today overlooking the same beautiful green lawn that sweeps down to the Rogue River.

Shortly after rebuilding the restaurant, Gary met Carole, an attractive and petite blonde. They married soon afterwards. Gary and Carole will celebrate their thirty-eighth wedding anniversary in 2005, and have five children, twelve grandchildren, and own an exquisite home on forty-two acres overlooking the ocean in Oregon. During this time, Gary Clawson bought, opened up, and sold several successful restaurants on the coasts of Oregon and California. He has done quite well with his business affairs, is a Christian, and was a millionaire early on.

As an example of his business instincts, when a buyer of one enterprise of his, this time a tavern, was thrown into jail, Gary cut a deal with the person, taking back the tavern in return for the bail money. A few months later, when a potential buyer couldn't make up his mind to buy it, Gary reached over, took the potential buyer's checkbook, ripped out a check and filled it in with an amount of money, handed it to the guy, and said "If you sign this check, you now own a tavern." The man did. To find another buyer of one of his businesses, Gary called up the car dealers in one part of Oregon, knowing that this one candidate liked fancy new cars. He finally found an auto dealer who remembered the man, got the telephone number, called him up, and visited him to try and sell him the business. Instead, Gary ended up buying the first of his successful seafood restaurants.

Aside from the various restaurants he has bought and successfully operated, Gary bought other investments, as well. As just one example, he bought a "fixer-upper" 50-foot wooden-hulled boat, built in 1928, because he always wanted it, once owned by royalty. After restoring it to its initial luxurious condition, he sold it at a substantial profit. In the 1990s, Gary bought the Crescent Hotel in Eureka Springs, Arkansas, and refurbished it; this elegant hotel is part of the rich regional history of the area.

Gary Clawson survived the tidal wave not just because he wasn't afraid of the ocean due to his snorkeling and undersea diving. He lived because he had survival instincts that you can't get from going to college. Years later, when Gary was vacationing in Hawaii, high unexpected waves engulfed his wife. He swam over to Carole and managed to get her safely back to the beach. While doing this, he swallowed ocean water in gulps from the swollen breakers. Turning around while gasping, he discovered that his sister, Ginny, was also in trouble. Gary took in water from another large swell that broke over him, then from another, and watched the waves breaking over his sister. He swam over in the rough seas to Ginny, pushed her head above water, as his went down, when a swell would break over them. Clawson was hyperventilating and said to himself, once again, "I'm not going to make this one." But he wouldn't give up and continued holding his sister up. Meanwhile, Ginny's husband saw what was happening from the beach, and he jumped into the surf with a floating plastic mattress. When he got to Gary, however, he started taking in water. Grabbing the mattress from him, Gary managed to drag Ginny to one end of it, his brother-in-law to the other, and then towed both back to shore. All family members survived this time, though Ginny needed to be hospitalized in intensive care for four days.

The "what ifs," however, have stayed with Gary. What if Nita and Earl Edwards had taken the cash box when they left the tavern after the first small flooding of water? It's conceivable that no one would have gone back. If that day hadn't been Bill Clawson's birthday, would they have simply turned around and left after getting the cash? What if Gary hadn't tried to save the two drowning persons? The group otherwise would have easily crossed Elk Creek and been on safe ground with time to spare. What if they had turned away from the trees and headed in the opposite direction, back towards Elk Valley Road and not across Elk Creek?

Gary reflected on this and then said:

> A terrible thing happened. What more can you say? We think we have control over our lives, but we really don't. People tell me that they couldn't have survived the deaths of their mom and dad, let alone the others. Well, you have to overcome it, since there is just no other choice. When you're faced with this type of tragedy, you just do it. You overcome.
>
> I've asked myself so many times before, "why this?" and "why that?" I was frozen blue when I dragged myself out of Elk Creek for the last time, but I didn't even catch a cold and everyone else died. All I know is that there's a sun, stars, trees, and oceans. I know something is out there, that something's happening, and I have a strong belief that there is a power. I have had these feelings for a long time, way back before anyone died. I know now that there is no answer, no answer at all. Things just seem to happen, the bad along with the good.

16

THE NEXT ONES

The Pacific Tsunami Warning Center was established on Oahu primarily to warn residents of the Hawaiian Islands. The 1964 Alaskan earthquake showed beyond a doubt that a warning system needed to be established specifically for Alaska and the U.S. West Coast. In response, the federal government created the U.S. West Coast/Alaska Tsunami Warning Center (WC/ATWC) in Palmer, Alaska, in 1967. A small, quaint town, Palmer is a one-and-a-half-hour drive north of Anchorage, Alaska, and was selected for the ATWC site because the area is geologically stable.

The WC/ATWC's responsibilities have been enlarged since its inception to include the responsibility for all Pacific-wide tsunamis, including all "tsunamigenic" sources, that could affect the coasts of California, Oregon, Washington, British Columbia, and Alaska. The National Oceanic and Atmospheric Administration's (NOAA) National Weather Service operates both the Pacific and the Alaska Tsunami Warning Centers.

A staff of four geophysicists and two computer/electronic specialists operate the WC/ATWC during normal weekday hours. After normal hours, two duty-personnel are on paid standby and must respond to the center within five minutes of any alarm. This facility is a large geophysical data acquisition and analysis center with access to the earthquake-sensing data from networks owned and maintained by it: the National Earthquake Information Center, Albuquerque Seismological Lab, IRIS/ISA-UC San Diego, California Institute of Technology, UC Berkeley, University of Washington, University of Alaska in Fairbanks, and other centers. It also operates and maintains fifteen remote-sensing tidal gauges positioned off Alaska and the Aleutian Islands, along with several other sites located off the U.S. West Coast, including British Columbia.

The center owns numerous pieces of electronic equipment with complete system backup, ranging from satellite dishes and sophisticated computer systems to seismometers, data telemetry systems, and display monitors. The present seismic-processing system utilizes advanced technology: currently Pentium IV PCs with Windows XP operating systems. All real-time processing PCs are networked together using the Windows XP peer-to-peer LAN system. Indeed, the systems are highly sophisticated with continually updated software specifically adapted to the center's requirements.

When an earthquake measures 7.1 or higher on the Richter scale, a tidal wave warning is issued as a matter of policy. Since the WC/ATWC typically can't tell if an earthquake in the 7.1 to 7.5 range will in fact generate a tidal wave, it has set the criteria for such a warning at 7.1 to be safe. When the intensity of an earthquake is between 6.5–7.1, the Center will issue a Tsunami Information Bulletin (TIB) to notify emergency personnel as to the occurrence of this large earthquake. Tide gauges in the immediate vicinity of the earthquake are immediately monitored to determine whether a tidal wave has been generated. With earthquakes smaller than 6.5 on the Richter scale, the center issues an informational message to the tsunami warning recipients.

When a coastal earthquake measures greater than 7.1 in the WC/ATWC's area of responsibility, a combined watch and warning is issued. In the message, the appropriate coastal areas are placed on a warning status, while those just outside of the warned area are placed on a watch status. The remaining areas, if any, are placed on an information status. Personnel at the Alaskan center monitor the distant tide gauges from the vicinity of the epicenter outward to determine if any unusual tsunami wave activity is present. If the wave activity is large and dangerous, the warning area is expanded and the watch area increased to include those areas just outside of the warned area. The WC/ATWC technicians continually observe

An 8.3 earthquake on March 9, 1957, in the Aleutian Islands generated a tidal wave that caused authorities to evacuate Crescent City. (Wallace and Lillian Griffin/Crescent City Printing Co.)

An 8.6 earthquake off the coast of Chile on May 22, 1960, caused a tsunami that flooded lower streets of Crescent City, sank three large fishing boats, and damaged other craft. (Wallace and Lillian Griffin/Crescent City Printing Co.)

The Good Friday, 1964, tsunami carried logs and debris over Front Street when the first wave flooded lower portions of the city. (Wallace and Lillian Griffin/Crescent City Printing Co.)

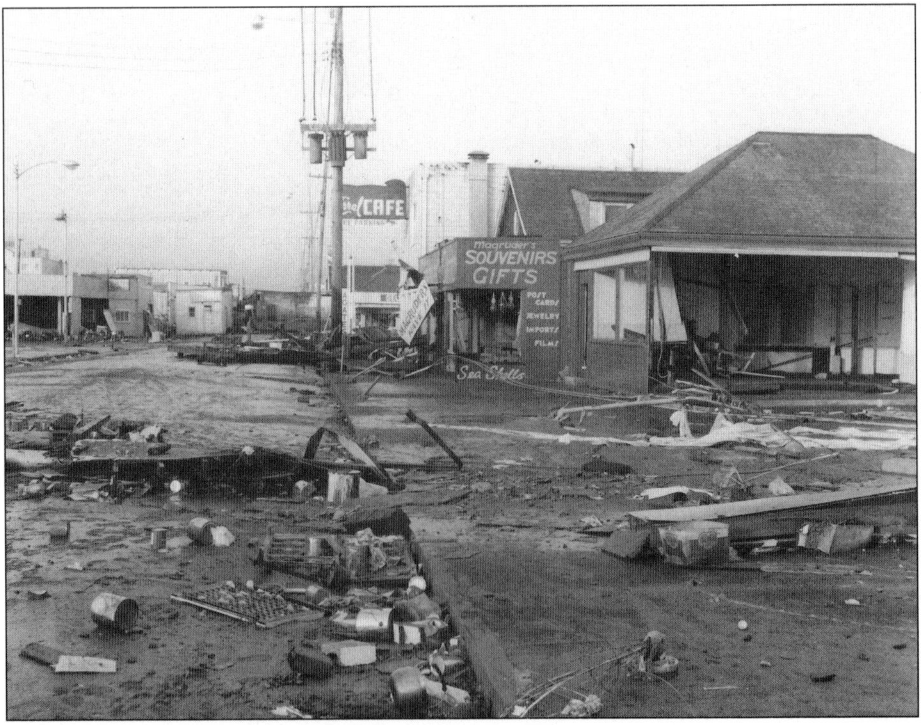

Later, that same intersection after the third and fourth waves. (Del Norte County Historical Society, Walt Harris Collection)

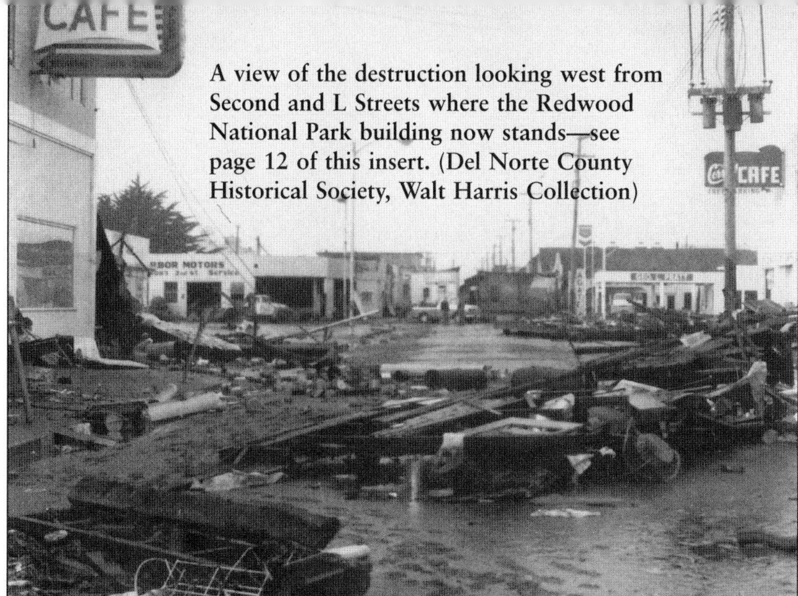

A view of the destruction looking west from Second and L Streets where the Redwood National Park building now stands—see page 12 of this insert. (Del Norte County Historical Society, Walt Harris Collection)

Rushing waters carried smashed structures far from their original locations. (Del Norte County Historical Society, Walt Harris Collection)

The office and one of the motel units from Van's Motel on Highway 101 South were spun onto that thoroughfare. (Del Norte County Historical Society, Walt Harris Collection)

The tsunami ruined over a thousand vehicles, strewing them around a five-mile-square section of town or leaving them sunk or floating in the harbor. (*top:* Del Norte County Historical Society, Walt Harris Collection; *center and bottom:* Wallace and Lillian Griffin/Crescent City Printing Co.)

Citizen's Dock afterwards.

The tidal wave deposited this boat and structures at Fourth Street, where O Street would be, or nearly two miles from where the boat was probably anchored. (Wallace and Lillian Griffin/Crescent City Printing Co.)

An aerial photograph with the intersection of A and First Street shown at far left. The currents swept away structures even at this far end of the city and bay, causing deaths, injuries, and obvious destruction. (Wallace and Lillian Griffin/Crescent City Printing Co.)

The tidal wave savaged the interiors of many structures that weren't outright mangled or swept away into the darkness. This interior shows the Ben Franklin store, located at Third Street and owned by Ernie Pyke. (Del Norte County Historical Society, Walt Harris Collection)

The blazing infernos at Highway 101 South included the Texaco Bulk Plant, auto agencies, and two gasoline service stations. The heat literally caused vehicles to melt. (*top:* Wallace and Lillian Griffin/Crescent City Printing Co.; *center and bottom:* Del Norte County Historical Society, Walt Harris Collection)

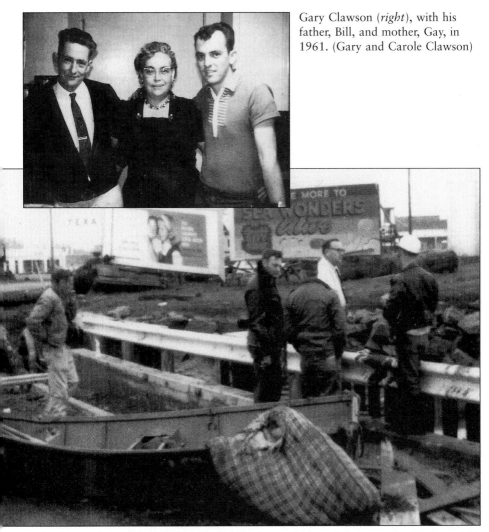

Gary Clawson (*right*), with his father, Bill, and mother, Gay, in 1961. (Gary and Carole Clawson)

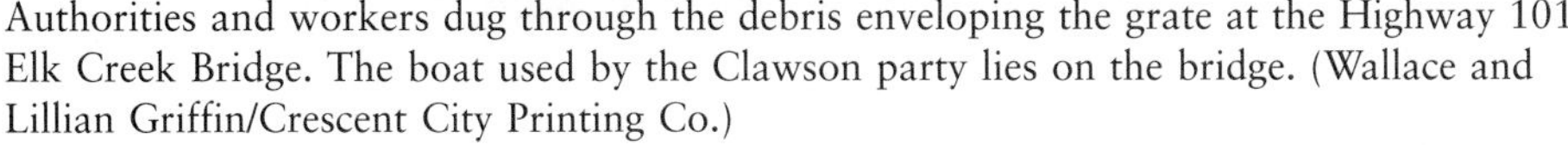

Authorities and workers dug through the debris enveloping the grate at the Highway 101 Elk Creek Bridge. The boat used by the Clawson party lies on the bridge. (Wallace and Lillian Griffin/Crescent City Printing Co.)

The reconstructed Elk Creek Bridge, twenty years later and showing the confining grate. (Wallace and Lillian Griffin/ Crescent City Printing Co.)

Viewing inland, the destruction and remains of the municipal swimming pool under construction are evident. (Del Norte County Historical Society, Walt Harris Collection)

Sause Pier after the tidal wave. (Wallace and Lillian Griffin/ Crescent City Printing Co.)

The ocean stormed over the breakwater, rolling over dozens of boats, leaving shells and broken masts behind. (Del Norte County Historical Society, Walt Harris Collection)

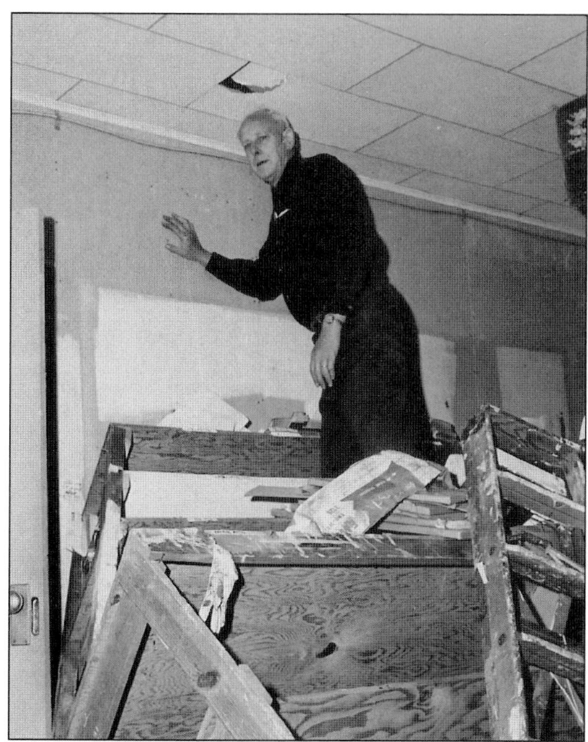

Cozy Collins, manager of Daly's Store on Third Street, positions himself under the hole that the currents pushed his head through. (Wallace and Lillian Griffin/Crescent City Printing Co.)

A resident patrols inland and north of where second street ends. (Wallace and Lillian Griffin/Crescent City Printing Co.)

Once streets were cleared, the demolition of what was left of the inner city could begin. (Wallace and Lillian Griffin/Crescent City Printing Co.)

Bonfires blazed for weeks, as trucks continually hauled down the remains of destroyed structures. (Wallace and Lillian Griffin/Crescent City Printing Co.)

The Hamilton Brothers lumberyard at the end of Second Street became another "elephant" dumping ground. (Del Norte County Historical Society, Walt Harris Collection)

The Hamilton Brothers lumberyard twenty years later. (Wallace and Lillian Griffin/Crescent City Printing Co.)

Now housing the Chamber of Commerce, this building was constructed on the beach side of Front Street, between J and K Streets. (Wallace and Lillian Griffin/ Crescent City Printing Co.)

As part of the redevelopment program, the Redwood National Park building was constructed between Front and Third Streets, between K and L. (Wallace and Lillian Griffin/Crescent City Printing Co.) The scene as it was before redevelopment can be seen on page 3 of this insert.

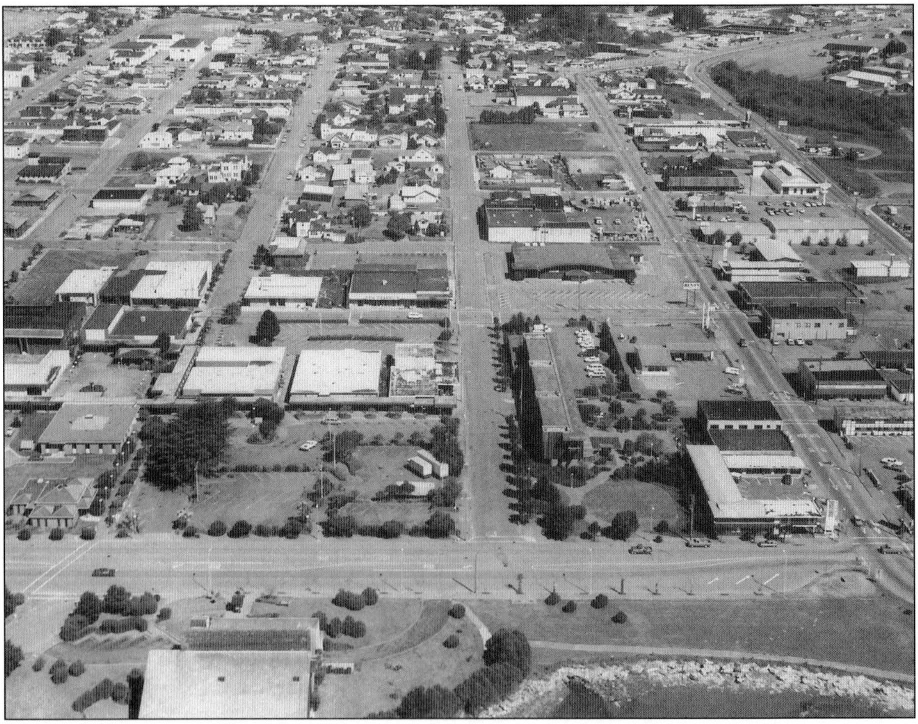

An aerial view of Crescent City twenty years after the tsunami hit. An area of fifteen square blocks between Fourth Street and Front, from H to M Streets (in lower middle to left of picture), was designated for urban renewal. Long slender structure in lower middle is the Redwood National Park building. (Wallace and Lillian Griffin/Crescent City Printing Co.)

The Tsunami Landing mall was constructed in the redevelopment zone. Today it houses a number of small businesses from what was once Second Street from H Street east to K. (Dennis M. Powers)

Historically a seafaring town, Crescent City is still home to hundreds of pleasure and commercial fishing boats. (Dennis M. Powers)

In response to the death and destruction brought about by the 1964 Alaskan earthquake and tsunamis, the West Coast/Alaska Tsunami Warning Center was created three years later in Palmer, Alaska. (West Coast/Alaska Tsunami Warning Center/NOAA/National Weather Service)

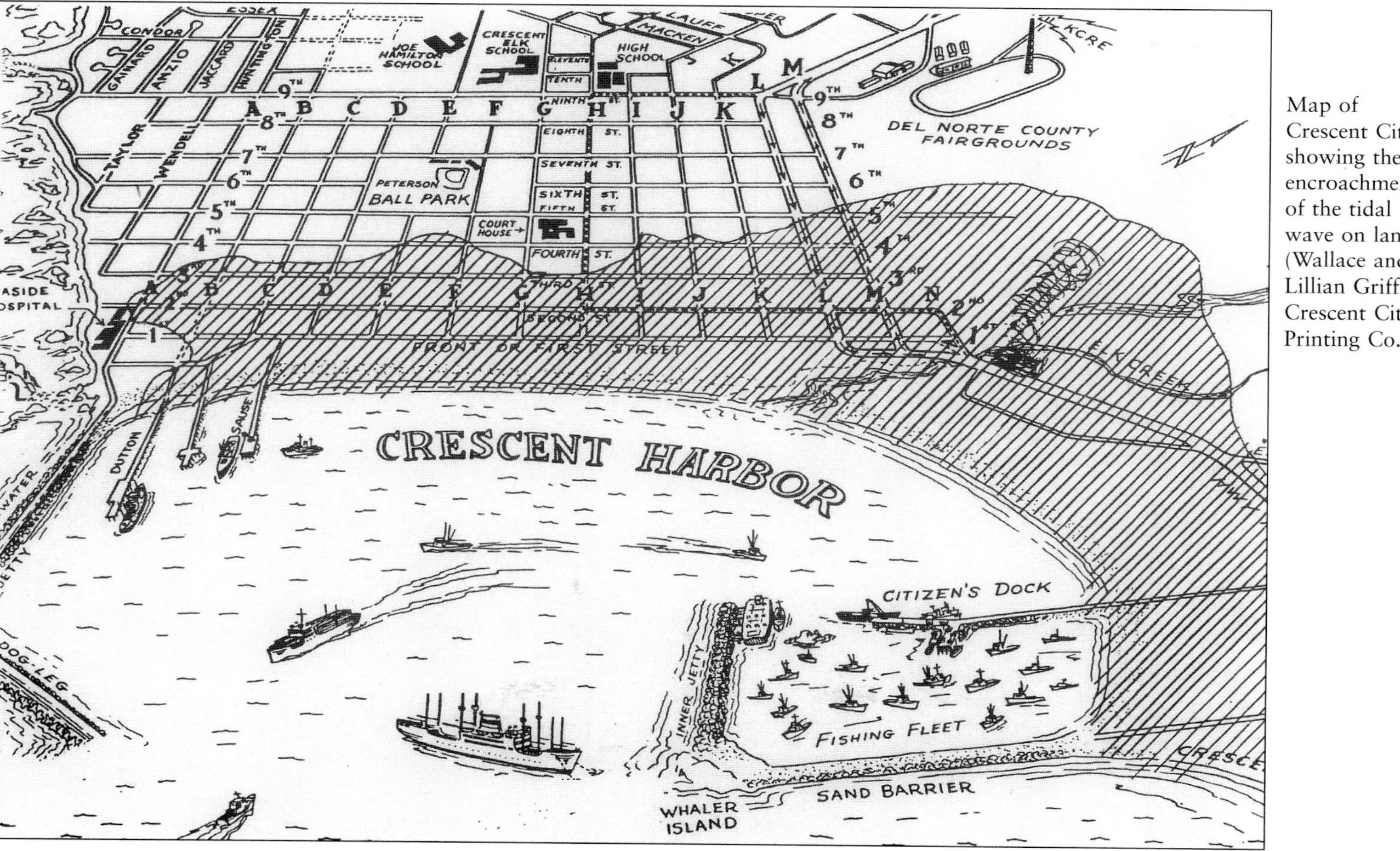

Map of Crescent City showing the encroachment of the tidal wave on land. (Wallace and Lillian Griffin/ Crescent City Printing Co.)

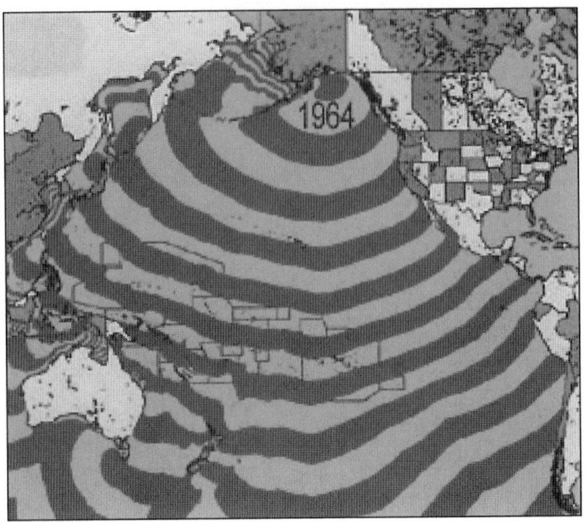

Map of the 1964 Alaskan earthquake showing the tidal wave positions in one-hour increments. The tsunami struck Crescent City less than four and a half hours after the earthquake occurred. (Pacific Marine Environmental Lab, WC/ATWC/NOAA/National Weather Service)

Trehearne's department store, located between Second and Third Streets. (Del Norte County Historical Society, Walt Harris Collection)

tide-gauge wave activity throughout this entire time period, passing information onto coastal emergency personnel to keep them abreast of the changing situation. If the warning is continued or expanded, the WC/ATWC calculates the expected tsunami arrival times at various coastal locations and immediately transmits this critical information to local, state, national, and international agencies, as well as to the media. If the tide gauges show no unusual activity, or negligible activity, the Alaskan center cancels the warning/watch.

The WC/ATWC issues its warnings and messages in various ways, including over the National Warning System (NAWAS), NOAA Weather Wire Satellite system (NWWS), dedicated FAA teletype (NADIN2), and the National Weather Service (WS), among other channels that it utilizes. When necessary, the center transmits its warnings and information by secondary means such as e-mail, its Web page (wcatwc.gov or wcatwc.arh.noaa.gov), telephone, and digital-pager messages.

NAWAS is an instant voice communication system, and emergency personnel actually hear messages read verbally over the NAWAS phone system. These emergency sites range from U.S. Coast Guard stations and federal agencies to state and county government levels on the U.S. West Coast, Alaska, and Hawaii. The NWWS satellite system transmits a printed message to the affiliated agencies, while the FAA teletype system sends a printed copy to different governmental offices, military installations, and foreign countries.

Since 1981, the WC/ATWC has issued ten regional tsunami warnings. Its staff responds to 250–300 earthquakes annually, or about five each week, that activate this alarm system. Four-fifths of the warnings issued occurred after normal working hours. Over the last several years, the Alaskan center has cut its average response time (the time it takes to issue a warning from the time of sensing the earthquake's start) from ten minutes down to its present six minutes due to technological and software advances brought about by its former director Tom Sokolowski (who retired in 2002), along with his staff and its present director, Paul Whitmore.

An operator generates a computerized tsunami warning by selecting from a menu of different statement options. The software program automatically composes the appropriate message with the earthquake's location, magnitude, and origin time. The tsunami's ETA, or estimated time of arrival, at its coastal areas of responsibility is included automatically in the message, as well, along with any other general information that's available. It is possible to overlay the earthquake's epicenter onto computerized maps, indicating the quake's position within the Pacific Basin, the country, region, and even city-areas, along with historical tidal-wave data and forecasted tsunami wave heights, for any potential tsunamigenic event.

Once the staff issues a warning, personnel monitor the nearest tide gauges to confirm the existence or nonexistence of the tsunami and its degree of severity. The WC/ATWC has access to more than one hundred tide sites throughout the Pacific Basin, due to the interconnections with its own stations and those of national tsunami warning centers maintained by other countries along the Pacific Rim (such as Japan, Indonesia, the Philippines, and Australia). All of these countries, including the United States, have joined the NOAA Tsunami Warning System to exchange earthquake/tsunami data and cooperate in the issuance of regional and global tidal-wave warnings. The U.S. National Ocean Service (NOS) owns and operates most of the tide gauge instruments located around the Pacific Rim.

The Alaskan center maintains or connects to systems with both seismometers (measuring an earthquake's direction, intensity, and duration) and tide gauges (measuring tide changes). These gauges measure tide flows at specific moments, collect the information, and then transmit this data at regular intervals. Most of these gauges, however, do not give the ability to look at what's happening at a specific instance or in real time. Although these instruments obtain data in near-real time, difficulties in transmitting this information can translate to hours of delay before there can be access to Pacific-wide tide gauge data. This delay problem does not exist for the WC/ATWC's eight real-time tide gauges in Alaska.

However, there are two problems with tide gauges. First, they cannot determine a tsunami's energy when it hits a distant shore. In other words, they can show the tsunami's relative wave height at a specific location, but can't forecast that height at other coastal locations or how destructive it will be. This "damage potential" depends upon the target's offshore terrain and composition (its "bathymetry"), configuration of coastal geography, slope of the coastal land, presence of underwater reefs or cliffs, among other factors. This fact increases, of course, the danger of false alarms being issued. Second, delays from fifteen minutes to three hours exist when receiving data from non-real-time tide stations—the great majority of instruments in use—due to technical differences between gauges and the information collection, transmission, and reception systems.

Regardless of the equipment in use, determining the intensity or destructiveness of any tsunami is still an art, and research efforts focus on how to become more qualitative or accurate when forecasting wave heights for coastal communities. The WC/ATWC and its counterpart in Hawaii, the PTWC, do a good job in immediately issuing warnings to protect coastal populations in harm's way. The problems then become not knowing the tsunami's intensity at specific locations, a generally unaware public, the difficulty in getting information out to everyone, and people in coastal areas simply disregarding what's told them. Although warning centers continue to partner with the coastal states' emergency officials to educate coastal populations in becoming aware of tsunami hazards, it is still up to the people in our sizeable coastal populations to react wisely and safely—because another large tsunami like this one will happen again. This is especially true for areas where people are caught in the middle of a violent earthquake and an offshore tsunami.

CRESCENT CITY adopted measures after 1964 and over time to decrease the odds of another devastating tidal wave. Reconstruction projects built up its beach area, constructed more protecting tetrapods in the harbor, planted more trees on shore, and built stronger breakwaters. Disaster officials and Bill Parker discarded the teletype warning system in favor of a real-time system, causing Crescent City to be hooked up to NAWAS's direct voice-message system, and the town instituted a general alarm system. The harbor tide gauge transmits data to the city's civil defense headquarters, and even the smallest of wave motions register there. Now, two citywide sirens are in place, one at the harbor and another located inland at Ninth Street.

Officials activate and test the siren system regularly, so residents are constantly reminded of the system and risks of tsunamis. The weekly tests take place mostly in the winter to minimize scaring the tourists, and the newspapers inform people about test times. A continuous siren means an attention signal is being issued, and people are to tune into local radio stations for further information. An alternating tone indicates a tidal wave alert, advising everyone to evacuate immediately and stay away for at least two hours. The attention tone is always sounded first.

Officials have prepared inundation maps indicating the areas with the greatest risks of being struck, and road signs are in place showing the safest routes to take. Geologists give lectures at school classes, warning students about tidal waves and what to do when an emergency is sounded. Crescent City takes steps to inform its residents of evacuation plans and what to do when an alarm occurs. Many of its residents have gone through previous tidal wave alerts and evacuations, although people still grumble over whether these "false alarms" are worth it—especially people new to the area.

However, many other coastal communities on the West Coast don't do this, despite federal legislation that was enacted. They aren't as tsunami-wary or educated in "tsunami common sense" as Crescent City residents. "They just don't know what one's like," said one old-timer. Unfortunately, even Crescent City faces the danger of apathy. Those who endured the Good Friday tidal wave are slowly and unfortunately dying away, and the new generation does not take the precautions as seriously. Short of constructing a twenty-five-foot-high reinforced-concrete seawall around the total length of its bay, Crescent City is still at risk, due to its magnetizing attraction for tidal waves. In fact, some local residents believe that the current landfill barrier will simply redirect another tidal wave with more intensity and destruction into other parts of the city, including the now built-up Highway 101 South beach section with its restaurants, motels, tourist attractions, boat and manufacturing facilities, then upwards again into the downtown section.

SINCE 1964, significantly large, destructive tidal waves have surged throughout the world. Some eighty-five tidal waves were reported worldwide during the 1990s, and ten destructive tsunamis in this period alone claimed more than 4,000 lives. The tidal waves that struck Flores Island, Indonesia, in 1992 killed more than 1,000 people; most of them didn't know that the earthquake could produce an even more threatening sea wave, so they didn't flee to higher ground. The 1998 tsunami that lashed several small villages on islands offshore of Papua New Guinea killed over 2,200 people—monstrous thirty-foot waves crashed three times over narrow sand spits that were only three feet over sea level and crowded with villages, homes, and people. The waves began surging over the sandy beaches only fifteen minutes after the quake first hit.

Both of these earthquakes struck close to home, causing savage uplifting or undersea landslides and creating powerful tsunamis that in minutes raced over land, wrecking structures, and drowning hundreds and hundreds of unsuspecting people. The New Guinea earthquake measured a relatively small 7.1 for tidal wave purposes—but the epicenter was located only nineteen miles offshore, and the ocean bottom undulated savagely up and down there.

Closer to the Americas, a tidal wave caused by an earthquake offshore from Nicaragua in 1992 was particularly dangerous because most of the people in the surrounding areas didn't even feel the quake. It was a "silent one" where the seismic energy producing the characteristic earthquake rumblings never made it onshore to the mainland. These short energy waves die out quickly as they spread away from the epicenter. A relatively "modest" 7.0 magnitude quake caused tsunamis to surge onto land, killing 170 people and leaving 13,000 homeless.

Regardless of what tsunami warnings are in place, scores of people can be killed and injured and vast amounts of property destroyed. However, there is no question that fatalities are significantly reduced by education programs, effective warning systems, media announcements when evacuation becomes a necessity, and trained authorities who know what to do when there isn't much time. In Okushiri, Japan, a 7.8 magnitude earthquake located twenty miles offshore in 1993 caused fifteen- to thirty-foot waves to crash ashore less than five minutes after the earthquake stopped. The surges washed completely over seawalls that had been constructed after past tsunami disasters, destroying buildings, starting raging fires, and killing 239 people. The experts believed the death toll would have vastly exceeded Papua New Guinea's disaster had the town not issued the quick and accurate warnings that it did. Many residents heeded them in fleeing pell-mell to higher ground.

Some twenty (or nearly 15 percent) of the 150 tsunamis hitting Japan over the last century have damaged property or killed people. On the other hand, tidal waves slamming into Indonesia have caused death or destruction there over the last one hundred years in more than 50 percent of its thirty-four tsunamis. Experts believe that Indonesia's lack of warning systems, education programs, or protecting land improvements translate into the more severe destruction and casualties figures.

Over half of all tidal wave deaths in the Hawaiian Islands occur at Hilo, Hawaii, due to its location in the "zone of danger." Consequently, this city, like Crescent City, takes tsunamis seriously. Maps indicating the most likely tsunami inundation zones and safe areas are in every telephone book; road signs clearly mark evacuation routes. Radio and television broadcasts spring into action when a warning has been issued, and sirens pierce the air in all low-lying areas. Tsunami-education classes are given to the public, and disaster officials have the absolute power to take whatever steps are necessary to safeguard the public after a warning has been issued.

But neither Crescent City nor Hilo are densely populated communities. Contemplating an earthquake-caused tidal wave with its strike direction pointed at the heart of Los Angeles, San Francisco, or New York City leaves people simply shaking their heads. If a tidal wave surged into such a major populated area, there would be a disaster of incalculable proportions, not to mention the tens of thousands of vacationers who jam onto tiny sandpits of coastal land during the summer months, starting from Southern California to north of Seattle, Washington.

FROM THE Aleutians to Peru, Japan, and Hawaii, earthquakes centered in different countries since 1964 have created tidal waves that coursed through the Pacific and down the U.S. West Coast. As one example of the frequency with which tsunamis occur on the Pacific Coast, Crescent City experienced six tidal waves that were one foot or less during the late 1960s, four during the 1970s, and two during the 1980s. Surges as high or higher were reported during this period in other coastal communities on the U.S. West Coast, although thankfully there were no reports of damage or injuries.

The Loma Prieta 6.9 magnitude earthquake that struck the San Francisco area in 1989 caused widespread destruction and deaths. However, as the quake's motion was side to side, not up and down, this tremor did not generate significant tidal-wave action. A subsequent one-foot tidal wave was measured in Monterey Bay, just south of San Francisco, but no damage or injuries occurred.

A 7.1 earthquake in 1992 off Northern California and Cape Mendocino caused speculation as to whether this area was beginning to stir. The quake's epicenter was six miles inland and caused millions of dollars in damage in the near-coastal towns of Ferndale, Del Rio, Fortuna, and Scotia. As with the Loma Prieta earthquake, no significant underwater landslides occurred, nor was there any uplifting of the ocean's bottom. However, wave fluctuations up to four feet occurred in Crescent City's harbor, and the actual wave runup was three feet higher than normal. Damage to boats and shoreline structures was reported outside of Crescent City.

Seismologists noted that the Cape Mendocino earthquake was significant, because it was generated at the southern end of the Cascadia Subduction Zone. Numerous experts believe that this offshore region is capable of generating large tsunamis.

GIVEN THAT the present technology in issuing tsunami alerts cannot differentiate between whether a destructive tsunami, or just a mild wave, is heading onshore, the problems proliferate as to false alarms and how a disbelieving public will behave. Since tsunami centers must always err on the safe side, they end up issuing a far greater number of "false alarms" than the public is willing to accept. Various studies have concluded that over three-quarters of all tidal wave warnings end up as a false alarm. This high number puts the "Peter crying wolf" fable into reality. Coastal residents and even their disaster personnel end up not believing the warnings that they receive. These false alarms cause local economies to be disrupted, and the alarm itself subjects people to the risk of injury.

For example, an unnecessary evacuation of Honolulu in 1986 shut down the entire island of Oahu, costing Hawaii an estimated thirty million dollars in lost business and wages. The largest tidal wave that day on all the islands (including the Hilo side of Hawaii) was two feet high. A 1994 earthquake in the Kuril Islands, north of Japan, brought severe damage in the Kurils and Japan; however, the tsunami was nearly undetectable on the U.S. West Coast, where numbers of coastal communities had dutifully carried out their evacuations.

Crescent City has received its fair share of tsunami alerts and evacuations since 1964. In 1986, a magnitude 7.6 earthquake in the western Aleutian Islands generated a tidal wave with a miserly eight-inch runup at Adak, Alaska. The ATWC issued a tsunami warning, and Crescent City decided to take the safe route. It issued a tidal-wave warning, and the downtown areas were ordered to evacuate at 7:30 P.M. Local radio stations blared, "Earthquake off the Alaskan coast."

The highways filled with people heading out of town, and all of the sixty fishing boats fled for the safety of the deep ocean under the escort of the Coast Guard cutter *Cape Cross*. All available firemen, civil defense workers, city police, highway patrolmen, and sheriff's deputies were called in. Fire trucks and police cruised the city. The authorities even arrested one accountant at work for not leaving when the emergency was declared, and he was handcuffed, booked, then released later from county jail. Numbers of evacuees stayed at the Del Norte County Fairgrounds on high ground until the all-clear notice sounded. The tidal wave was three inches high when it came into Crescent City, and the authorities ordered the end of the alert at 11:20 P.M. It was certainly better to be safe than sorry, but these false alarms do add up over time. People then disregard them, leaving them vulnerable when the "big one" rolls in.

Authorities issued alarms and ordered the evacuation of people from low-lying areas for the Loma Prieta and Mendocino earthquakes. Notwithstanding these emergency declarations, some people didn't evacuate and stayed in their homes or businesses. The tidal waves generated were insignificant and no injuries or damage occurred. These false alarms were like the ones experienced by Crescent City before the 1964 Alaskan earthquake—then the big tsunami roared in.

An earthquake north of Japan triggered another tsunami alert in Crescent City in 1994. The quake and the ensuing waves killed sixteen people in Japan. The Pacific Tsunami Warning Center in Hawaii issued a tsunami warning for the entire Pacific Rim, including the U.S. West Coast and Canada. In this case, Crescent City didn't order an evacuation. Harbor and downtown activity continued as before. When the five small tidal waves cruised into the bay, the highest wave measured two and one-half feet. There was no damage or injury and other alerts have followed since then.

The residents of tiny Cannon Beach, Oregon, located near the Washington border, still remember one 1996 evacuation. The people, including the city's Police Chief and City Manager, felt what seemed to be a strong earthquake tremor, so the Chief of the Fire Protection District activated the district's tsunami warning system. The sirens wailed and a loud warning broadcasted that ordered all people to leave the area immediately. Desk clerks told motel guests to evacuate, and police and fire officials moved emergency vehicles to higher ground. An estimated 3,000 people evacuated. The all-clear alert sounded a half-hour later, after geologists advised that what they had felt wasn't an earthquake.

The improvements and warning systems in effect at Crescent City have narrowed down the odds of it being caught by surprise again from an Alaskan earthquake. However, an offshore submarine slide at the Humboldt-Del Norte coastline would be substantially different. Residents would only have a window of minutes—from five to thirty minutes, depending upon the earthquake's epicenter—in which to move inland sufficiently far to escape an ensuing tsunami. That isn't much time.

Even though the tidal waves generated caused only minor damage, the Mendocino Coast earthquake was severe enough for federal authorities to act. Congress in 1997 allocated 2.3 million dollars to create the National Tsunami Hazard Mitigation Program. Alaska, Hawaii, California, Washington, and Oregon joined with NOAA, the U.S. Geological Survey, and the Federal Emergency Management Administration (FEMA) in a program that attempts to minimize tsunami threats to their coastal towns.

First, these states are to create computerized tsunami inundation maps for various coastal cities and localities indicating the areas more likely to be flooded by a tidal wave. Emergency authorities are to concentrate their efforts in these low-lying areas to get the necessary warnings out to their residents, identify the best evacuation routes, and determine which areas would be hit hardest. The basic objective is that people should know ahead of time where the safest areas are and how to get there with a minimum of confusion.

A second objective is educating coastal communities so that residents who hear the warning will recognize it and leave immediately for higher ground. Many still don't know that you can't outrun a tidal wave, or "if you can see one, then you're too close" and are in serious trouble. Tsunamis can occur anytime and race up the rivers and streams that empty into the ocean. A small surge at one beach can be a giant tidal bore at another. People need to know that a strong earthquake in a low-lying coastal area is a natural warning by itself, and that a tidal wave is not just one wave that passes through, but a series of powerful surges over a longer time period. Approaching sea waves can raise or drain coastal waters, exposing interesting-looking tide pools, but this is definitely not the time to explore them. People need to know this ahead of time, not discovering their mistake after it's too late.

A third objective is to develop real-time reporting stations. Seismometers measure earthquakes, not tsunamis. Coastal tide gauges were specifically designed to measure tidal waves, and although they can measure tsunamis close to shore, they can't predict their effect in faraway countries. As false alarms undercut credibility, NOAA has been experimenting with deep-ocean reporting stations that can reliably track tsunamis and report back in real time.

One proposed deep-ocean system consists of three integrated units: a pressure-sensitive recorder deep on the ocean floor, a transmitting buoy on the surface, and a satellite communication system. Highly sophisticated sensors are anchored to the seafloor below, able to detect the increased pressure from any additional volumes of seawater passing by. This is a prime characteristic of tidal waves, and the device can detect a near-microscopic, one-millimeter change in sea level. Ships and storm waves don't trigger the sensors, because their pressure changes are not transmitted that far down. When a sensor picks up a tidal wave, it will immediately send signals to a surface buoy that's located up one mile or more on the surface. The buoy transmits that data via satellite to the warning stations. Presently, there are problems in the transmission of this data through the ocean to the buoy, but researchers believe they have solved this problem by using alternative transmission systems.

Additionally, authorities under the National Tsunami Program are upgrading earthquake-monitoring equipment, so that they can more accurately pinpoint offshore tidal-wave-producing earthquakes and measure their size. They are also working to improve the communication among the different emergency networks and decrease communication delays, thereby enabling tsunami-warning centers to react faster when issuing their warnings.

The installation by various coastal towns of the blue-and-white tsunami hazard and evacuation route signs is one of the first indications to the general public of this increased awareness. These signs warn and remind residents and tourists alike about the dangers in low-lying areas. The route signs identify the best ways to get to higher ground.

The warning signs usually depict a person running from a giant wave, with the message, "Tsunami Hazard Zone. In case of earthquake, go to high ground or inland." Typically, tsunami disaster planning is done in conjunction with an earthquake drill under the area's earthquake preparedness office. These steps are good to take, but they miss one important point. The authorities should add to the signs: "If you're close enough to read this, then it could be too late."

Coastal states also have enacted their own specific legislation. For example, Oregon restricts the construction of critical buildings (i.e., fire stations, hospitals, and schools) in low-lying areas with tsunami risks. It requires coastal schools to participate in three earthquake and tsunami drills a year, and to show state-created tsunami-educational videos, one for kindergarten through third grade and another from fourth grade through high school. A school curriculum with activities planned around these tsunami videos has also been developed.

Educational products that alert coastal residents about the hazards have been developed in other states, as well, ranging from bookmarks and decals with information to refrigerator magnets and coffee mugs. Stickers with tsunami information are on hotel-room doors in low-lying inundation areas. Large interpretive signs about tidal waves are displayed in various popular tourist communities. Laminated cards for adults and coloring sheets for children are placed on restaurant tables in selected establishments and areas, as U.S. coastal states take various steps to comply with this federal legislation.

As part of this, the National Weather Service created a "Tsunami-Ready" designation for coastal cities. To receive this award, cities must develop inundation maps of at-risk low-lying areas; post evacuation routes and tsunami-hazard zone signs; and create an emergency plan outlining how emergency personnel are brought together, the public will be alerted, and everyone is to be evacuated in an orderly way, among other conditions. At this time, ten coastal communities have received this award, including four in Alaska (Seward, Homer, Sitka, and Kodiak City), three in Washington (Ocean Shores, Long Beach, and the Quinault Indian Tribe Reservation), Cannon Beach in Oregon—and, yes, Crescent City, California. In mid 2004, the University of California at Santa Barbara in California became the tenth entity so designated.

However, these steps are still woefully insufficient. Given the large numbers and range of populated coastal cities up and down both U.S. coasts, ten communities over a five year period does not show a widespread endorsement of this program. Although the approaches are laudable, the amounts of money involved for starters are not nearly enough. Simply consider for one moment what's being done in your area or where you or friends vacation by the sea. Counties and states still don't earmark scarce funds for events that occur rarely, and people still don't take the information seriously.

GIVEN THE "we can do it" attitude of Crescent City after the 1964 tsunami hit, the American public got off cheap. Today, an equivalent tsunami would run into the hundreds of millions of dollars—and if this happened to Los Angeles or New York City today, the financial bill would be in the billions. The deaths and injuries would be staggering. Next, add in the litigation, court costs, and class action legal settlements, and you have a financial and legal nightmare for the rest of the United States.

Whether caused by earthquakes located in countries far away or the even more dangerous nearby underwater tremors, tsunamis have pounded into California, Oregon, and Washington over the last three centuries. Extensive property damage and injuries continue to occur, although to date relatively few fatalities have resulted except for the Crescent City disaster.

In 1812, an earthquake destroyed Mission San Juan Capistrano, near San Diego. Two more earthquakes occurred that day, the second and largest one with an estimated magnitude of 7.7. These quakes destroyed the Mission and Presidio of Santa Barbara in Southern California, located ninety miles north of Los Angeles, as well as Mission San Buenaventura in Ventura, a town twenty-five miles to the south of Santa Barbara.

The ensuing tidal wave heights have been a source of discussion ever since. Some accounts placed them at thirty to thirty-five feet in Santa Barbara and ten feet or more in Ventura. Other eyewitnesses placed them at half that much. In any event, the experts agree that at least a "moderate" tidal wave had been created and surged over land. They believe that the Santa Barbara event was triggered by a submarine landslide brought about by the earthquake.

In 1923, twenty-foot waves hit San Pedro Channel, off Los Angeles, believed to be the result of an earthquake and tsunami from Japan; one man drowned while trying to save his companion. In 1927, a 7.3 earthquake occurred forty miles northwest of Santa Barbara where Vandenberg Air Force Base is now located. This tremor caused considerable damage on shore and was also felt strongly at sea, generating tidal waves up to six feet high. One surge washed over and destroyed Southern Pacific's railroad tracks for "many yards," as well as totally inundating the station.

A 5.2 submarine earthquake in 1930 in Santa Monica Bay off Los Angeles generated a twenty-foot wave at Santa Monica. One man drowned and lifeguards had to save numbers of people who were swimming or wading at the time. The 1946 Alaska tidal waves, 1960 Chile tsunami, and the 1964 disaster were discussed earlier. Given these and the numbers of earthquakes that rumble in the Alaska-Aleutian zone over time, it's quite likely that other tsunamis similar to the 1946 and 1964 occurrences will take place. In fact, James F. Lander, who wrote the definitive books on U.S. tsunamis—*Tsunamis Affecting the West Coast of the United States: 1806–1992* and *United States Tsunamis (including United States possessions), 1690–1988*—believes that there is an 84 percent chance that a magnitude 7.4 or greater earthquake will occur somewhere in this zone before the year 2008. As more time passes between these disastrous events, the odds increase that we will experience another one sooner rather than later.

Seismologists particularly suspect the Cascadia Subduction Zone as being a prime candidate for such an event. This 750-mile long fault runs parallel to the West Coast's heavily developed coastline, from Northern California to British Columbia. Some seismologists believe that this fault could generate the largest earthquake ever experienced by the United States. Experts have identified historical sand deposits carried significantly inland into Washington by tidal waves created in the northern portion of this zone. Its earthquake danger is believed to be comparable to that of inland Southern California and its well-publicized San Andreas Fault.

The Washington and Oregon coastlines lie along several plates that are constantly colliding. The Juan de Fuca, Gorda, and Explorer Plates are moving at a rate of 1.5 inches (four centimeters) per year. These plates and others are thrusting under the North American Plate. If these plates lock up as they try to move past each other, tremendous energy would build up that could be released only by sizeable earthquakes.

Geologists are certain that a huge tidal wave crashed over an inland Indian encampment five hundred years ago on the Oregon coast. Studies have indicated that both Washington and the Oregon coastlines have been shaken by as many as thirteen huge earthquakes in the 7.0 to 9.0 magnitude-range during the last 7,000 years. Some of these tremors generated tidal waves that were calculated to be higher than forty feet over land. Every few hundred years, earthquakes centered on or adjacent to the Cascadia Subduction area and California generate massive mega-tsunamis.

Several studies further conclude that a superquake in the 8.5 to 9.0 Richter range occurred in 1700, when the Juan de Fuca Plate slipped further underneath the North American Plate. The quake savagely shook the coasts of what are now the states of Washington and Oregon towards their border. The resulting thirty-foot tidal wave swept inland into those states, depositing ten times as much sand on shore as the 1964 Crescent City tsunami left behind. The sea waves surged across the Pacific, causing damage with six-to-nine-foot high waves to three villages on Japan's coast, after traveling 5,000 miles in ten hours. Although this was the last global tidal wave generated off the Northwest coast in the Cascadia Subduction Zone, the experts believe that another large one will be generated over time. Seismologists debate how large an earthquake-generated tsunami would be in this area and what its effects would be, since this zone neighbors large populated cities such as Seattle, Portland, and is geologically close to San Francisco.

An earthquake centered offshore this zone would cause a momentous tidal wave to crest tens of feet high and roar in fifteen to twenty minutes later into very populated areas. The property damage would be in the billions of dollars—or more. The numbers of people killed or injured would be inordinately high.

Unfortunately, warnings don't mean much if residents don't take them seriously. Many coastal communities aren't like Crescent City and don't employ a continuous program of tidal wave warnings, alarms, and drills. This is not done in Seattle, San Diego, or other large metropolitan centers. Even given an effective warning that's taken seriously, the number of people needing to be evacuated from these widespread and highly populated areas is too vast to be accomplished in time.

Think of the catastrophic casualties and destruction if such an earthquake occurred offshore from San Francisco or Los Angeles, and the waves roared up those bays in the middle of the night. Or if another Alaskan earthquake occurred like the Good Friday one. Think what would happen if such a wave caught a supertanker and pushed it over the docks into the skyscrapers lining these cities. Or a serious tsunami like the thirty-foot-high, five-mile-wide, and twenty-mile-long Papua New Guinea monster swept into Seattle or New York City.

According to the experts, however, the possibility of offshore earthquakes generating tidal waves on the U.S. East Coast is "remote" and not as likely as off the West Coast. The East has suffered few effects from tidal waves, because its underground plates aren't in the same torturous conflict as the West Coast. The Continental Shelf along much of the East Coast also apparently gives a moderating effect to any tidal waves that are generated. For example, a 7.5 magnitude earthquake in Charleston, South Carolina, in 1866 was the largest reported on the East Coast, but this quake didn't produce any tidal waves. However, other East Coast earthquakes have produced tidal waves.

Scientists are still studying a 7.2 magnitude earthquake that occurred in Eastern Canada in 1929. This was Canada's most destructive quake, creating a tidal wave that slammed into Lord's Cove and other coastal towns, killing twenty-nine people and causing extensive damage. The quake was located 150 miles south of Newfoundland on the southern end of the Grand Banks, where the Continental Shelf drops sharply down into a deep canyon. The earthquake was centered twelve miles beneath that sloping sea bottom. This created small tsunamis that surged into Atlantic City, New Jersey, and Charleston, South Carolina, among other places, but no fatalities or severe injuries were reported.

Earthquakes centered in or around Puerto Rico have created tidal waves that also have hit the East Coast. A 7.5 magnitude quake in 1918 produced small tidal waves that were detected in Atlantic City, some 1,350 miles away. A smaller quake in Puerto Rico in 1922 created a two-foot tsunami that hit Galveston, Texas.

A non-earthquake-caused landslide in 1926 created a tidal wave that crashed into the city of Bernard on Mt. Desert Island off the northeastern coast of Maine. Bass Harbor suddenly emptied, and an initial ten-foot wave crested in, followed by two smaller ones. These surges threw fifty fishing boats inland. No one was injured, although falling cakes of ice nearly killed two men when their boat suddenly grounded on land. Nearby Corea, Maine, experienced the same high waves with boats torn from their moorings, lobster traps smashed, and "thousands of flounder" deposited far inland.

Recently, geologists and researchers have been studying Cumbre Vieja, a volcano on the island of Las Palmas. This island is located at the western end of the Canary Islands, which lie off the African coast. Scientists developed a computer model that indicates severe eruptions from this volcano could trigger enormous landslides into the sea, in turn generating massive tidal waves that would travel to distant continents. Reminiscent of the Alaskan-triggered tsunamis that hit coastal communities around the Pacific Rim, these islands are in the Atlantic Ocean, however, with the anticipated tidal waves pounding the Atlantic Coast seaboard—from Florida to New York City, as well as European coastal cities, including those in England. The difficulty, of course, is predicting when such eruptions would occur. But no area of the world is really safe from tsunamis.

In fact, earthquakes have generated tidal waves off the entire U.S. coastline. For example, geologists discovered an unusual layer of gravel in an outcropping along the Gulf Coast of Texas. This was located so high in the strata, some two hundred feet high, that a monstrous tidal wave was quite likely created by a volcanic eruption or a massive landslide such as the one that hit Lituya Bay in Alaska in 1958. That earthquake-induced landslide created a tsunami subsequently measured to be 1720 feet (525 meters) or five hundred feet higher than the 102-story Empire State Building. Although limited to this specific bay, that local tsunami caused every tree on the landside to be severed or uprooted from the ground, neatly limbed and debarked, the soil completely scoured down to bedrock.

IN ONE WAY, Crescent City never recovered from the tidal wave that ripped through its midsection. As Wally Griffin observed, "Many people lament the passing of the quaint old town look, and our downtown buildings don't seem to invite onlookers for any length of time."

However, Crescent City is still "Comeback Town, U.S.A." with the way it overcame the immense devastation of the tsunami. According to longtime local residents, however, the older, tidal-wave generation's attitudes are dying out. This could also be a function of the times, increased population, technology, and the deaths of people who once considered most around them to be their friends.

Crescent City then was a small town of basically hard working, strong-minded, church-going peoples who got along—had to get along—despite the differences that all of us have. They were forced together to try and rebuild their lives and community. These "Generation Fifties" folks, their strong work ethic, and an "I won't give up" attitude brought about the rebuilding of their town—starting that very first morning when people saw the destruction.

As to the impact of another major West Coast tsunami, Bill Parker observed:

> I can't believe that another tidal wave would have the low amount of deaths that we experienced in Crescent City, especially if it hit at a San Francisco or Seattle. So many curious people were down at the beach in San Francisco Bay during our 1964 tidal wave, that according to their Civil Defense Director, if the tsunami had been like we had at Crescent City, they would have lost tens of thousands of people. Just think about the millions of people who live there and who would be trying to get, let's say, over the Golden Gate Bridge in an evac-

uation. Afterwards, trying to feed all of these people is mind-boggling. You would have the food, but there wouldn't be enough loading docks or trucks to get them into the hands of everyone. Further, the streets would be destroyed or covered with debris. It would be a madhouse.

There is a sculpture and plaque commemorating the eleven people who died in the Crescent City tidal waves. In the middle of Tsunami Landing, the city constructed a Tsunami Memorial to honor those who died. A circular bricked area, filled with stone, supports the metallic sculpture in its middle. There is also a monument at Beverly Beach State Park in Oregon, memorializing the four McKenzie children who died there. However, time dims memories, as those who experienced this calamity or knew the victims pass from the scene.

Thirty years after the Crescent City disaster, the experience of Southern Californians on October 4, 1994, is ominous. Tidal-wave fever in San Diego escalated that day, when the WC/ATWC issued an alert advising coastal cities of a possible tsunami that would arrive at 5:17 P.M. that day. It issued the warning when a major earthquake rumbled under the ocean floor, 650 miles north of Tokyo; eleven-foot waves caused flooding along the Japanese coast, and residents in the low-lying areas of Hawaii evacuated. Crescent City issued a tidal wave alert, but didn't order an immediate evacuation and watched nervously for further signs.

This event in Southern California ranked right up there with the San Diego Chargers football team. Sightseers immediately converged on the beach, piers, boardwalks, and breakwaters to "see the tsunami." Dozens of surfers jumped into the ocean's swells so that they could say they surfed one. Photographers fought for space on the hills overlooking the ocean for that one great shot. At an exclusive restaurant overlooking the ocean, only one customer called to ask if she should change her dinner plans—and she didn't. In fact, one oceanfront restaurant received several calls from people who wanted to make dinner reservations in time to watch the tsunami's arrival. The hostess jokingly told them to bring lifejackets.

When the tsunami arrived, the waves were negligible. Disappointed people called it the "little tsunami that couldn't." One twenty-four-year-old man thought about printing souvenir T-shirts that would read, "I survived the San Diego tsunami of '94." First issued at 9:00 A.M., the warning was canceled at 3:30 P.M. The local Coast Guard then canceled its contingency plans to fly their Falcon jets and rescue helicopters to an air station located on higher ground.

Experts believe that the 1994 tsunami false alarm underscored the public's misunderstanding of tidal waves, showing that people don't take warnings seriously, no matter what form they take. People will continue to build new homes in low coastal areas with the best ocean views, and developers build subdivisions on or by the beach. Coastal towns proliferate and grow in size with retirees and younger couples with children. Residents and tourists alike still jam harbors to see tidal waves, even when a full-scale alert is in effect. On the entire U.S. West Coast, including Crescent City, two generations have grown up without having seen forty-foot boats smash through buildings, or a broken small body dug from an inland swamp.

Earthquakes and undersea landslides meanwhile continue to cause tsunamis. An 8.4 earthquake in 2001 near the southern coast of Peru caused a one-foot-plus tidal wave to rise off Crescent City. An 8.0 earthquake on September 25, 2003, near Hokkaido, Japan, caused another one-foot-high tsunami to head into the city's harbor. In both cases, the highest rises occurred there of all coastal locations on the U.S West Coast. Measurable rises, moreover, were also created in both instances up and down the entire West Coast, from Alaska to Mexico.

In Crescent City, one photograph shows twenty children standing on top or around a huge redwood log thrown inland by the 1964 tsunami. The children at the bottom have their hands raised, and the log's width is twice that. Tourists come to town and have their pictures taken next to the tsunami's landmarks and high-water marks. They shop at "Tsunami Landing," constructed on the graveyards of the buildings that the tidal waves destroyed.

People forget the lessons of the past and that tsunamis know no boundaries. They can occur without any warning, on a beautiful sunny day, and suddenly roll in from an offshore or even faraway earthquake. A tsunami can happen anytime, nearly anywhere, next month, even tomorrow.

A "big one" will happen again, and it unfortunately will be worse than Crescent City's experience then. The only question is when—and who will suffer this time.

INDEX